THINKING MATTER

Materialism in
Eighteenth-Century Britain

THINKING MATTER

MATTER

Materialism in Eighteenth-Century Britain

By John W. Yolton

University of Minnesota Press, *Minneapolis*

Published by the University of Minnesota Press,
2037 University Avenue Southeast, Minneapolis, MN 55414
Printed in the United States of America.

Library of Congress Cataloging in Publication Data

Yolton, John W.
Thinking matter.

Bibliography: p. 209
Includes index.
1. Materialism — History — Addresses, essays, lectures.
2. Philosophy, English — 18th century — Addresses, essays, lectures.
I. Title.
B1302.M37Y64 1983   146'.3'0941   83-6507
ISBN 0-8166-1160-2
ISBN 0-8166-1161-0 (pbk.)

The University of Minnesota
is an equal-opportunity educator
and employer.

To

Shadia Drury

Stephen Ford

Sylvana Tomaselli

John Wright

Contents

Preface

The research from which this study grew was begun in the early 1970s, while I was still at York University in Toronto, Canada. That original project called for writing the history of the way of ideas in the seventeenth and eighteenth centuries. My earlier work on Locke had examined some of the reactions to Locke's use of the term 'idea' by his contemporaries. My *Locke and the Way of Ideas* (1956) discussed a few writers reacting to that term, whose work and life extended into the early years of the eighteenth century. Research at Oxford during 1968–69 on my *Locke and the Compass of Human Understanding* (1970) began to uncover other related eighteenth-century texts. I became aware of the pervasiveness of the term 'idea' in both centuries. There were few studies which even tried to trace the history of that term, its uses, its interpretations, or its role in accounts of perceptual knowledge. I began to formulate a research program for another book, but I did not have much time for a full-scale assault on the vast amount of books, tracts, and pamphlets that needed to be read and analyzed. A detailed and careful inventory of the term 'idea' was required.

It was clear that what was needed was a critical examination of the works of such major figures as Descartes, Arnauld, Malebranche, Leibniz, Locke, Berkeley, Hume, Hartley, Reid, with an eye to their use of the term 'idea'. Theories of perception, philosophy of mind, cognitive psychology: these were the areas in need of attention.

Working with one of my graduate students, Peter J. White, on his thesis, "A Study of the Psychology of Cognition in John Locke" (Ph.D., York University, 1972), gave me a chance to begin my explorations. Seminars and classes that I offered at York also helped me expand my study of these topics. Two papers embodied some of this early research: "Ideas and Knowledge in Seventeenth-Century Philosophy" (*Journal of the History of Philosophy*, XIII, 1975), and "On Being Present to the Mind: A Sketch for the History of an Idea" (*Dialogue*, XIV, 1975; my presidential address in 1974 to the Canadian Philosophical Association). Then in 1974–75 a sabbatical leave from York, spent at Oxford, enabled me to plunge into the project in depth.

What emerged from the early stages of work on this project was the importance of a phrase and a principle, both of which appeared in almost all the books and pamphlets which employed the term 'idea'. The phrase was 'present to (or with) the mind'. The principle was "no thing can be or act where it is not." The principle was used for cognitive as well as for physical action: no cognition at a distance. Both the phrase and the principle used spatial concepts, even when the writers using them tried to avoid the literalism of the location talk for mind. If physical objects cannot be 'present with the mind', something else—ideas—must be present, because what is known must be present with the mind. Commitment to the principle led many writers to apply the term 'extension' to mind (most of whom insisted, however, that the mind was not extended in the way bodies are). Some writers also distinguished the extension of body from the extension of space: Locke speaks of the expansion of space in contrast to the extension of body.

These concerns with the extension and location of mind were also applied to God: God is everywhere (omnipresent); he is, Newton said, present to all things and space is, as it were, the sensorium of God, just as our brain is the sensorium of our ideas. The analyses of perceptual acquaintance, of mental activity, of our knowledge of body and cognitive access to the world were intertwined with other concerns and interests relating to the nature of thought, its connection (causal or otherwise) with the physiological mechanism of the body.

Thus, from my readings in the way of ideas from Descartes to Reid, I soon saw that there was another important theme in need of attention: the concept of human nature, implicit or explicit, in many of the writers (both known and little known) whose use of the term 'idea' I was tracing. One powerful focus for this interest in human nature in eighteenth-century Britain came from what appears to be only a passing remark made by Locke in his *Essay*, that there is no contradiction in the notion that God might superadd to matter the power of thought. The immediate reactions to this remark gave Locke notice that he had touched a sensitive orthodox nerve. The subsequent reactions to and the attacks upon this remark extend to the end of the century. The arguments Locke anticipated against this possibility of thinking matter (for this is what his suggestion was seen to imply) were extensive throughout the century in Britain. Both writers who supported the conceptual point—that, for all we know, God is able to give the power of thought to a material substance—and those few who accepted the implication and tried to explain what it would be for thought to be a property of the brain, were warmly attacked by the defenders of immaterialism: those who insisted that there is a soul that is immaterial, that thought is and can only be a property of the soul, that no organization of matter and motion could ever produce thought, and that God could not, without essentially changing the nature of matter, make matter think. The arguments flow back and forth in the century. The issue was (so the immaterialists believed) whether man has an immortal soul with spiritual attributes, or whether man is a complex bit of organized matter sharing the attributes of all bodies. The immaterialist insisted that the very possibility of moral action, and, of course, of ultimate rewards and punishments, depended upon their view of man as a two substance creature, body and soul.

From a research program for studying the history of the term 'idea', I was thus led into this other area. The two areas are related in a number of ways, but it has turned out better to treat them in separate volumes. The history of the way of ideas is presented in a companion to this volume, under the title, *Perceptual Acquaintance from Descartes to Reid*.

The story of the thinking matter controversy in eighteenth-century Britain is largely the story of reactions to Locke's suggestion. While Hobbes and Spinoza are routinely cited as the arch materialists, it is to Locke's suggestion that most of the reactions were directed. In tracing this story, we shall find that the scientific view of matter played an important role, as did the various notions of space, extension, place, and the underlying physiological mechanism of the body. The story of thinking matter in eighteenth-century Britain is thus broader than the metaphysical possibility Locke suggested. It is not, however, the full story of materialism. That story starts before Locke's suggestion. Cudworth showed the ancient roots of the controversy, in his *The True Intellectual System of the Universe*, a work that may have supplied Locke with his formulation of the possibility of thinking matter. In Locke's century, thinking matter was a notion that emerged from some of the Cartesian writings, especially over the issue of animal machines. Hobbes's form of matter and motion explanations, together with Spinoza's metaphysical doctrines, focused attention on the possibility of a materialist account of man and the world. Leibniz plays a role in the story too, as do most prominently Diderot and the *philosophes*. There are also social, political, and religious ingredients to the the materialism-immaterialism controversy.

My study does not concern itself with these larger components of materialism. The justification for narrowing the scope is that the thinking matter debate in eighteenth-century Britain has not been much discussed, many of the writers I present have not been studied, and the links between the metaphysical and moral concerns within this debate and the scientific concepts of matter have been little noticed, nor has much of the fascinating writing on what we today know as the philosophy of action been known.

It is nevertheless important to keep in mind that the thinking matter controversy was part of a larger context and of a larger development in other countries. For those who wish to acquaint themselves with some aspects of this larger framework, I can recommend the following books.

Some of the earlier reactions to Locke's suggestion have been discussed in my *Locke and the Way of Ideas* (1956), especially in chapter IV, section 3. Some of the same questions about active forces in matter that are linked with the thinking matter controversy fired a debate in biology and physiology, the debate between 'preformationists' and 'epigenesists'. This debate has been effectively presented by Shirley A. Roe, *Matter, Life, and Generation: Eighteenth-century Embryology and the Haller-Wolff Debate* (1981). Also, Jean Mayer's long introduction to his edition of Diderot's *Eléments de physiologie* (1964) is a very good account of the background physiology of the period and of Diderot's concept of human nature.

There are several studies of the different concepts of matter in the eighteenth century, especially of the ways in which those concepts relate to the possibility of active forces in matter. Robert E. Schofield's *Mechanism and Materialism: British Natural Philosophy in an Age of Reason* (1970) and Arnold Thackray's *Atoms and Powers: An Essay on Newtonian Matter-Theory and the Development of Chemistry* (1970) are highly recommended. For a more limited treatment, Ernan McMullin's *Newton on Matter and Activity* (1978) is carefully done and very convincing. Alexandre Koyré's *From the Closed World to the Infinite Universe* (1957) should be standard reading.

A work of much different scope is Carolyn Merchant's *The Death of Nature: Women, Ecology, and the Scientific Revolution* (1980), especially chapters 7-11. The social implications of and the direct involvement in social change by a number of the writers discussed in my study are presented in a fascinating work by Margaret C. Jacob: *The Radical Enlightenment: Pantheists, Freemasons, and Republicans* (1981). Her earlier work, *The Newtonians and the English Revolution, 1689-1720* (1976) is also relevant.

A work that touches on some of the same issues as are discussed here is Ben Lazare Mijuskovic's *The Achilles of Rationalist Arguments: The Simplicity, Unity, and Identity of Thought and Soul from the Cambridge Platonists to Kant* (1974). Mijuskovic recognizes the central role played by Cudworth's formulation of doctrines in the eighteenth-century arguments about the soul, the person, and the nature of thought.

No part of this study has been published previously, but some sections have formed the basis for papers presented to several groups. Chapter II was first presented to the Washington Philosophy Club in Washington, D.C., in the spring of 1979, under the title: "Locke's Mechanical Bird and the Eighteenth-Century Automatical Man." This same paper was later read to the Philosophy Club at Rutgers University, Newark, and most recently, in the fall of 1981, a revised version was given as a public lecture at the Folger Shakespeare Library in Washington, D.C. The entire study formed the basis for a twelve-week seminar, with the title, "Space and Time, Matter and Mind: The Development of Materialism in Eighteenth-Century Britain," given under the auspices of the Folger Institute of Renaissance and Eighteenth-Century Studies. That seminar, with its very special interdisciplinary membership, provided just the right environment and audience, at just the right time, to enable me to refine and clarify the study. I would like to thank John Andrews and Susan Zimmerman for making my stay and my wife's at the Folger so pleasant during that period, and for making the weekly trips from New Jersey to D.C. so worthwhile. I would also like to thank the members of that seminar for their spirited participation and for their helpful responses.

The research program, which has now yielded two books, this one on thinking matter and the companion study on perceptual acquaintance, was begun, as I have indicated, while I was at York University. A number of graduate students worked with me there on various related aspects of these two studies. The project was originally planned as a single study. Even though it has now taken the form of two separate books, I want to dedicate both books to four of those students, students who now are friends and colleagues in intellectual history. These four students also represent for me other students, and many happy, fruitful years, at York University. Through their work at York and in correspondence and personal visits since, they have stimulated my work, reacted to it, and encouraged it. They are beginning, and will continue, to make contributions to our understanding of historical figures and doctrines.

Shadia Drury's paper, "The Relationship of Substance and Simple Natures in the Philosophy of Descartes" (in *New Essays on Rationalism and Empiricism, Canadian Journal of Philosophy*, Supplementary Volume IV, 1978), as well as her recent work on natural law in relation to concepts of human nature, are products of her studies at York. Stephen Ford's Ph.D. thesis at York, "Imagination and Thought in Descartes" (1977), was an important analysis of Descartes's heavy use of the faculty of imagination in the *Regulae* and other writings. That thesis really should be published. Sylvana Tomaselli introduced me to some of the French *philosophes*, especially Diderot, as we worked through some of the British writers, e.g., Hume and Hartley. Her doctoral studies at Cambridge, England are pursuing the concept of human nature in some eighteenth-century British and French authors, especially in Hume and Diderot. John Wright has been involved with both my studies more than anyone else. We have worked closely together over the years. His exciting book on Hume, *The Sceptical Realism of David Hume*, has just appeared. The fruits of his related study in eighteenth-century views on mental illness should appear before too long.

I would like to thank my research assistant at Rutgers University, Mr. James G. Buickerood, who has provided excellent help in checking references and quotations and in tracking down books. As well, the comments of two readers for the University of Minnesota Press on the penultimate draft of this study have called to my attention a number of places in need of clarification.

For works in French, where there is not a standard English translation, I have supplied translations of my own. References to books discussed are given in the text, with full bibliographical information given at the end of the volume. For the more obscure writers, I have supplied, where it is known, some brief information about them.

I am grateful especially to my wife for her usual outstanding assistance. The detailed bibliography is entirely her work.

THINKING MATTER

Materialism in
Eighteenth-Century Britain

Introduction

The seventeenth and eighteenth centuries in Great Britain are marked
by a general and persistent concern about threats to orthodoxy in
religion. Many doctrines and views were seen as threatening: theories
about the origin and nature of human knowledge, metaphysical claims
about the nature of the world, claims about human nature, about the
person and action. Locke's views in most of these areas were seen by
many of his contemporaries either as attacks on traditional religion or
as lending themselves to others who *were* interested in undermining
religion. Labels such as 'Socinian', 'deist', even 'atheist' were attached
to Locke. Hobbes was another writer whose doctrines were considered
antireligious. In his case, it was what was taken to be the materialism
of his doctrines that was attacked. The mechanisms of the Cartesian
account of matter and of the physiology of the human body were also
frequently viewed as leading to and aiding materialism. If explanations
of human action can be given in terms of the mechanism of the body,
some people thought, then mind or spirit may be short-changed, or
even ignored.

There were two ways in which mind was ignored. If matter is inert
and passive, and if that kind of matter is seen to be dominant, there
seems to be no room for mind or spirit. The result is mechanism, automatism, and necessity. On the other hand, if matter is thought to have
active principles inherent in it, or if it is receptive to such principles

3

imposed upon it, once again there is no need for spiritual or mental causality in the workings of nature. A more extreme version of this second alternative is that thought is retained in the account of the world, but it becomes a property of matter, either inherent or imposed. For the orthodox in religion, it was important that there be two substances, one material, the other immaterial. The immateriality of the soul was a necessary condition for immortality. Any suggestion that the two substances be reduced to one (i.e., to material substance) eliminated the soul. Locke's account of the person located the identity of self in consciousness, not in an immaterial substance. Many viewed that account as disconnecting the property of thought from its substance. A property without a substance was a hard enough notion for the traditionalist, but when Locke also insisted that we do not know the essence of material or of immaterial substance, such scepticism, coupled with his account of the person, could only be seen as tantamount to locating both extension and thought in *one* substance. Such a notion sounded to many of Locke's contemporaries (and to many in the eighteenth century) suspiciously like Spinoza's.[1] When readers of Locke's *Essay concerning Human Understanding* came across his suggestion that there was nothing contradictory in the notion that God could add to matter the power of thought, the case of materialism against Locke was sealed.

Locke's suggestion that matter might be made to think revived and reinforced the fears many held of Spinoza and of Spinozism. Hobbes was frequently linked with Spinoza, but it was the particular doctrine in Spinoza's philosophy, which identifies substance with the world, that focused those fears. It was not without reason that Spinoza was described as "the most famous atheist of our time,"[2] for not only did he predicate thought and extension of one substance: that one substance was identified with God. The world was material and God was that world. The material world that was God was also eternal and infinite.

When Locke discusses the claim that matter is eternal (4.10.18), he has in mind an older claim, one that said there are two eternal beings: God and matter. Locke explains that people were led to this claim in part because of the difficulty of conceiving how something could come from nothing. This problem, and a series of closely related issues, had been thoroughly and repetitiously presented and discussed by Cudworth in 1678, in his *The True Intellectual System of the Universe: Wherein, All the Reason and Philosophy of Atheism Is Confuted; and Its Impossibility Demonstrated*. For Cudworth's contemporaries, this work must have been a major source book of ancient versions of materialism, as well as for the array of arguments to combat it. His book was originally planned to deal only with liberty and necessity, but he was led in time to give attention to the metaphysical underpinnings of the necessitarians, especially the democratic corporealists or atomists. Atheism for Cudworth is closely linked with materialism. The atheist's principle is cited as "whatsoever is not Extended, is Nowhere and Nothing" (p. 9). He identifies four different kinds of atheism.

First, the *Hylopathian* or *Anaximandrian*, that derives all things from Dead and Stupid Matter in the way of *Qualities and Forms*, Generable and Corruptible: Secondly, the *Atomical* or *Democritical*, which doth the same thing in the way of *Atoms* and *Figures*: Thirdly, the *Cosmoplastick* or *Stoical Atheism*, which supposes one *Plastick* and *Methodical* but *Senseless Nature*, to preside over the whole Corporeal Universe; and Lastly, the *Hylozoick* or *Stratonical*, that attributes to all Matter, as such, a certain *Living* and *Energetick Nature*, but devoid of all *Animality*, *Sense* and *Consciousness*. (pp. 134-35)

That Cudworth's description of the four forms of atheism spans inert, passive, senseless matter and matter endowed with active principles, is especially interesting for the study of eighteenth-century British materialism. The active principles invoked by eighteenth-century Newtonians (and by Priestley) differ from those used by the Hylozoick or Stratonical materialists discussed by Cudworth, but the explanatory scope of old and new active principles was equally threatening to religion. The really fascinating version of active principles in matter was the attempt to include among such principles thought, volition, and consciousness. The thinking matter controversy in the eighteenth century reflects and repeats many of the same points, and the opposition's arguments are similar to those made by the ancients whom Cudworth discusses.

In the object of his attack, in the arguments pro and con, Cudworth's work anticipates many of the books and pamphlets, including the Boyle lectures, in his own and the next century. Most of the side issues too are similar. An inventory of some of the issues raised by Cudworth will serve to introduce the eighteenth-century debates over materialism.

(a) The Nature of Matter for the Corporealists

In what Cudworth refers to as the 'Atomical Physiology', body is nothing but extended bulk. No properties are attributed to it "but what is included in the Nature and *Idea* of it, *viz.* more or less Magnitude with Divisibility into Parts, Figure, and Position, together with

Motion and Rest" (p. 7). No part of body can move itself. The explanation of the appearances, of perceived qualities, was done entirely by reference to the simple "Elements of Magnitude, Figure, Site, and Motion (which are all clearly intelligible as different Modes of extended Substance)." No reference is needed to substantial forms, to intentional species or corporeal effluvia coming from objects, nor to "any other kind of Motion or Action really distinct from Local Motion (such as Generation and Alteration)." Matter on this view is senseless, sluggish, and inactive. The only causation in such a system is mechanical, the impact of particles.

(b) Incorporeal Principles

Cudworth points out that even those who try to say all there is is matter in motion have to admit that appearances belie such a claim. Thus some account of the appearances must be given. As soon as an attempt is made to save the appearances, it is difficult not to recognize the "Phancies or Phantastick *Idea's*" produced by the figure and motion of matter to be themselves other than "Modes of the *Bodies* without us" (p. 29). The "Ancient Physiologers" tried, Cudworth says, to treat these products as mere fancy, since their goal was to resolve "all into *Mechanism* and *Phancy*" (p. 32). Their claim was that "from those different Modifications of the small Particles of Bodies (they being not so distinctly perceived by our Senses), there are begotten in us, certain confused *Phasmata* or *Phantasmata*, *Apparitions*, *Phancies*, and *Passions*, as of Light and Colours, Heat and Cold, and the like, which are those things, that are vulgarly mistaken for real Qualities existing in the Bodies without us; whereas indeed there is Nothing Absolutely in the Bodies themselves like to those *Phantastick Idea's* that we have of them; and yet they are wisely contriv'd by the Author of Nature, for the Adorning and Embellishing of the Corporeal World to us" (p. 33). Bodies were thus considered in two different ways: "as they are Absolutely in themselves, or else as they are Relatively to us."[3] Cudworth insists that the second way of considering body forces us to recognize those 'phancies' and ideas as modes of cogitation, and cogitation requires an incorporeal substance (p. 29).

Cogitation too must be explained. That "*Life* and *Understanding* are not Essential to Matter as such," and that "they can never possibly rise out of any *Mixture* or *Modification* of *Dead* and *Stupid Matter*" were truths that Cudworth asserts over and over. He does not believe that "the *Democritick* and *Epicurean*" went so far as to identify thought with matter. They were neither so 'Sottish' nor so 'Imprudent' as a

"Modern Writer hath done, to maintain, that *Cogitation*, *Intellection*, and *Volition*, are themselves really Nothing else, but *Local Motion* or *Mechanism*, in the inward *Parts* of the *Brain* and Heart" (p. 761). The reference is clearly to Hobbes. Cudworth argues repeatedly that such a reduction extends to men what Descartes claimed for animals: it makes men "Really Nothing else, but *Machines*, and *Automata*" (p. 761; cf. pp. 50, 844, 846, 850).[4]

The reductionist thesis is the strongest version of materialism, but Cudworth worked just as diligently to discredit the lesser thesis, that thought could be produced by matter in motion. Since "there is Nothing of Soul and Mind, and Reason and Understanding, nor indeed of Cogitation and Life, contained in the Modifications and Mechanism of Bodies," to claim that thought rises out of bodies would be to say something, some 'entity', can come from nothing. Cudworth's response here is colored by his acceptance of the principle that properties require substances. If cogitation were produced by matter—a substance without anything of thought in its nature—that cogitation would have to come with a substance, an incorporeal substance. Such a substance would be the 'real entity' created by corporeal substance.

One possible way to avoid violating the *ex nihilo nihil fit* principle would be to say that "Senseless Matter may as well become Sensitive, and as it were [be] kindled into Life and Cogitation" (p. 46). After all, light and heat are generated in bodies which before were devoid of such qualities. To this attempt, Cudworth replies that light and heat in bodies are never more than the agitation of insensible particles. Unless we want to say thought is no more than an appearance, a fancy, for sentient creatures (as perceived light and heat are), the difference between particles in motion and perceived light will not help the corporealist sustain the thesis that senseless matter can become sensitive.

Still another possibility is to say that matter as such has "an Antecedent Life and Understanding" in it—that part of its nature is sensitive. A *reductio* (one often repeated by later writers) faces the Stratonical corporealist over this thesis: if matter did have as part of its nature life and understanding, "then every Atom of Matter must needs be a Distinct Percipient, Animal, and Intelligent Person by it self" (p. 72). The consequence would be that "every Man would be . . . a Heap of Innumerable Animals and Percipients." Besides this absurdity, this Hylozoick alternative adulterates the very "*Notion of Matter*," giving it properties of two different kinds of substance. Life and understanding are neither essential to matter, part of its nature, nor can they rise out of any mixture or organization of matter. (See also pp. 848, 850, 871.)

(c) Self-Activity and Intentional Causality

In rejecting these attempts to link thought with matter, Cudworth believed he was undermining the grounds for atheism. On the positive side, he argued for an intelligible world, the true intellectual system, to which man belongs. As a grounding for this intellectual world, he advocates something like the Hylozoist's life: what he called a 'Plastick Nature'. He rejected the Hylozoist's life because that life was blind, directionless. All of the corporealists rejected final causes, claiming that "every thing comes to pass *Fortuitously*, and happens to be as it is, without the Guidance and Direction of any *Mind* or *Understanding*." The corporealists "banish all *Mental*, and consequently *Divine Causality*, quite out of the World" (p. 147). Order and organization cannot, Cudworth insists, come about through chance, or by mechanical causation. "Mind and Understanding is the only true Cause of Orderly Regularity, and he that asserts a *Plastick Nature*, asserts *Mental Causality* in the World" (pp. 154-55). Fortuitous mechanism versus final or intending causality: that is the central debate Cudworth has with all materialists. His concept of a plastic nature embodies the sense of plan, intention, and order that is present in the world. It is a force and a presence. Since God does not act immediately in the world (certainly not all the time), His plan and His intention are monitored and guided by that force (pp. 149-50). This force, which Cudworth sometimes seems almost to personify, "doth not comprehend the *Reason* of its own *Action*" (p. 158). He contrasts the actions of the plastic nature with expressly conscious action. The metaphysical categories for Cudworth are two: "*Resisting* or *Antitypous Extension*, and *Life*, (i.e. Internal *Energy* and *Self-activity*;)" (p. 159). The category of Life divides into two again: that which "either acts with express Consciousness and *Synaesthesis*, or such as is without it." It is the latter that is his 'plastick nature', a phrase that designates "all *Action* distinct from *Local Motion*." It is the energy of nature. It is cogitative but unconscious. This force is responsible for the action of matter, it is what begins action. 'Vital Autokinesie' is the phrase Cudworth uses in characterizing this internal energy (pp. 159, 844-45). Ultimately it is God from whom such self-initiation derives, but all cognitive beings have the ability to initiate actions. It is this internal energy, present in nature and in man, which catches an important difference between the causality of human action and the causality of body:

The *Action* of an *Extended Thing* as such, is nothing but *Local Motion*, Change of Distance, or Translation from Place to Place, a meer Outside and Superficial thing; but it is certain, that *Cogitation*, (*Phancy*, *Intellection*, and *Volition*) are no

Local Motions; nor the meer *Fridging* up and down, of the Parts of an Extended Substance, changing their *Place* and *Distance*; but it is Unquestionably, an *Internal Energie*; that is, such an *Energie* as is *Within* the very *Substance* or Essence, of that which *Thinketh*; or in the Inside of it. (p. 831)

By virtue of such internal energy, man is able to act on extended body, can even penetrate it and coexist in the same place as that body.

(d) Space and Extension

The sense in which a thinking substance can coexist in a place with an extended substance was an important issue for understanding both the mind's relation to the body as well as God's presence to all things. Body can exist only in space, point for point; but mind, which is indivisible, "can at once both comprehend a Whole *Extensum* within it, and be All of it in every Part thereof" (p. 832). This principle—later to be mocked by Hume—was often used by the immaterialists in the eighteenth century. Just as the human soul is in every part of the body, so God is in the whole universe and in every part, but neither the soul nor God exists in a place in the way body does. God is everywhere but nowhere. Many writers who accepted the existence of incorporeal substance still felt that that substance had some kind of extension, although not bodily extension.

Those who argued for space without body also often said that space was also extended. As mind was said to be able to penetrate body, so space devoid of body was said to be penetrable and intangible (p. 769). Some of the atheists attacked by Cudworth resisted making space something separate from body, saying that it was "only *Singular* Body" (p. 700). This debate too recurs in the eighteenth century: is space something real or only an abstracted idea? The interpretation of God's omnipresence and God's relation to space was closely tied to this debate. Sometimes God is said to be present to all things by knowing them: omniscience is omnipresence.

A somewhat similar question arose over how finite mind can know body. Cudworth warns against mistaking our fancies for the things themselves, seemingly denying a direct knowledge of body (p. 768). On the other hand, he is very clear about not confusing direct local (i.e., physical) contact with cognition of body. The soul, he says,

Conceives *Extended* things themselves, *Unextendedly* and *Indivisibly*; for as the *Distance* of a whole *Hemisphere* is contracted into a narrow Compass in the Pupil of the Eye, so are all Distances contracted in the Soul it self, and there Understood *Indistantly*; For the *Thought* of a Mile *Distance*, or of Ten thousand Miles, or Semidiameters of the Earth, takes up no more *Room* in the Soul, nor Stretches it any more, than does the Thought of a *Foot* or *Inch*, or indeed of a *Mathematical Point*. (p. 827)

Not only is thought inappropriate for matter as a property; the properties of matter—size, shape, location—do not apply to thought (p. 828).

Cudworth's concern in these various issues was not only to protect the metaphysics of theism: there was a strong moral motive behind his exhaustive attack on the various forms of corporealism. He charged some of the corporealists with intentionally pursuing their philosophy in order to take *"away all* Guilt *and* Blame, Punishment *and* Rewards," thereby *"rendering a* Day of Judgment, *Ridiculous" (Preface to the Reader).* Eighteenth-century defenders of orthodoxy made this same charge against those whom they saw as 'deists', a term used by some writers as a thinly disguised accusation of 'atheist'. Any suggestion that man is not composed of two substances, that thought might be a property of a highly organized bit of matter such as the brain, or that the complex physiology of our bodies could account for human actions, was attacked, often for the reasons Cudworth gives in his Preface.

In some cases, those later attacks on materialist doctrines confronted the issue of thinking matter, asserting boldly, as Richard Bentley did in his second Boyle lecture: *Matter and Motion Cannot Think* (1692). Bentley's subtitle identifies the concern: "A Confutation of Atheism from the Faculties of the Soul." In other instances, the issues identified by Cudworth are placed in the wider context of *A Demonstration of the Being and Attributes of God* (1705), Samuel Clarke's highly popular Boyle lectures. Clarke announces on his title page that he sees Hobbes and Spinoza as the enemies. Anthony Collins also became a threatening person to Clarke; the exchange between Clarke and Collins drew much attention in the early years of the century. Clarke's lectures had reached a fourth edition by 1716, and it was frequently cited and defended. Another extended commentary on the running battle between materialist and immaterialist is found in Edmund Law's notes to his translation of a popular and respected work, William King's *De Origine Mali* (1702). Law's notes take up much space throughout his 1731 translation of King; in them Law discusses most of the issues in the debate, the same issues high-lighted by Cudworth earlier. Collins was attacked by Law, as was Pierre Bayle, and many other lesser-known figures appear in Law's notes. Another translated work, this time of Cumberland's *De Legibus Naturae* (1672), contains a long appendix paraphrasing and summarizing the Clarke-Collins exchange (*A Treatise of the Laws of Nature*, 1727, translated by John Maxwell). Still later in the century, many of the issues over space and extension, the nature of matter, thought as a property of the brain, and active principles, figure in Hume's dramatic *Dialogues concerning Natural Religion* (1779).

These are just some of the more prominent sources for the debate in the eighteenth century over what was viewed as a growing materialism. The term 'Free-thinker' was associated with this materialism, a term given prominence by Collins's *Discourse on Free-thinking* (1713). This work was heavily attacked by Bentley in his *Remarks Upon a Late Discourse of Free-Thinking* (1713), and also by Berkeley in the pages of *The Guardian*.[5] Three other journals played an important role in the growing controversy. Later in the century, *The London Review* and *The Monthly Review* carried reviews, citations from, and comments on (including letters to the editor) many of the books in this controversy. *The London Review* particularly gave extensive attention to Priestley's writings on mind and matter, and to his edition of Hartley.

One of the more important journal coverages of this long debate was Jean LeClerc's *Bibliothèque Choisie*. Published in Holland in duodecimo, written in French, LeClerc's journal kept his continental readers well informed of British publications. It was also read in England. From 1703 to 1713, LeClerc ran review after review of all of the central books. He took as his basic text Cudworth's *True Intellectual System*. Beginning in volume I for 1703, he reviewed that work, then presented in six subsequent issues, through 1706, long translations of sections and chapters from it. In all, ten articles were devoted to presenting Cudworth. These articles consumed 653 pages of his journal. For a work published in 1678, LeClerc's attention to it in the early years of the eighteenth century gives some indication of the importance of and the interest in the issues and doctrines Cudworth dealt with.[6] LeClerc's occasional "Remarques de l'Auteur de la B.C." are all on the side of orthodoxy.

In addition to this coverage of Cudworth through reviews and translations, there is a long two-part review-extract of Nehemiah Grew's *Cosmologia Sacra* (1701), in the very first volume of the *Bibliothèque Choisie*. A third part of this review is found in volume III. Grew's work is of interest to LeClerc in part because of Grew's notion of a *vital principle* in bodies. In volume V LeClerc devotes an article to comparing Cudworth's plastic nature and Grew's vital principle, in response to some critical comments by Bayle on both writers. In volume IX LeClerc replies to more comments on Cudworth by Bayle.[7]

LeClerc's attention to this controversy over the nature of matter and thought was not limited to Cudworth and Grew. In volume III he remarks on Bayle's objections to Locke's account of substance, particularly as they relate to thinking matter. LeClerc defends Locke against what he takes to be Bayle's misreadings. He reviews Clarke's Boyle lectures (in volume XXVI, 1713) as well, and the exchange Clarke had with Collins. The same issue also contains a review of several other books stemming from the Clarke-Collins exchange. Another important contribution to the defense of immaterialism reviewed is Humphrey Ditton's *A Discourse Concerning the Resurrection of Jesus Christ* (1711), with special attention given to its appendix on matter and thought.

With this indication of the kind of attention accorded some early eighteenth-century books in the defense of orthodox metaphysical views, with an understanding of the prominence given Cudworth's early study, and with hints of Locke's role in the eighteenth-century developments, we are now ready to examine in detail some of the many pamphlets written to defend or attack the materialist claims. The themes, the arguments and counter-arguments, even much of the vocabulary were established by Cudworth. These were given a more succinct statement by Locke, in the context of a system of thought which straddled orthodoxy and change. We shall start with Locke's suggestion that God could superadd to matter the power of thought. We shall follow the reactions to this suggestion by some of Locke's immediate contemporaries. We shall listen to fears of the automatism that would ensue if some of the new views about substance and about man were accepted. We shall follow Hume's rather satirical portrayal of the immaterialist-materialist debate. We shall also discover that interwoven with much of this controversy were certain scientific views about the nature of matter. If matter should turn out not to be the inert, passive, sluggish stuff described by Cudworth—if its nature should prove to be closer to force than passive particles—then the possibilities for materialism change drastically, as they did in the hands of Priestley. Closely related to these topics is an interest in the nature and possibility of human action: do I move my arm? If so, how is that possible, given the detailed workings of my physiology? In this context we shall examine some of the very many works, both medical and religious, that describe the mechanism of the body.

Notes

1. Pierre Bayle read Locke this way; see his *Réponse aux questions d'un provincial*.

2. LeClerc, *Bibliothèque Choisie*, t. XXVI, p. 293. Even as late as 1771, in the *Encylopaedia Britannica*, the article on "Religion or Theology" places at the head of a list of twenty-two groups which the "theologian will have to combat," the "Atheist, with Spinoza at their

head." Margaret Jacob has recently observed: "By the early eighteenth century 'spinozism' denoted a multitude of intellectual heresies, yet all possessed a common thread. Spinozism brought together all philosophy, ancient and modern, that possessed a tendency to unify, divinise or animate the universe, also more generally, that offered a deterministic philosophy of man and nature" (*The Radical Enlightenment* (London: Allen & Unwin, 1981), p. 48).

3. The similarity of Cudworth's language here to that of Boyle and Locke when writing about qualities is striking.

4. Cudworth took issue with Descartes's account of animals as machines, insisting that they do have sense. "But on the contrary, if it be evident from the *Phenomena* [as Cudworth thought it was], that Brutes are not meer *Senseless Machins* or *Automata*, and only like *Clocks* or *Watches*, then ought not *Popular Opinion* and *Vulgar Prejudice* so far to prevail with us, as to hinder our Assent, to that which sound Reason and Philosophy clearly dictates, that therefore they must have something more than *Matter* in them" (p. 863).

5. A. A. Luce attributes numbers 27, 35, 39, 49, 55, 62, 70, 77, 83, 88, 89, and 126 to Berkeley. There are critical comments against free-thinkers in other issues as well: 3, 125, and 130. O'Higgins also reminds us that Jessop has suggested that the sixth Dialogue of Berkeley's *Alciphron* was written with Collins in mind. (James O'Higgins, *Anthony Collins: The Man and His Works* (The Hague: M. Nijhoff, 1970).)

6. Cudworth's book was republished in a shortened version in 1706, in a full Latin translation in 1733, and in a two-volume edition (edited by Thomas Wise) in 1743. (See Lydia Gysi, *Platonism and Cartesianism in the Philosophy of Ralph Cudworth* (Bern: H. Lang, 1962).) The Latin translation by Mosheim was reviewed in two issues of the *Bibliotheque Raisonnée* in 1734.

7. Bayle entered the debate through various notes in his *Dictionnaire*, in his *Continuation des Pensées Diverses*, and in his *Réponse aux questions d'un provincial*. In these latter two works are found discussions of Grew, Cudworth, and Locke.

Chapter I

Locke's Suggestion

In writing about the limitation of human knowledge, Locke offers as an example the following:

We have the ideas of *matter* and *thinking*, but possibly shall never be able to know whether any mere material being thinks or no: it being impossible for us, by the contemplation of our own *ideas*, without revelation, to discover whether Omnipotency has not given to some system of matter, fitly disposed, a power to perceive and think, or else joined and fixed to matter, so disposed, a thinking immaterial substance: it being, in respect of our notions, not much more remote from our comprehension to conceive that God can, if he pleases, superadd to matter a faculty of thinking, than that he should superadd to it another substance with a faculty of thinking. . . . (4.3.6)

Both alternatives are, as far as human knowledge goes, equally probable. There is, moreover, "no contradiction in it that the first eternal thinking being should, if he pleased, give to certain systems of created senseless matter, put together as he thinks fit, some degrees of sense, perception and thought." We can have no certainty of knowledge that, e.g., pleasure and pain are not "in some bodies themselves, after a certain manner modified and moved," any more than we can have certain knowledge that such perceptions are "in an immaterial substance upon the motion of the parts of body." The second alternative is beyond our ability to understand because, "as far as we can conceive," body is only able to strike or affect body by impulse and motion. How motion can produce sensations or ideas is as much beyond us as is the possibility of ideas and perceptions being properties of matter. Since we must allow that God "has annexed effects to motion, which we can no way conceive motion able to produce, what reason have we to conclude that he could not order them as well to be produced in a subject we cannot conceive capable of them, as well as in a subject we cannot conceive the motion of matter can any way operate upon?" Having indicated the noncontradictory nature of both alternatives, Locke is careful to add: "I say not this that I would any way lessen the belief of the soul's immateriality," although he is convinced that "all the great ends of morality and religion are well enough secured without philosophical proofs of the soul's immateriality." The issue of materialism had been linked with the question of the nature of the first eternal being, i.e., God. In the passage I have just cited, Locke pointed out that he had proved elsewhere in the *Essay* that "it is no less than a contradiction to suppose matter (which is evidently in its own nature void of sense and thought) should be that eternal first thinking being," that is, God. In his discussion in this later passage (4.10.10-17), Locke reveals his own view of matter as well as his opinion of those who would make men themselves to be matter thinking.

In 4.10.10, Locke says that if there must be something eternal (the claim he shared with the materialists), it is obvious that "it must necessarily be a *cogitative* being." Matter cannot produce a thinking intelligent being: this is just as impossible to conceive as that "nothing should of itself produce matter." All matter is dead and inactive. Can we then conceive how, e.g., a pebble could "add motion to itself, being purely matter, or produce any thought?" If matter is ever in motion, motion too must be eternal, if all there is is matter. If we suppose motion eternal, it is still not possible for incogitative matter and motion to produce thought, "whatever changes it might produce of figure and bulk." It is, Locke insists, as easy to "conceive matter produced by *nothing* as thought to be produced by pure matter." If we suppose matter divided into *very* minute parts, which some writers imagine as "a sort of spiritualizing, or making a thinking thing of it," those parts are still matter and can operate on each other only by impulse: "you may as rationally expect to produce sense, thought, and knowledge by putting together in a certain figure and motion gross particles of matter, as by those that are the very minutest that do anywhere exist. They knock, impel, and resist one another just as the greater do, and that is all they can do."

The argument thus far in 4.10.10 is summarized by Locke as follows:

"So that if we will suppose nothing first or eternal, *matter* can never begin to be; if we suppose bare matter without motion eternal, *motion* can never begin to be; if we suppose only matter and motion first or eternal, *thought* can never begin to be." Therefore, since there is thought, the first eternal being must be cogitative. Locke suggests that even the materialists, the men devoted to matter (perhaps he has in mind the Spinozists),[1] recognized the demonstration of an eternal knowing being, but they then ignore or forget the 'knowing' and insist that all is matter. (4.10.13) If these men of matter say there can be

eternal matter without any eternal cogitative being, they manifestly separate matter and thinking and suppose no necessary connexion of the one with the other, and so establish the necessity of an eternal spirit, but not of matter: since it has been proved already that an eternal cogitative being is unavoidably to be granted. Now if thinking and matter may be separated, *the eternal existence of matter will not follow from the eternal existence of a cogitative being*, and they suppose it to no purpose. (Ibid.)

Setting aside this internal inconsistency in the materialist claims (i.e., their separating matter from thinking), Locke goes on to raise a series of objections to such materialism (most of which were subsequently raised in the eighteenth-century disputes arising out of Locke's suggestion). (1) Do they suppose that every particle of matter thinks? Locke says they would not like the notion of "as many eternal thinking beings as there are particles of matter" (4.10.14). But this conclusion is unavoidable, Locke thinks, for "if they will not allow matter as matter, that is, every particle of matter, to be as well cogitative as extended, they will have as hard a task to make out to their own reasons a cogitative being out of incogitative particles, as an extended being out of unextended parts, if I may so speak." (2) Perhaps only one atom of matter thinks. Such a supposition "has as many absurdities as the other, for then this atom of matter must be alone eternal or not. If this alone be eternal, then this alone, by its powerful thought or will, made all the rest of matter. And so we have the creation of matter by a powerful thought, which is that the materialists stick at" (4.10.15). (3) A third possibility is that "it is *some certain system of matter*, duly put together, that is this thinking eternal being" (4.10.16). There is an important difference between bits of matter (i.e., individual corpuscles) and those same bits organized into a system of interrelated parts, as in a living plant or body, or even the organized matter of the brain. Locke thinks this is the most favored alternative among those who would make God a material being. It is also a view "suggested to them by the ordinary conceit they have of themselves and other men, which they take to be material thinking beings." But this supposition of a system of incogitative parts ascribes "all the wisdom and knowledge of that eternal being only to the juxtaposition of parts," which is absurd. "For unthinking particles of matter, however put together, can have nothing thereby added to them but a new relation of position, which it is impossible should give thought and knowledge to them." (4) Thinking, on this materialist assumption, could only be a function of the motion of the parts of the system of matter. But this makes all thought accidental, "since all the particles that by motion cause thought, being each of them in itself without any thought, cannot regulate its own motion, much less be regulated by the thought of the whole: since that thought is not the cause of motion (for then it must be antecedent to it and so without it), but the consequence of it whereby freedom, power, choice, and all rational and wise thinking or acting will be quite taken away; so that such a thinking being will be no better nor wiser than pure blind matter" (4.10.17). No particle of such a system of matter could "know its own or the motion of any other particle, or the whole know the motion of every particular, and so regulate its own thoughts or motions, or indeed have any thought resulting from such motion."

Locke is thus firmly of the opinion that thought cannot be a property of matter if all there is is matter and motion. He also clearly believes thought not to be a property of matter, but he insists that it would be possible for God—that omnipotent, eternal, cogitative being—to add to a system of matter the power of thought. This latter is not just a logical possibility; it is not self-contradictory to say God might add such a power: it is also a real possibility we should recognize, given the limitation of our knowledge of matter and mind.

It was not this suggestion alone that raised a storm of protest and discussion right through to the last years of the eighteenth century: it was, in addition, Locke's comment that immateriality was not necessary for immortality. Both to Locke's suggestion and to this added rider, Stillingfleet was not slow to rise. Stillingfleet had said that, if matter thinks, matter and thought would be confounded, and hence the essence of matter destroyed. Responding to this remark, Locke distinguished *matter* from *particular instances* of matter, i.e., animals, plants, etc. Matter is a solid, extended substance. If nothing more is added to it, it will stay just that. But to some parts of that matter, God adds motion, to other parts of matter he adds life, to others he adds sense and spontaneous motion. In none of these instances is the essence of matter destroyed (*Mr. Locke's Reply to the Bishop of Worcester's Answer to His Second Letter*, in *Works*, IV, p. 460). That is, "the properties of a rose, a peach, or an elephant, superadded to matter, change not the properties of matter; but matter is in these things matter still." Why then, Locke asks, do some men object to the notion of going "one step further, and say, God may give to matter thought, reason, and volition, as well as sense and spontaneous motion?" The seeds for later writers to say this is precisely what man is—a system of matter with sense, spontaneous motion, thought and reason—were thus present in Locke's elaboration and defense of his suggestion.

Locke invokes a general principle in this argument (a principle frequently denied by others): adding properties to matter does not destroy the essence of matter, so long as matter is still an extended solid substance (pp. 460-61). If adding properties to matter did destroy the essence of matter, then plants and animals would not be material. Plants are wholly material, yet they have properties not contained in *matter as matter*. (p. 462) Rude, senseless matter is distinguished from animals, matter with sense, motion, etc. Some parts of matter do in fact have additional properties. This distinction between matter as matter and matter modified by sense, motion, life, and other properties will bother some later critics of Locke's suggestion, but in his reply to Stillingfleet, Locke expands on the distinction by an example. God, he suggests, first creates a substance, e.g., a solid, extended substance. Now, must God give that substance any other properties besides solidity and extension? Locke thinks God could leave it at that; he could, for example, leave that substance inactive and inert. Nevertheless, such inactive, extended substance is still a substance, an existing substance, "for action is not necessary to the being of any substance, that God does create" (p. 464). Next, suppose God creates (again, *de novo*) another substance, this time an immaterial one. Again, God need not add anything more to it than the 'bare being'. However, the parallel with material substance does not hold, for while the first substance God creates in this supposition is one with two properties, solidity and extension, the immaterial substance next created does not seem to have any other properties than 'bare being', an odd sort of property. The notion of a substance with only bare being is not very clear.

M. R. Ayers[2] comments on this passage that the doctrine invoked by Locke is an ancient one: "quite generally, to whatever substance God gives a being, it is possible that," as Locke says, he should "leave it in a state of inactivity." God can, on this doctrine, "always create its essence without putting it into operation." But the example of immaterial substance used by Locke in his remarks to Stillingfleet does not seem to have an essence; its only property or attribute (if indeed this is an attribute or property) is bare being. The difficulty of conceiving of such a substance may be due to the lack of a standard account of immaterial substance. There were two available accounts of material substance, one which identified its essential property as extension, another which used the corpuscular theory. While it may startle us to hear Locke suggesting that motion is not part of the essence of matter, or at least that it is a quality which could be superadded by God to the extended parts, we can at least make sense of a material substance without motion.[3] Ayers is probably correct to see in this example the Aristotelian distinction between separable and inseparable accidents: "The latter are attributes which all members of the species possess throughout their existence but which, unlike properties, do not flow from the essence."[4] Locke is saying to the Bishop that thought could be, or perhaps even is, a separable accident, attachable by God to either material or to immaterial substance. What are the inseparable accidents of immaterial substance? There seems to be no answer in Locke's remarks.

The distinction to which Ayers has called our attention may help explain an otherwise odd remark made by Locke in a letter to Limborch. Locke had been drawn by Limborch into constructing an argument demonstrating the unity of God. In that argument, Locke characterized God as a being infinite, eternal, and incorporeal. Limborch informed Locke that the person to whom he wanted to show Locke's argument was a Cartesian, and, he said, "it is well known that the Cartesians dislike the word 'incorporeal' as negative and affirming nothing positive; they on the other hand substituted the word 'thinking', and glory in its excluding any idea of body."[5] Limborch suggested that Locke might recast his argument, using the phrase 'incorporeal or thinking', when describing God. To this suggestion, Locke replied that

the term 'incorporeal' or 'immaterial' would not on that account [on the account of the person to whom it was to be shown being a Cartesian] have to be omitted from the definition of God since whoever wants to think rightly about God ought to remove all matter or corporeity from him. 'Thought' certainly does not do this, whatever the men devoted to Descartes' opinions suppose to the contrary.[6]

If thought does not remove all corporeity from God (or from whatever substance to which it belongs or is added), the reason must be that thought is a separable accident or attribute (separable from substances other than God) and that incorporeity is characterized by other accidents or properties. What those separable accidents might be, Locke does not say and, I suppose, would not claim to know.

Nevertheless, his inability to say what an immaterial substance is, or even to use a ready-to-hand hypothesis about its nature, renders his response to Stillingfleet on this point somewhat obscure.[7] What he wants to say about that immaterial substance is clear in one point: whatever its nature, God need not make it active. Neither of the two substances created by God thinks, neither has the power of self-motion. Why, then, cannot God give thought or self-motion to either substance? To deny that God can do so is to deny God's omnipotency (p. 465). He cannot "make a substance to be solid and not solid at the same time," but "that a substance may not have qualities, perfections, and powers, which have no natural or visibly necessary connexion with solidity and extension, is too much for us . . . to be positive in." What we can say is that thinking is not "within the natural powers of matter" (p. 468).

This distinction between the natural power of a substance and other attributes that can be joined or added to that substance is, as Ayers says, a version of the separable-inseparable accident distinction. The language of *natural* powers was frequently used by writers in the eighteenth century. John Norris says (*A Philosophical Discourse concerning the Natural Immortality of the Soul*, 1708) that the soul can be immortal but not naturally so. A natural property, Norris tells us, flows from that of which it is a property. If it belongs to that thing because of some external will or power, the property is *positive* (p. 5). 'Nature' is the same for Norris as 'essence.' He argues that the soul is immortal positively, not naturally.[8] Peter Browne (in *The Procedure, Extent and Limits of Human Understanding*, 1728) uses the terminology of natural properties to draw the conclusion that, "if Thinking were *Natural* to Matter, then every *Particle* and every *System* of it would think," a conclusion Clarke pressed earlier (p. 166). Locke is making a suggestion similar to that of Norris, but about material and immaterial substances: neither has thought or self-motion naturally, but either could be made so by an act of God. Thought would then be not a natural but a positive property of whichever substance God added that property to. Locke is not saying this is in fact the way creation occurred; he is not saying the soul is not naturally a thinking substance. He simply thinks we do not know enough about the soul to say whether thought is a natural or a positive property of either kind of substance. He repeatedly tells Stillingfleet that he would be pleased to have a proof that the soul is immaterial, but he does not find any such proof, either in Stillingfleet's writings or elsewhere.

In a sermon preached in 1692, Richard Bentley (*Matter and Motion Cannot Think*) seems to make the soul's life and motion a positive attribute: they are "wholly owing to the Power of God" (p. 12).

Bentley does not mention Locke, although his arguments and ex-amples repeat some of those found in Locke's discussion. He writes against the Epicureans, who make the universe and man the result of a concourse of atoms, and against the Aristotelians, who make the world eternal. He thinks it self-evident that there is something in our composition "that thinks and apprehends, and reflects and deliberates, determines and doubts, consents and desires" (p. 13). The soul also "receives various sensations and impressions from external objects and produces voluntary motions of several parts of our Bodies." These faculties of sensation and perception are not inherent in matter as such. If they were, "Every Stock and Stone would be a percipient and rational Creature" (p. 14). Moreover, "every single Atom of our Bodies would be a distinct Animal, endued with self consciousness and personal Sensation of its own" (p. 15). If any bit of matter thinks, every bit must: an argument that is repeated many times throughout the eighteenth century.

Thus, since the notion of perceiving atoms is absurd (morcover, out of such a group of perceiving atoms, we could not get a single mind), the only way matter could have sensation would be if that sensation were the result of some modification of matter, of some "organical Disposition." This notion that thought is a property of a system of matter suitably organized is, Bentley says, the opinion of "every Atheist and counterfeit Deist of these times." Bentley argues that "no particular Species of Matter, as the Brain and Animal Spirits, hath any Power of Sense and Perception" (p. 16). No motion super-added to matter can produce sense or perception, hence no specific motion of animal spirits in muscles and nerves can do so either. The atheists (i.e., the materialists) speak of our bodies as rational machines. But not even God's omnipotence can create cogitative body. This is so because of the incapacity of the subject, the body, not because of the power of God. Bentley invokes the current notion of secondary qualities as relative to perceivers, in support of his denial of such qualities to body. "No sensible Qualities as Light, and Colour, and Heat, and Sound, can be subsistent in the Bodies themselves abso-lutely considered, without a relation to our Eyes, and Ears, or other Organs of Sense" (p. 18). These qualities are only "Ideas and Vital Passions in us that see and feel"; they are not inherent in our bones, blood, or brain; they are passions of some other kind of substance, i.e., of an immaterial substance.

The same arguments appear in Bayle's *Dictionnaire* under his article on Dicearchus. Dicearchus had attacked the notion of the immortal-ity of the mind. In remark C, Bayle says this view is not worthy of a philosopher. Dicearchus held that the mind is not distinct from the body and that it is a 'vertue' or property equally distributed among all living things. If mind is not distinct from body, it is, Bayle points out, essential to body. From this, it follows that the property of sensing does not cease with the death of the body: every part of the body carries its own life and mind. Moreover, Bayle believes this line of thought leads to the ascription of feeling to all bodies and all parts of bodies. What must be established is either that "the substance which thinks is distinct from body, or that all bodies are substances which think."

Bayle suggests someone might object that 'feeling' can be a modification of body, not an essential property. Thus body could, without losing any essential property, cease to feel or sense when it was no longer living or enclosed in a "living machine." To this objection, Bayle replies that this is absurd, for all the modifications that we know of are such that, when one ceases, another *of the same kind* takes its place, a figure can be changed only by another figure, one color by another, etc. Thus, if the animal spirits (those active agents in the physiology of the eighteenth century), when outside a nervous system, do not have the feelings they have when in such a system, they could lose those feelings only by acquiring other feelings. Nor can motion bring about changes other than changes of motion. Thus his general conclusion about sensation or feeling: "any body which once feels, always feels."

In Remark L of the same article, Bayle considers an objection someone made to Remark C.[9] The objector suggested that Dicearchus says that living differ from nonliving bodies only in that their parts are figured and arranged in a certain way. The objector compared this with Descartes's view of animals as machines: if a dog differs from a stone, it is not that the dog has a body and a mind, while the stone is only a body; it is rather that the parts of the dog are arranged to form a machine, while those of the stone do not make a machine. Bayle objects that such a view would reduce man to the condition of a machine. The human mind would not be distinct from the body, "but it is only a construction, a mechanical disposition of several parts of matter." But these parts of the body, the atoms, do not by themselves (on this supposition) think or feel. Thus it is still inconceivable for Bayle that when organized in a system of matter they could think or feel: the arrangement of atoms or of bones and nerves cannot make a substance, that had never thought, begin to think. This view of the living machine reduces the arrangements of the bodily organs to diversely modified movements, as in a clock. If the wheels of a clock did not have an impenetrable extension before being assembled, they could not work the clock after assemblage. In the same way the organs of the body could not produce thought, "if each organ before being put in place did not actually have the gift of thought." Thought cannot be made out of movement, which is all the properties the parts of the body are capable of. Thought is distinct and different from all figure and change of situation. It is absurd to think that by putting together some veins, arteries, etc., as one puts together the pieces of a machine, one would be able to produce feelings, or sensations of color, odors, sounds, love, hate.[10]

In Britain the reactions to Locke's suggestion added little to the points contained in Bayle's Remarks, but those reactions were extensive throughout the century. Sometimes Locke was misinterpreted as favoring the view that matter does think. One of the more famous misreadings of Locke on this point was that of Samuel Clarke. In his first reply to Leibniz (*A Collection of Papers, Which Passed between the Late Learned Mr. Leibnitz, and Dr. Clarke*, 1717), Clarke wrote: "That Mr. *Locke doubted* whether the *Soul* was *immaterial* or no, may justly be suspected from some Parts of his Writings. But herein he has been followed only by some *Materialists*, Enemies to the *Mathematical Principles of Philosophy*; and who approve little or nothing in Mr. *Locke*'s Writings, but his errors" (pp. 10-11). Earlier Henry Lee (*Anti-Scepticism*, 1702) says that the 4.3.6 passage in Locke's *Essay* "insinuates . . . that 'tis as probable that our Souls are Matter, indued with the Faculty of Thinking, as Immaterial Substance*" (Preface). Later in this same work, Lee says that Locke might as well have said "that the Soul of Man may be only thinking Matter, or Matter organized as our Bodies are" (p. 246). On this philosophy, Lee says, "Man may be only a Species of Machines." Other writers found Locke's suggestion stretched the bounds of conceivability beyond the powers of God. John Broughton (*Psychologia: Or, An Account of the Nature of the Rational Soul*, 1703)[11] had no trouble conceiving that God could suspend the laws of gravity (iron might swim), but he could not conceive that matter could think (pp. 26-27). What cannot be conceived, he asserted, is a contradiction. God cannot do what is contradictory. Broughton wrote in defense of the immateriality of the soul, mainly against William Coward.[12] He insisted that there is no connection between thought and extension; you cannot infer the one from the other. His objection was that *matter* cannot think, but he allows that God could change (i.e., replace) every particle of matter into a thinking, immaterial being (p. 59).

One reaction found frequently throughout the century is that God would not give "the Faculty of one Being, to any other Being to whom that Faculty does not naturally belong" (B. Hampton, *The Existence of the Human Soul after Death*, 1711). Hampton found Locke's suggestion monstrous. Will any man, he appealed, "that is not a Coxcomb, say that a single Atom thinks? And then if our atom can't think, it is certain that a Composition of them can't think; for Thought is the Operation of an entire indivisible being, and not of a Compound of things" (pp. 27-28). There is no principle of spontaniety in matter, either for self-movement or for thought (p. 33). He agreed with Locke that we do not know what the pure naked substance of matter or spirit is, but we know well the accidents of both. Where the accidents are so different, as thought and extension are, the substances must also differ (pp. 34-35). "The degrees of Matter don't alter the kind, Matter is Matter still, tho' of a finer Mould; and if Matter can't think, it is impossible by all the Chemistry of Nature, to extract thinking and reasoning Spirit out of it" (pp. 35-36). As Bentley had said, if any composition of matter thinks, all parts of it must think.

Robert Jenkin (*The Reasonableness and Certainty of the Christian Religion*, 1708) had used Bentley's argument in saying that if it was part of the essence of matter to think, all matter would think: there would be no reason why the brain rather than a trenchard should think (p. xxv). The same dictum is repeated by Isaac Watts (*Philosophical Essays*, 1733): "If Extension has the Property of thinking, every Part of Extension must either have that Property in itself, or must do something towards it in the whole" (p. 18 n.). This notion that parts contribute to give the whole new properties was just what Collins seized upon in his debate with Clarke, to argue in favor of thinking matter.[13] Watts missed this point, citing Clarke and Bentley among others as having proved that matter cannot think. The several essays in Watts's collection (on space, substance, perception, and ideas, the powers of spirit to move bodies) show a heavy indebtedness to Malebranche, especially to the occasionalist denial of any real interaction between mind and body, or any efficacy of second causes. God's presence and intervention in the workings of nature Watts offers as the explanation for the phenomena we observe.

Another follower of Malebranche, P. Barnabite Gerdil, wrote the most sustained discussion of and attack on Locke's suggestion. (*L'Immaterialité de l'Ame, Demonstrée contre M. Locke*, 1747)[14] Gerdil's book is important for British thought, not only because of his discussion of Locke: he has extensive comments on Newton and Newton's followers. It was these latter who, in making gravity an intrinsic property of matter (which Newton himself did not do, as Gerdil carefully remarks), moved in the same direction as Locke's suggestion. For if active properties such as attraction and thought are or even could be properties of matter, the source of activity in nature need not be traced to God and to God's laws. This reaction by Gerdil to Locke and to the Newtonians marks his general Malebranchian position. Not all of his comments on Locke's suggestion carry the Malebranche stamp; most start from a firm claim about the essence of matter. Gerdil thinks that Locke's concept of matter probably contained, though in a quiet and hidden way, more than just solidity and extension. The notion of an unknowable substratum or essence makes it difficult for Locke to say matter cannot move itself or even think. It is this basic limitation of our knowledge of body that, Gerdil thinks, leads Locke to entertain his suggestion. For Gerdil, were God able to add to matter the power of thought, this would be to give to the solid parts of matter a certain size, figure, movement and relation such that from these, thought could result (p. 30). To believe this possible would be to obtain thought from the juxtaposition of particles. Thought would be a real perfection added to matter, and this is not possible. In order for God to add the power of thought to matter, he would have to add some degree of being and reality to matter. A *purely* material being cannot think, a point he believes even Locke admits (p. 125). To add this power or perfection to matter would be really to create another substance (p. 126).[15]

Throughout, Gerdil appeals to one standard argument: faculties are not substances, they are modes of being of a substance. They result from the essence of the substance. Any faculty which does not result from (and which cannot be deduced from) the essence of a thing, cannot be a faculty of that thing. Since Locke himself admits that thought does not result from the essence of matter, it follows that Locke's suggestion is impossible. This argument is in the background of Gerdil's discussion of Locke's exchange with Stillingfleet on this question of thinking matter. When Locke tries his example of God creating a substance and then adding properties to it—e.g., movement—Gerdil remarks that movement "is perfectly deducible from extension, which is the essence of matter" (p. 147). Divisibility is "a consequence of extension," and mobility is a consequence of divisibility. When Locke goes on to say that God then adds vegetation and life to the substance, Gerdil replies that these qualities depend only on a certain arrangement of the parts of matter. Thus they do not require anything beyond the essence of matter (p. 148). When Locke continues with his suggestion that perhaps God created two substances, one material, the other immaterial, and then decided which of these substances to give the power of thought to, Gerdil seizes upon the notion of 'power'. If this power is something distinct from the substance, then it becomes a substantial form, which Locke would not accept. If it is a quality, then we are back to Gerdil's main argument: God is not able to give to a substance any quality which does not depend upon and is not deducible from the essence of that substance (pp. 159-60).

The criticisms and objections to Locke's suggestion did not change as the discussions developed in the eighteenth century. References to the continuing debate were well summarized and documented in Philip Doddridge's *A Course of Lectures on the Principal Subjects in Pneumatology, Ethics, and Divinity* (1763) (pp. 204-06). Doddridge cites Watts's essays for putting the case against Locke. A much better source to cite, one of the more articulate objections to Locke's suggestion, was Malcolm Flemyng's *A New Critical Examination of an Important Passage in Mr. Locke's Essay* (1751). Flemyng recognizes that Locke said God is immaterial and that matter is not in its own nature (i.e., naturally) capable of thought, nor even able to put itself in motion (p. 9); but free-thinkers have made ill use of Locke's suggestion that God could add to matter a foreign property, i.e., thought. Flemyng thinks that, even on Locke's own principles, there is a contradiction in his suggestion, for if thought is added to matter, it would cease to be matter (p. 11). "The Nature of everything stands possessed, if not actually, yet potentially, of every Property that is deducible from the essential Attributes of that thing, and every other Property is not only foreign to, but incompatible with it" (p. 12). If God tries to superadd to matter a property incompatible with its nature, matter could not receive that property; if it could, it would be "both what it is, and what it is not, at the same time." In reference to Locke's attempt to separate matter as such from particular instances of matter, Flemyng calls 'matter as such' a being of reason. It is impossible "for any Parcel of Matter to exist, without other Properties. . . . Whatever exists really is a concrete Individual, and is possessed of all the Attributes that concur to constitute it the very thing it is" (p. 14). The notion of the essence of matter as such is an 'abstracted idea'. The claim that a rose or a peach could have added to its matter properties that are above the essence of matter is a contradiction: it would be to make the peach both "more than Matter, and no more than Matter, at one and the same time" (p. 18). When Locke, in that reply to Stillingfleet, goes on to imagine God adding to some parts of matter the properties of sense and spontaneous motion, Flemyng remarks that it may look as if Locke's talk of adding extra properties to body will leave the essence of body untouched. But Flemyng insists that "The

Question is not, whether Matter in Man, or Man's Body, be truly Matter, or not; but whether the whole living, thinking, rational Man be only a Parcel of organised and agitated Matter, and therefore framed only of one Kind of Substance" (p. 21).

Flemyng then switches to a different line of argument. He now supposes some system of matter to which God intends to superadd thought, according to Locke's supposition in his reply to Stillingfleet. Flemyng's argument now makes an odd assumption, namely that God's *intention* to add thought to matter is sufficient for that property to be added. God need not do anything more. If God does *act*, Flemyng assumes that it will only be to create a new substance. Thus, Flemyng reasons, either thought must follow upon God's intention, without any new act of volition or power, or God needs a new act. If the first (no new act is required), then Locke contradicts himself. If the latter, Locke seems to establish a distinction where there is none (pp. 25-26). The first alternative would mean that matter and motion would produce thought, since no new act of God has intervened. "The Structure and Mechanism of the Machine, in this case, may be as properly said to produce Thought, as a Clock or a Watch rightly framed, and wound up, may be said to point out the Hours, or one Billiard Ball to produce Motion in another" (p. 27). If the second alternative is the case (a new act of God is required), then "a new cogitative Substance" is created "and joined to the corporeal Machine, and not barely Thought superadded to matter as a Property or a Mode" (p. 28).

In his *Letters concerning the English Nation* (1733), Voltaire indicates the strength of the reaction to Locke's suggestion, but he remarks that the opponents of Locke need only ask one question: "is the suggestion a contradiction?" Voltaire recognized that Locke's point is simply that we do not know how matter operates, so it *might* be made to think. But Voltaire's comparison of the soul to a clock would not have allayed the fears of many. The soul, he says, is "a Clock which is given us to regulate, but the Artist has not told us what Materials the Spring of this Clock is compos'd" (p. 79). Locke's suggestion echoed down the years of the eighteenth century, attacked here, cited there, reinforced and expanded towards the end of the century when Priestley seized upon the Boscovician concept of matter as power and force. Before Priestley's new materialism came on the scene, a number of writers struggled to articulate the notion that to a suitably organized system of matter, thought might indeed be a property. But how to conceive of this without turning man into a machine?

Notes

1. There were other earlier writers who advanced similar views. See Bayle's article on Spinoza in his *Dictionnaire*. In his *Letter to the Right Reverend Edward Lord Bishop of Worcester* (Stillingfleet), Locke cited Cicero, Vergil, and even passages from the Scriptures to show that other respected authorities distinguished subtle matter from gross matter, identifying the former with the soul (*Works*, 1823, volume IV, pp. 33-34).

2. "Mechanism, Superaddition, and the Proof of God's Existence in Locke's *Essay*," in *The Philosophical Review* XC, 1981, p. 230.

3. Writing about Boyle, Margaret Jacob makes a similar point. "Although motion appears to be a property of matter, in fact matter in its natural state is inert, only the laws of force give it movement, and force in the universe derives from spiritual agencies and ultimately from the will of God" (*The Radical Enlightenment*, p. 71).

4. M. R. Ayers, "Mechanism," p. 228.

5. Letter to Locke, 22 March/1 April 1698, *Correspondence*, Letter 2410, vol. 6, p. 354.

6. Locke to Limborch, 4 April 1698, Letter 2413, ibid., p. 365.

7. Robert South wrote Locke that "you presse and drive him [Stillingfleet] to the Wall in a more than ordinary manner, where you Argue about the Capacity of matter's having a faculty of Thinking added to it." South said Locke's *Reply* was "One of the Exactest books you have wrote: and may well stand Second to the Essay itself" (South to Locke, 18 June 1699, ibid., Letter 2597, p. 644).

8. Norris adds a further distinction: once the soul is created, its immortality follows from its nature, its immortality is then *consequentially* natural.

9. Vartanian suggests that this objection was "a figment of Bayle's prudence" (*Diderot and Descartes: A Study of Scientific Naturalism in the Enlightenment*. Princeton: Princeton University Press, 1953, p. 226). Sorting Bayle's own views from the various arguments presented in his comments is not necessary for my purposes. What is important is to see the objections, real or fancied, put to the question of thinking matter.

10. Bayle, in Remark M of this same article, refers to the Locke-Stillingfleet debates on this topic. Even though he calls Locke "one of the most profound metaphysicians of the world," he clearly disagrees with Locke: immateriality is necessary for immortality. Bayle describes Stillingfleet as "one of the most knowing men in Europe."

11. The term 'rational soul' was meant of course to single out man's soul. Some of the discussion of whether animals had souls use the term 'sensitive soul'. The issue over animal or man machine involved the question of a *rational* soul.

12. See for example, Coward's *The Grand Essay* (1704).

13. See below, pp. 39-41.

14. Gerdil was also the author of a detailed discussion of Locke's attack on Malebranche. See his *Defense du Sentiment du P. Malebranche sur la Nature, et l'Origine des Idées contre l'Examen de M. Locke*, 1748.

15. Jenkin made the same point: if God could make matter think, this would be because he changed the nature of matter (*The Reasonableness and Certainty*).

Chapter II

The Automatical Man

In his *Traité de l'homme*, Descartes describes some of the mechanical statues he undoubtedly saw in the caves and grottoes in the "gardens of our Kings," apparently at Fontainebleau or at Saint-Germain-en-Laye. These were hydraulic automata that moved, spoke, even played musical instruments. He describes how, upon entering one of these caves, you would unknowlingly trigger a mechanism by stepping on a set of tiles. If, for example, you tried to approach a bathing Diana, she would run and hide in the roses. If you sought her behind the roses, Neptune would ward you off with his trident, or a sea monster would spit water in your face.[1] Jaynes suggests that Descartes's youthful visits to these caves were the original inspiration for the notion of animals as machines.[2] Leonora Cohen Rosenfield has called attention to Descartes's fascination as a young man with mechanistic systems. He even proposed "the invention of a man-machine to be actuated by magnets."[3] Professor Rosenfield also cites Father Poisson, who tells us that Descartes "planned the construction of two machines simulating beasts, one a flying pigeon and the other a pheasant hunted by a spaniel."[4] Automatical beasts, planned or fancied, have a long history; they were in vogue in France during Descartes's time. In his edition of *Traité de l'homme*, Florentias Schuyl mentions some of the classical contrivances: "the flying pigeon made by Architas of Tarento; the wooden eagle of Regiomantanus; . . . the wooden statue of Venus of Dedalus, that was supposed to have become animated when quicksilver was infused into the veins."[5]

Descartes takes such contrivances as the model for the human body. He also cites clocks, artificial fountains, mills, and other machines made by man, machines that are self-moving once started. The supposition on which his *Traité* is constructed is that of an "earthen machine" made to look like a human body, having all the internal mechanism for making the statue walk, eat, breathe, and in general copy "whichever of our own functions can be imagined to proceed from mere matter and to depend entirely on the arrangement of our organs."[6] Descartes was not suggesting that man *is* a machine; he was only attempting to give the details of the mechanism of the body. He did of course think animals were automata. In France, 'l'homme machine' waited for La Mettrie, although Vartanian has shown how much the French *philosophes* from Diderot to La Mettrie borrowed from Descartes's detailed study of the physiology of the body, both animal and human.[7] The debate in France over the issue of the souls (if any) of animals was sometimes a stimulus, at other times a cover, for the development of a materialism of living organisms, a development that culminated in La Mettrie's bold work, *L'Homme machine* (1748).

In Britain this view never reached a full statement like that of La Mettrie; and it developed along a somewhat different path. Locke's suggestion provided a strong impetus toward materialism, but it was not the only one.[8] There are at least three discernible strands in the development of materialism in Britain: Locke's suggestion of thinking matter; Collins's insistence that organized masses of matter can have properties that none of the individual parts has; and the change in the scientific concept of matter, from passive corpuscles to active forces. Reactions to the first two of these strands frequently involved the fear that man would be viewed as a machine, as a piece of clockwork. Closely related was the debate over animals: do they reason or are they machines?

Voltaire (in his *Letters concerning the English Nation*, 1733) indicated the dilemma facing those who opposed Locke's suggestion.

Beasts have the same organs, the same Sensations, the same Perceptions as we; they have Memory, and combine certain Ideas. In case it was not in the Power of God to animate Matter, and inform it with Sensation, the Consequence would be, either that Brutes are mere Machines, or that they have a spiritual Soul. (p. 81)

Peter Browne (*The Procedure, Extent and Limits of Human Understanding*, 1728) discusses some of the problems for those who took the latter alternative of Voltaire's conclusion. Such writers were "so embarrassed in thinking how to dispose of those *Irrational Immortal* Souls after the Dissolution of their Bodies, and what sort of Immortality to contrive for them, that they imagine them all to return into the great Soul or Spirit of the World; or by a *Metempsychosis* to pass into the bodies of succeeding Animals" (p. 173). Browne thinks that if animals are granted souls, they must have the same immortality as do the souls of humans, "since we cannot with any Sence of Consistency distinguish two *Different* Kinds of Immortality for created Spirits." While Browne himself takes the first of Voltaire's alternatives—brutes are mere matter (p. 165)—he adds an important qualification: "they are a System of Matter under a *Certain Modification*, and *Contexture*, and *Motion* of its Parts, by which they are adapted and disposed to receive certain Impressions from external Objects" (p. 169). He assigns sensation or sensitive perception to brutes, such perception being a property of that system of matter. Sensation in brutes is not conscious; it is just one material substance striking another (p. 159). Instinct in animals plays the role of reason and knowledge. Impressions are made upon the imagination of brutes and then they move. These "Ideas or first Impressions in their Imagination" are "more strong, and lively and durable, than they are in Man" (p. 161). Brutes are not self-moving; they move *of* themselves, "as a *Clock* can't in any Propriety of Speech be said to move itself, tho' it moves of itself by the Force of Spring, or Weight, or Pendulum" (pp. 162-63). Just as motion and sound are properties of the mechanism that is a clock, so sensitive perception and movement are properties of the system of matter that is an animal.

Browne objects, though, to those persons who, "to avoid the Souls of Brutes being immaterial, will have them to be no other than a more refin'd and complicated sort of *Engines* or *Instruments*; and call them mere *Machines*, or *Puppets*, or *Clockwork*" (pp. 171-72). His point here is that God's artifice and contrivance is not limited to wheels, screws, and springs:

As if God could not, after an *Inconceivable* manner, work up a System of mere Matter into a Brute; and by a curious Disposition and Contexture of all its Parts, vastly out of the reach of our Comprehension, could not render it in a peculiar manner susceptible of such Motions and Impressions from external material Objects, as may be the impulsive Cause of all that variety of Actions we see in them. (p. 172)

Browne draws a distinction between the view that animals are machines and the view that they are a *system* of matter. What God creates is a complex system of matter capable of responding and moving, even of giving us the impression that, e.g., the dog recognizes its master, but in fact possessing none of the conscious, cognitive predicates. Such cognitive properties are not natural to matter, even to a *system* of matter. It was because of this fact that Browne rejected Locke's suggestion as "trifling and frivolous" (p. 165). The suggestion, he thought is without meaning, since it amounts to the question: "Whether God can *Alter* the very Nature of Matter, so as that it shall be Matter and no matter at the same time?" (p.166) Browne appreciated the distinction used by Collins—between mere matter and an organized system of matter—but he just as firmly rejected the possibility that God could add thought to the latter as to the former.

Writing in the same year as Browne, the author of *Two Dissertations concerning Sense and the Imagination*[9] allows that animals may have ideas; but he is quick to point out that he rejects the notion of some writers, that "to have an *Idea*" is "the same thing with an Act of *Understanding*" (p. 170). To deny ideas to brutes can only be done, he insists, if "we should suppose them to be mere Engines or Machines." Animals even have memory and imagination, so Mayne appears to go further than Browne. What he denies of animals is that they understand or are self-conscious. Not being conscious, brutes "cannot be *Rational* or *Intelligent*" (p. 169). Mayne cites "an established opinion among some Men," that the instinct of animals "is true genuine *Reason* and *Understanding*, and does not differ from the *Mind's Reason* in its *Kind* and *Nature*, but only in *Degree*." A dog "remembers, and hath Instincts of a very high and extraordinary Nature" (p. 201). Mayne defines instinct as "nothing else but the Power and Force of their *Imaginations*, working upon, and actuating their Souls, according to the particular Frames and Constitutions of their several Beings, as the Divine Power and Wisdom, to which nothing is impossible or difficult, hath thought fit to order and direct" (p. 172).

We are more familiar with Hume's version of this definition of instinct, where Hume applies it to animals and to men: "reason is nothing but a wonderful and unintelligible instinct in our souls, which carries us along a certain train of ideas, and endows them with particular qualities, according to their particular situations and relations" (*Treatise*, p. 179). In the *Enquiry*, Hume speaks of "instinct or mechanical power" (p. 108). He is concerned to argue that philosophical theories of thinking have been too fancy, too intellectual, making human actions much too dependent upon conscious thinking, intending, and reasoning. Experience—custom and habit, nature—often takes the place of *conscious* reason. There is inferring, conjecturing, storing of knowledge in animals and man, which is far short of consciousness.

(See *Enquiry*, pp. 105-6.) Thus the difference between man and brutes for Hume is minimized. Even the human body is said to be "a mighty complicated machine" (*Enquiry*, p. 87).[10]

Not many writers in this controversy over thinking matter, even those who accepted Locke's suggestion, so explicitly echoed Descartes's *Traité de l'homme*. It was easier to limit the machine talk to animals. Thomas Morgan, M.D. (*Philosophical Principles of Medicine*, 1725) opts firmly for this side of the dilemma:

> That the animal Body is a pure Machine, and that all its Operations and Phae-nomena, with the several changes which happen to it, are the necessary result of its Organization and Structure, is now generally known, and confirmed beyond all contradiction by the modern Observations and Improvements in Anatomy. (p. vii)

Morgan speaks of "this curious piece of Machinery" when writing of animals. He also refers to "the animal Automaton." This automaton is constructed for self-preservation and is "under a sort of mechanical necessity of regulating its own Motion." The self-regulating and self-restoring features of the animal machine are evidences of God, for in man-made machines there is no such mechanism (p. ix). This self-restoring mechanism is referred to as a "natural necessary *Conatus* or Effort in the animal Machine" (p. ix).

Humphrey Ditton (*A Discourse concerning the Resurrection of Jesus Christ*, 1712) was typical of many writers who saw the dangers for man in the view of animals as automata. Ditton insists brutes are not mere automata or machines; their actions *"plainly show Thought and Design"* (p. 517). To treat them as machines, "one may venture to account, every whit as well, for most of the ordinary Actions of Mankind, by *mere Clockwork*." To say animals are machines means they are "mere Matter, aptly set together with Springs and Wheels, and other instruments of Motion" (p. 518).

Ditton wrote with Locke, among others, in mind; for despite the correctness of Voltaire's reminder—that Locke only claimed his suggestion was not self-contradictory—it was Locke who drew out the machine analogy between the bodies of animals and men. Locke was careful to find criteria for distinguishing animals from men. While he allowed that brutes "have several *Ideas* distinct enough," yet they do not compare their ideas any "farther than some sensible Circumstances annexed to the Objects themselves" (*Essay*, 2.11.5). Nor can brutes add ideas together as men do: a brute may (as with a dog) "retain together several Combinations of simple *Ideas*, as possibly the Shape, Smell, and Voice of his Master," but brutes do not compound ideas to make complex ones (2.11.7). Abstracting, one of the more important mental operations for Locke, is "not at all in them" [brutes]. It is in fact "the having of general *Ideas* . . . which puts a perfect distinction betwixt Man and Brutes" (2.11.10). Animals do not have general ideas, they do not make use of general signs. They do, however, have some reason, but their reasoning is with particular ideas only (2.11.11).

Locke even confronted the question whether animals were "bare Machines (as some would have them)" (2.11.11). He granted that "Sound may mechanically cause a certain motion of the animal Spirits, in the Brains of those Birds [when learning tunes], whilst the Tune is actually playing; and that motion may be continued on to the Muscles of the Wings, and so the Bird mechanically be driven away by certain noises, because this may tend to the Birds Preservation" (2.10.10). But such a mechanical explanation will not work for the phenomenon of a bird hitting the notes right, getting nearer and nearer to "a Tune play'd yesterday," especially when learning a tune is unrelated to the bird's preservation. The birds must have sense and memory at least, so that they have an idea of the tune, which serves as a "Pattern for them to imitate."

Nevertheless, the body of the animal or bird is for Locke very much like a machine. In his discussion of identity and diversity, Locke distinguishes between a mass of matter and living plants or animals. Identity of the former lies only in "the Cohesion of Particles of Matter any how united," while identity of living organisms consists in "such a disposition of them [particles] as constitutes [e.g.] the parts of an Oak; and such an Organization of those parts, as is fit to receive, and distribute nourishment, so as to continue, and frame the Wood, Bark, and Leaves, *etc.* of an Oak, in which consists the vegetable Life" (2.27.4). It is the *organization* of the particles of matter which distinguishes one plant or tree from another; that organization through time *is* the individual life. We shall find that it is this notion of an organized mass of matter which becomes important for several writers in the eighteenth century who argued against the immateriality of the soul. Important in this connection, both for the eighteenth-century development of materialism and for the links with the Cartesian animal machine, is Locke's application of the concept of an organized mass of matter to animals. "The Case is not so much different in *Brutes*," Locke writes in the section after his account of sameness of life in plants and trees,

but that any one may hence see what makes an Animal, and continues it the same. Something we have like this in Machines, and may serve to illustrate it. For

Example, what is a Watch? 'Tis plain 'tis nothing but a fit Organization, or Construction of Parts, to a certain end, which, when a sufficient force is added to it, it is capable to attain. If we would suppose this Machine one continued Body, all whose organized Parts were repair'd, increas'd or diminish'd, by a constant Addition or Separation of insensible Parts, with one Common Life, we should have something very much like the Body of an Animal, with this difference. That in an Animal the fitness of the Organization, and the Motion wherein Life consists, begin together, the Motion coming from within; but in Machines the force, coming sensibly from without, is often away, when the Organ is in order, and well fitted to receive it. (2.27.5)

The animal machine Locke here describes has sense and memory and some kind of reason, but it is the organization and motion of the parts (both sensible and insensible) that constitute the life of the animal. Sense, memory, and reason are products of, even predicates of, matter and motion.

To my knowledge, few in Britain objected to Locke's strong endorsement of this Cartesian understanding of animals, but it may have influenced some to take the next step in predicating human consciousness and reason of organized matter in motion. Locke himself continued in the very next section following the above account, to apply such a view to man:

This also shews wherein the Identity of the same *Man* consists; viz. in nothing but a participation of the same continued Life, by constantly fleeting Particles of Matter, in succession vitally united to the same organized Body. He that shall place the *Identity* of Man in any thing else, but like that of other Animals in one fitly organized Body taken in any one instant, and from thence continued under one Organization of Life in several successively fleeting Particles of Matter, united to it, will find it hard, to make an *Embryo*, one of Years, mad, and sober, the same Man, by any supposition, that will not make it possible for *Seth*, *Ismael*, *Socrates*, *Pilate*, *St. Austin*, and *Caesar Borgia* to be the same Man. (2.27.6)

Locke was rejecting the same *soul* as sufficient to make the same *man*. He was searching for some way of excluding the possibility that "those Men, living in distant Ages, and of different Tempers, may have been the same Man." Locke turns to matter for the answer. There must be, he argued, something "in the Nature of Matter, why the same individual Spirit may not be united to different Bodies."

Locke thus provides a strong formulation of the animal machine concept and of its extension to man, at least to the body of man.[11] He also discounts the notion that an immaterial substance is necessary for identity of person. He still pays lip-service to the two-substance view, but it is sameness of consciousness that holds our identity. He views consciousness as intimately related to the organized matter of the body. It is this linkage of consciousness to body that is reflected in the eighteenth century. There were in Great Britain a number of writers from early in the eighteenth century who were urging a concept of man, not as mind and body, but as a single unit, the living organism. Locke is not always cited in these writings, but the influence of his concept of person and man is present in many of the tracts written in that century. The automatism and machine-like features of the body were also used. For example, Henry Layton, a prolific but not overly impressive pamphleteer, urged the automatic model for man in a number of his tracts. He was fascinated, as was the young Descartes, with mechanical contrivances, especially with those ancient ones mentioned by Schuyl in his edition of Descartes's *Traité de l'homme*. Layton was fond of drawing out the stories associated with these contrivances. He cites Architas's pigeon or dove, made at Tarento, "which would Fly high into the Air, and there make divers Doubles and Turns, and then return to the Place which she parted" (*Observations upon a Short Treatise Written by Mr. Timothy Manlove*, 1697, p. 34). In another work, *Observations upon a Treatise intituled Psychologia* (1703), Layton refers to two other mechanical contrivances, Regiomantanus's Eagle and his Fly. The Eagle was made of wood with "Wings displayed, cover'd neatly with Feathers, and Fashion'd with a Beak and Talons thereto Annexed." Springs were installed in the structure so as to make it fly. When the Emperor Charles V visited Nuremberg, this Eagle flew "from the Tower of its Station to the City Gate, and thence a Mile from the City where the Emperor was to be received." The eagle hovered over the Emperor and followed his procession for a while and then returned to his tower. Layton tells us also how the same artisan who made the eagle that had so charmed the Emperor, also made a large fly out of iron. At a state banquet, with the prior agreement of the Emperor, the artisan let the fly creep out of his sleeve at one end of a long table and then fly the length of the table past all the guests, circle the Emperor and return to the artisan and disappear in his sleeve. This again was all done with springs and screws (pp. 66-67). In both events—the flight of the Eagle, the shorter flight of the fly—Layton says that the people watching thought they were seeing a real bird and a real fly. Layton cites these as examples of how we cannot infer from appearances to the internal mechanism.

These wondrous automata were not, of course, ever constructed. They are cited by authors before Layton.[12] Layton wrote as if he thought they did in fact exist and do the things he describes. His point was that if, as apparently he thinks, people were taken in by these automata—believing them to be real, even refusing to believe they were machines—then man as made by God could equally be mechanical, though not made of wood, iron, springs and screws.[13] In his account of man, Layton agrees that there can "be no Spontaneous Local Motion nor self moving Powers, without a Spiritual Efficiency," but he does not think that that efficiency need be immaterial. He speaks of death dissolving "the Machine of the Person." He does not want to say that matter thinks, but rather that intellect springs out of the combination of body and blood, blood being the vehicle of life (*Observations upon a Treatise Intituled Psychologia*, p. 14). He rejects the notion of a human nature common to man as such, a substance. Such a notion is "only a bare Notion of the Mind" (p. 36). Extension and thought are "the Natural Properties of the Human Person," not of different substances. There is nothing in man that thinks and wills: it is the man himself that does these things (*Observations upon a Sermon Intituled, A Confutation of Atheism*, 1692). God makes use of "Matter and motion to produce Effects, that must always be wonderful in our Eyes," just as Regiomantanus's Eagle and Fly were wonderful to the people who saw them perform. (See also *Observations upon Dr. Nicholls' Book*, 1763.)

In this last mentioned tract, Layton was replying to one of his many critics. Layton assures Nicholls that he does not make matter and motion think. It is not the parts of man that are intelligent, but the whole man. By their natural powers, matter and motion are incapable of thinking. Nor can man produce thought by mixing matter together. Those automata he was so fond of citing did not think. But Layton does not see how we can say God cannot produce thought out of matter and motion. If man can make music result from pipes and other bits of matter as in an organ, where none of the parts can produce music, God surely, "by the Acting of a Material Spirit," can produce life, sensaton, thought via the finely made organs of the body (p. 6). Nicholls had said that Layton made men a curious piece of clockwork. Layton replies that man is an *intelligent* piece of clockwork.

Another, anonymous critic (his remarks are printed, along with Layton's replies, in *Arguments and Replies, In a Dispute Concerning the Nature of the Human Soul*, 1703) said that Layton had not proved that the combination of blood and inflamed spirit produces thought. Nor had Layton shown why this combination produces thought in man but not in animals. Layton replies by admitting that he has not proven his claim, but neither have his critics proven that thought arises from an immaterial principle (p. 8). To explain why the combination of blood and inflamed spirit should produce thought in men but not in animals, Layton cites "the more apt and perfect Composition of the Organical Parts of their Bodies." He admits that his reasoning is speculative and rests on uncertain arguments; but he thinks he has made the soul's materiality more probable than its immateriality.

A second letter in this same collection (by the same or a different critic) claims that all Layton has shown is that "Mechanical Powers may be sufficient for performing many of the lower Operations of the Soul, and instances in Automata; but he neither has produced, nor can produce one single Instance of an automaton that has been able to perform any single Act of Perception of any, even the most ignoble kind, that of Sensation, much less of Intellection" (p. 37). Even an especially fine machine cannot perform *"an Operation that is more than Automatical."* This critic expands on this point:

The most Automatical Powers can go no further than to continue that one Motion into which the Machine was put at first by the weight of the Spring. Thus one motion may be directed with the greater variety as the Workmanship of the Engine itself is more fine and curious. But no subtilty of the Artificer can enable it to give a new Motion to itself distinct from that which was impressed on the Engine when it was first made. (p. 37)

The "automatical pidgeon" that keeps on course no matter what allurements or deterrents meet her, is quite unlike a real pigeon. Reaction is not the same as perception; reacting to stimuli differs from perceiving objects. Animals are able to vary their behaviour depending upon conditions; they receive information from without, "where it is that their Food and their other Necessities are to be had, which Information I call Perceptions" (p. 38). New motions in animals are the result of these perceptions. Animals are not predetermined by mechanism.

Ditton made the same point about the difference between reaction and perception (*A Discourse concerning the Resurrection*). His proposition III says that *"A Power of Sensation or Perception of Objects, is never to be accounted for, by any Pressure or Endeavour, any Action, Reaction or Resistance, of the Corporeal Organs"* (p. 494). Ditton cites Hobbes on phantasms, for the sense and nature of animals. He also refers to Descartes's treatise on man and his *Principles* as putting forth materialism (p. 496). He insists that motion produces reaction in sense organs, but this is not perception. "How is this Reciprocal Agitation of an *Eye* or an *Ear*, my apprehension of the Thing seen or heard?" (p. 497) He finds no *"Similitude nor Relation between mere*

Vibrations or Undulations of *some fine Threads or Fibrillae in the Machine, and that Acquaintance which I have with an Object, in what I call an Act of Perception.*" Motion cannot account for perceptual discrimination.

Replying to *his* critic, Layton accepts what is said about mechanical contrivances made by men, but he does not think it has been shown that God could not make a machine such as man (p. 51). If God made Adam's brain cogitable, that would not, as Dr. Nicholls charged, have changed Adam's brain into a spirit. God "can make Matter Cogitative, without changing it into the Nature of a Spirit; . . . God can, by Matter and Motion fitly organis'd, produce Intellect and Thought in a proper Subject" (*Observations upon Dr. Nicholls' Book*, p. 41).

Throughout, Layton stresses that no single part of our body thinks; it is the whole man that thinks. It was precisely this point, the difference between the properties of the parts of matter and the properties of the organized combinations of parts, that was the crux of an important debate between Samuel Clarke and Anthony Collins. In his Boyle lectures for 1705 (*A Demonstration of the Being and Attributes of God*), written specifically against Hobbes, Spinoza, and their followers, Clarke had accepted the Cartesian principle that nothing can communicate to another thing perfections that the first does not have. To suppose that perception and intelligence can come from matter violates this obvious truth. He insists that "Intelligence *is not* Figure, and Consciousness *is not* Motion" (p. 114), apparently assuming that the materialists he wrote against were reductionists. Hobbes's attempt to reduce ideas and perceptions to matter and motion was, Clarke says, an attempt to reduce one kind of thing to another, just as if we were to say blueness is really squareness (p. 152). But Clarke rejected the weaker thesis also: that some combination of matter and motion can produce thought. Accepting the physiology of animal spirits, he, like Layton's critic, saw mechanism in the materialist's account. He claimed that it was contrary to experience to say that "the Spirits by which a Man moves the Members of his Body, and ranges the Thoughts of his Mind, are Themselves moved wholly by air or Subtle Matter inspired into the Body" (p. 176). He compares this account of action to the movement of the wheels of a clock. He thinks, as many writers did, that we have the power to move our animal spirits, to affect our physiology. The materialist makes all our actions "as Necessary as the Motions of a Clock" (p. 180).

In *A Letter to the Learned Mr. Henry Dodwell; containing Some Remarks on a (pretended) Demonstration of the Immateriality and Natural Immortality of the Soul* (1707), and in a series of replies to various defenses by Clarke,[14] Collins argued that Clarke had not shown it to be a contradiction to talk of a power arising from matter, which does not belong to the parts of the whole. Not even a clock is the same as its parts. Collins sees just two possibilities: either all of the particles of a rose unite to "contribute to the Individual Power, which is the external Cause of our Sensations; or else God almighty superadds the *Power* of producing that sensation in us upon Union of the Particles" (p. 79). It is the same with the particles of the brain: either thinking necessarily flows from them or God superadds that power to them, "though singly and separately they may not have the power of Thinking." Collins finds no need to go to an immaterial principle distinct from the brain. In fact, the mystery of how by thinking I can move my hand is removed, "if Thinking in Man be nothing but a Mode of Motion, or Matter in Motion." For then, it is just as conceivable how thinking can move my hands as the spring of a clock can move the hands of the clock.

In his *Defence of an Argument Made Use of in the . . . Letter to Mr. Dodwell* (1707), Clarke argued that it is false to say a whole can have powers or properties not contained in its parts. He draws a three-fold distinction of qualities. (1) There are those qualities that are inherent in a substance. These qualities or powers (he uses both terms) are the sum or aggregate of "so many Powers or Qualities *of the same kind*, inherent in all its Parts" (p. 92). Magnitude and motion are examples of this first kind of quality. (2) There are other qualities that are vulgarly looked upon "as *Individual Powers*, resulting from and residing in the whole System, without residing particularly in each or any of its single and original parts" (p. 93). Examples of this second sort are sweetness and color. This vulgar view is wrong, Clarke says, since these qualities are only effects produced in us by certain figures and motion in the bodies. (3) There are still other sorts of powers, e.g., magnetism, electrical attraction, gravitation, which are in fact only names for certain effects. Clarke insists that thinking is a quality of the first sort, "truly and *really inhering* in the Thinking Substance it self" (p. 95). Hence, if matter thinks, every part of matter does.

In response (*A Reply to Mr. Clarke's Defence*, 1707), Collins points out that Clarke's inventory of kinds of quality begs the issue, for he assumes that "A System of Matter has, and can have only Powers of one sort or kind," those that are "only the Sum or Aggregate of Powers of the same kind" (p. 114). Clarke needs to demonstrate, Collins says, "that there can be no other Power in any System of Matter, but what is the Sum or Aggregate of Powers of the same kind." In a later reply, *Reflections on Mr. Clarke's Second Defence* (1707), Collins draws a distinction between two sorts of powers, only one of which (those he calls 'numerical') are powers inhering in systems of matter that are not the sum of powers of the same kind: "the Roundness of a Body is not the sum of the Roundnesses of the Parts; nor the Power of a musical Instrument to cause an harmonious Sound, the sum of Powers of the same kind in the Parts singly considered" (p. 203). Consciousness, or the power of thinking, is a mode of motion, belonging to the numerical powers of body; specifically, it belongs to the particles of the brain.

In commenting upon the Clarke-Collins dispute, the anonymous author of *A Philosophical Enquiry into the Physical Springs of Human Action* (1732)[15] notes that this dispute came down in the end to the question of whether "it was possible in any Instance, to predicate an *Individual Quality* or Attribute of a whole System, without predicating the same of every part in some degree" (p. 5). Clarke's attempt to meet Collins's answer to this question makes use of a distinction between inherent and extrinsical properties. Rotundity is extrinsic and hence can only apply to the whole but not to the parts; but consciousness is inherent and hence must belong to all the parts (p. 7). The anonymous author claims that, if he can show that all qualities are equally real or inherent, Clarke's case will fall (by, of course, making consciousness a property of all the parts—not the answer Collins wanted).

Quality is defined by this author as whatever can be predicated of a subject as *"resulting from its Texture and Frame"* (p. 8). He is not very clear about these two terms, texture and frame, but they seem to have provided a way of referring to the structure of matter. Locke's definition of 'primary quality' as being *in* bodies makes qualities real beings, this author claims. The primary qualities are no more in the substances than are colors, sounds, smells. The bulk, figure, situation, motion or rest, just as the color, etc., "are only the several *Manners*, under which the Body or the Object presents itself to us" (p. 11). All of these "are nothing more than that *peculiar Texture* and *Situation of the Subject*" (p. 12). Thus Clarke's distinction, like Locke's, fails: no qualities inhere in a subject.

The author of this work argues that the substance of man is nothing but a peculiar modification of matter; hence man's properties also (his ideas, his intentions) depend upon his frame and texture. He points to the prevailing notion that man has both an animal and a rational nature: "the former of which is admitted to be only *Matter*, under that peculiar Organization, and therefore *mechanical*, and subject to all the Laws of *Mechanism*" (p. 1). The rational nature is the result of an immaterial substance, limited to the material frame but subject to none of the laws of matter. This rational nature, on this view, is *"unsolid, penetrable, indiscerpible,* and *unchangeable*; and has a Power, free from all *Restraints* and *Impediments*, of *beginning, directing,* and *with-holding*, the Motions of the Body" (p. 2). This notion of the soul is, this author says, unphilosophical and false. Man's substance is nothing but matter "under a *peculiar Modification*" (p. 3). In support of this claim, he lists four propositions: (1) we have no ideas of substance but those received by the senses from external objects; (2) those ideas are only of matter; (3) we have no reason to think that any part of man is immaterial—besides, there is nothing in the nature of matter which is incompatible with thinking; and (4) matter is the subject of cognition, i.e., that in which cogitation inheres.

Another author, Samuel Colliber, who sided with Clarke (*Free Thoughts concerning Souls*, 1734), said that no single particle of the brain could be the sensitive or thinking faculty. Moreover, if with "our Modern Corporealists" we say the soul is a result of a composition of animal spirit particles in the brain, he remarks that even this is not possible because these particles, even in composition, are volatile and in perpetual motion, unlike our thought (p. 15). His conclusion is that "the Human Soul is no constituent Part of the Body, nor any thing resulting from or essentially depending on it" (p. 21). The soul is a substance simple and uncompounded, capable of receiving impressions from sensible objects and also capable of acting on the Animal Spirits.[16]

The Collins-Clarke debate was cited and commented upon by many writers.[17] Some sided with Collins, many with Clarke. In the background of these various discussions over thinking matter, from early in the century to late, is the image of the clockwork man. Materialists were said to "consider Men only as Matter under different Situations, and consequently as mere *Automata*, or *Pieces of Clockwork*."[18] John Witty (*The First Principles of Modern Deism Confuted*, 1707) suspected the motives of some who invoked the machine image for men. He said that the possibility of thinking matter has been made use of *"by the very Beaux*; first *to Argue themselves into mere Machines; and afterwards in Letters to the Ladys; to persuade 'em, for what ends 'tis not difficult to determine, out of their Immaterial and Immortal Souls"* (p. v). While not so sensational in his charge, Ditton shared the suspicions of Witty that there was a deist plot behind the growing materialism: "the idle Notion of Matter's Thinking" has been "industriously propagated by our *Modern Deists*." Those who follow this notion do so, Ditton charged, because they think there is no eternal punishment in another world.[19] These people view man as one substance, "the whole Man all of a Piece," just as Layton urged. The body on this view is, Ditton says, "evidently nothing but a Machine, or a mere System of Matter" (p. 473). The deists advanced the notion of thinking matter in order to undermine "the very Foundations of Christianity" (p. 474).[20]

In an appendix to a later work, *The New Law of Fluids* (1714), Ditton made a sustained critique of the controversy, elaborating on these same charges.[21] That it was in the interest of deists to argue for thinking matter is clear to Ditton. He opens his analysis by referring to "this Controversy, as managed by the *Deists*"; in maintaining "their Grand Hypothesis about *Matter's being a Thinking Substance*," they have retreated from one position to another in defense. Working from the *known* properties of matter, the deists argued that they could best explain all the phenomena of the human mind in terms of those properties. All talk of thinking substance being distinct from matter is, the deists charge, gibberish and "Metaphysical Trumpery" (p. 3).

When the deists had to retreat from the explanation in terms of the known properties of matter, Ditton continues, their next position of defense was in terms of the *unknown* properties and powers of matter. A third line of defense was to invoke "the Absolute Power of Almighty God, to endow Systems of Matter, with the Faculties of Thinking and Willing" (p. 6). Still another ploy resorted to is to suggest *"That no Contradiction results from our joyning the Ideas of Matter, and its Properties, with that of Thinking Substance: Therefore* (say they) *Matter may be thinking Substance"* (p. 8).

In turning to a survey of the responses made to these various notions, Ditton says that the hypothesis of thinking matter is the main centre for *"the Whole System of Modern Infidelity"* (p. 9). It is the deists to whom he refers (pp. 17, 19, 22, 23, 43, 49, 51, 53, 70). Ditton repeats some of the points made in the earlier work (his *Discourse*), about the impossibility that mechanism is the cause of thinking and willing (pp. 10-12). Of the appeal to unknown properties, he says that those opposed to the deist can equally say there may be unknown properties that make it impossible for matter to think (p. 18). The atheists and deists "have made the whole *Universe* a meer Lump of Matter; and *Man*, the most elegant and lovely Creature of all; they have complimented no higher, than to give him the Title of the best and finest Piece of *Clock-work*. They have divested us of all our *Intellectual* Powers, and made up our very *Souls* of *Wheels* and *Springs*; so that we are only a Set of Moving pratling Machines . . . ." (pp. 23-24). He goes on to say "these People have allowed the little *Engine* they call

Man, such a thing as *Brains*." But brains cannot reason, no more so than can wires and threads. Even though these unbelievers give man a voice to speak and legs to move, they "have made it impossible for him to *understand*" (p. 24). He also charges that the doctrine of thinking matter enables the deists to avoid the terrors of an after-life: it is, in fact, "*A Fence Against the Belief of Punishments in a Life to come*" (pp. 26-27). These people want to prove that the Gospel's a "*meer idle Tale*."

Ditton then examines the notion of a system of organized matter. A system, he says, is an order and arrangement of parts (p. 29). If the properties of thinking and willing depend upon the order and arrangement of parts, that means that, "without any *other Causality* intervening," it is the order and arrangement that produces the properties. Ditton argues that it is an odd notion that some properties of matter (e.g., figure, divisibility, cohesion) should not be affected by the dissolution of the formal system, while others (e.g., thinking, willing) are (p. 33). For this latter sort of properties, there is no other foundation "in the Nature of Things but this *meer Order and Relation*," so the argument runs. Thus, before we can ascribe thought to such an order, we ought to be able to specify the proper requirements for a system to produce thought, to indicate what changes will destroy it, etc. (p. 34). In other words, Ditton is taking this particular argument about the order and arrangement of the parts of a material system on its own terms: it lies with the *system as such*, not the system of matter under such and such conditions, or so and so qualified, to produce thought.

Ditton argues that unless these writers can specify precisely what sort of system and arrangement of parts produces thought, they will have to face the possibility that thought may be attached to all sorts of systems, even that system of a dead body (p. 37). If the deists try to specify the nature of the system that produces thought, they will end up referring to *known* properties, i.e., figure, size, force, motion, cohesion (p. 39). Thus they are forced to give up their appeal to *unknown* properties of matter. If the properties by which matter thinks do not depend upon a system, then matter will go on thinking when the system is dissolved (p. 42). If one responds that God steps in and removes the property of thinking from matter upon the dissolution of the system, then Ditton thinks the immaterialists can use the same appeal to God's intervention to support their claims.

Ditton's own views about matter are clear: "a Sum of proper *Nothings* or *No-influences*, being rang'd together" will not "make a real *Something* or *Some-influences*" (p. 57). That is, unorganized, inert particles of matter have no force or power, can exert no influence, and cannot produce anything new. To the ploy that God superadds thought to matter, Ditton refers to his earlier discussion in his other book. He sees only three possible meanings to this suggestion: (1) that God extraordinarily enables and empowers matter to think and will by means of known properties; or (2) God extraordinarily adds the "meer *Qualities or Powers* of Thinking and Willing" to a system of matter; or (3) God joins *"a real Thinking Substance*, with a System of Matter" (p. 61). The first possibility is a contradiction, and goes against the laws of the universe. The second (a) gives up pure materialism "Because 'tis supposing *some Powers* in the Universe, which are not reducible to *Matter and Motion*," being of a Divine origin; or (b) the future state is left unclear, for thought may continue on in the future as attached to matter even after the system is dissolved; or (c) it is nonsense to talk of qualities not attached to a proper substance. The third possibility gives up the claim, since it gives back a two-substance doctrine (p. 63).

Whether Ditton is correct in seeing a deist plot in the claim that matter can think, it is important to appreciate the disturbance to traditional views of human nature which this claim brought about. In particular, the concept of man as a spiritual substance seemed to writers such as Ditton and Witty to be giving way to that of man as a material substance. To say that this material substance still has the properties which the older view associated with the essence of man (thought, volition) did not satisfy Ditton; for it was difficult to understand how properties of thinking and volition could belong to the same substance that had such properties as extension and solidity. There were metaphysical arguments to show how such a combination was impossible. It was not, however, those abstract arguments that led to the rejection of Locke's suggestion. The force at work in those who reacted against that suggestion was the fear of the automatical man. This image of the man-machine had widespread implications. It accompanied the debates over liberty and necessity, which concerned many writers in the century: mechanism, automatism, clockwork were consistent with necessitarianism; immateriality, spontaneity, and indivisibility of soul were consistent with libertarianism. Thus the debate over thinking matter, the tensions between materialists and immaterialists, were the focus of many themes in eighteenth-century British philosophy. Immaterialism was on the side of the angels. Materialism was that "hideous hypothesis" that everyone identified with Spinoza.[22]

Notes

1. *Traité de l'homme*, in *Oeuvres philosophiques*, ed. F. Alquié (1963), t. 1, p. 390-91. The English translation is found in T. S. Hall's edition, *Treatise of Man*, with French text, translation, and commentary (Harvard University Press, 1972), p. 21.

2. Julian Jaynes, "The Problem of Animate Motion in the Seventeenth Century," *Journal of the History of Ideas* 31 (1970).

3. *From Beast-Machine to Man-Machine* (Oxford: Oxford University Press, 1940), p. 4. The reference is to Descartes's *Cogitationes privatae*, *Oeuvres*, eds. Adam and Tannéry, volume X, pp. 231-32n.

4. Ibid., from Nicolas Poisson's *Commentaire ou Remarques sur la méthode de René Descartes* (1670), Part V, p. 156.

5. Rosenfield, *From Beast-Machine to Man-Machine*, p. 246.

6. Hall's edition, p. 4.

7. Aram Vartanian, *Diderot and Descartes. A Study of Scientific Naturalism in the Enlightenment* (Princeton: Princeton University Press, 1953).

8. Vartanian points out that Voltaire popularized Locke's suggestion, but Vartanian discounts this suggestion as having any "deep influence . . . on the materialism of La Mettrie, Diderot, Buffon and D'Holbach" (ibid., p. 300).

9. This work is usually credited to a Zachary Mayne, but that is a very dubious identification. There is an earlier person with that name, listed in the DNB, but he is too early, nor does his interest or style of writing fit the author of this interesting and important work. For convenience, I cite the name 'Mayne' as the author.

10. It is important to note, especially for our discussion below of the concept of matter, that to this complicated machine of the body Hume ascribed, as he did to all matter, 'secret powers'.

11. Locke's critic John Edwards caught the link between the thinking matter suggestion and animal machines: "Some take occasion thence to believe, that Men as well as Brutes are no other than Engines and Machines, mere Neurospasts and Senseless Puppets. Others build upon this Notion the Conceit of *Thinking Matter*." (*Some Thoughts concerning the Several Causes and Occasions of Atheism, Especially in the Present Age. With Some Brief Reflections on Socinianism: And on a Late Book Entituled The Reasonableness of Christianity*, 1695). The OED gives the meaning of the term 'Neurospast' as "a figure or puppet moved by strings." The term also occurs in a sermon by Cudworth.

12. For a thorough discussion of automata, see *Le Monde des Automates, étude historique et technique*, by Alfred Chapuis and Edouard Gélis, 1928. These authors say of the eagle and the fly, that although some serious writers took them to be facts (among the writers they cite Gassendi), they believe the eagle to be a pure fiction (Volume I, p. 86). On the fly, they say that the first mention of it is in Peter Ramus (1599). They concede that both of these automata *may* have been constructible, but "it is the imagination of some authors which have given to their works the fabulous character more suitable to stories of the Round Table or to the legends from the orient" (p. 87). For a more recent reference to some other occurrences of automata, see "Descartes, the Sceptics, and the Rejection of Vitalism in Seventeenth-Century Physiology," by Philip R. Sloan, in *Studies in History and Philosophy of Science* (1977), pp. 1-28.

13. The same conclusion was drawn earlier in France by A. Dilly (*De l'âme des bêtes*, 1684). In summarizing Dilly's book, George Boas remarks that Dilly's book contains a chapter that presents "astonishing automata which show how close to life man-made machines may approach. If man can make these marvels, why should not his Maker make greater ones?" (*The Happy Beast*, p. 111) In England, John Norris (*An Essay Towards the Theory of the Ideal or Intelligible World*, 1704, volume II) repeats this question. After citing the water-driven machines known to Descartes, Norris remarks that if men can make such machines, why can't God make animal machines that resemble more closely what we take to be organisms with souls? (p. 86) Norris argues that from the appearances of thought-caused movements it does not follow that those movements are in fact caused by thought. He follows the Cartesians

in saying animals are machines. He thinks we have evidence in our own case that we are more than machines, though he admits that if matter could think, we would or could be matter.

14. This exchange took place in 1707–08. All the pamphlets, including Clarke's original *Letter* to Dodwell, were reprinted in 1731. My page references in what follows are to this 1731 edition. A large section of Clarke's *Second Defence*, a small section of Collins's *Reflections*, and a portion of a *Third Defence* are presented in Maxwell's English translation of Cumberland's work on the law of nature: *A Treatise on the Laws of Nature* (1728). This summary can be found in an appendix to Maxwell's edition. For the full bibliographical reference to the Clarke-Collins exchange, see the useful study by James P. Ferguson, *The Philosophy of Dr. Samuel Clarke and Its Critics* (1974). There is also a useful discussion of the main point between Clarke and Collins in "Clarke, Collins and Compounds," by Robin Attfield, *Journal of the History of Philosophy*, 15 (1977).

15. For some account of the identity of the author (Samuel Strutt?), see Margaret C. Jacob, *The Radical Enlightenment*, p. 174.

16. In another work, *The Known God* (1737), Colliber says the human soul is neither matter nor spirit but a being of middle nature. He cites some of the other views then current. Some hold that the soul is unextended and unsolid and hence not qualified "for External Sensation or Local Motion in a separate State" (p. 64). Others stripped the soul of its substance, reducing it "either to a Pure Act without an Agent, or to a mere Complication of Active Powers, without any Proper Subject." Still others said the soul is in every part of its body. Colliber rejects the notion that thought can be produced from matter or from blood and animal spirits (p. 67).

17. The Clarke-Collins-Dodwell exchanges were carefully reviewed also in a series of articles by LeClerc in his *Bibliothèque Choisie*. See volume XXVI, 1713.

18. *An Enquiry into the Immateriality of Thinking Substance*, by William Windle, 1738.

19. *Discourse* (1712). Samuel Clarke does not link these views with deism, but he does warn that talk of the soul being *naturally* mortal (as some of those defending the view that thought might be a property of matter did) leads the libertines to believe they can escape eternal punishment.

20. Materialists and deists were also frequently identified as 'Freethinkers.' The term 'freethinker' or 'freethinking' had various meanings and connotations. Chambers gives the descriptive meaning as "A Class of People, . . . whose Character is, not to profess any particular Form, or System of Religion; but only to acknowledge the Existence of a God, without rendering him any external Worship, or Service." (See his *Encyclopaedia* (1728) entry under 'Deist'.) *The Guardian* (no. 130) gives the meaning used by those who saw it as a cover for atheism and materialism: Free-thinkers "have often declared to the world, that they are not actuated by any incorporeal being or spirit; but that all the operations they exert proceed from the collision of certain corpuscles, endued with proper figure and motion." Motion is mistaken for thought. The term also has associations with the developing Free Masons. Margaret Jacob has identified Collins and Toland as active Masons. She says that "Fairly good evidence also suggests that the first encyclopaedia of the eighteenth century was complied by a Freemason, that is, E. Chambers . . . ." (*The Radical Enlightenment*, p. 10). Professor Jacob also points out that Strutt had close associations with a number of known Freemasons, Toland's *Letters to Serena* being mentioned in his preface, While I am concerned in this study with the arguments for and against materialism, as those arguments revolved around the notion of thinking matter, we should not forget what Professor Jacob has shown: that the sect of Freemasons was closely associated with pantheism and materialism, especially of a Spinozist form. Of Locke, Professor Jacob remarks that while "English Masons claimed Locke as one of their own," the evidence for Locke's membership as a Mason is very dubious. (See p. 118.)

21. The Appendix carries a separate title page: *Matter Not a Cogitative Substance: Or, The True State of the Case About Matter's Thinking: with Some Considerations and Reflection Thereon, Tending to the Compleat Settling of That Point*, by Humphrey Ditton, 1713.

22. Of course, the work of and reactions to La Mettrie's *L'Homme machine* (1747) reflects the same concerns with mechanism and mechanical men. In his edition of this work, Vartanian mentions the influence on the thinking about the nature of man in France, of "the repeater-watch" and other "ingenious automata so popular at the time, such as Vaucanson's famous flutist and duck, which embodies the engineering equivalent of the man-machine theory and undoubtedly prepared the imagination of La Mettrie and his contemporaries for the idea of psychological automatism" (*La Mettrie's L'Homme Machine: A Study in the Origins of an Idea*, 1960, pp. 67-68). Vartanian also quotes from an article in the *Bibliothèque raisonnée* for 1744, which discussed these machines. As Layton did earlier in England, the writer of this article suggests that it is difficult not to think these machines have a mind, at least an animal mind, directing their activities. He suggests that more knowledge of the brain may show us that that material organ does activate men (pp. 68-69). The book under review in that article was *Recherches Philosophiques*, by St. Hyacinthe. On the question of thinking matter, the reviewer grants that we may not be able to say it is of the essence of matter to think, but we can say that it is able to think "when it is disposed and arranged in a certain way which God alone knows perfectly, since he is the Author and Creator of that admirable thinking machine" (*Bibliothèque raisonnée*, volume 32, 1744, pp. 48 et seq.).

Chapter III

Hume and the Hideous Hypothesis

Hume in the section of the *Treatise of Human Nature* (1739) on the immateriality of the soul (I.IV.V), started by challenging the concepts of substance and inhesion. These concepts are no more clear, he says, for immaterial than they are for material substance. Hume believed he had shown that we have no *impression* of substance; hence, given his principle that ideas are derived from impressions, we can conclude that we have no *idea* of substance. If the reply be that we have a *definition* of substance which explains what a substance is, Hume pointed out that the usual definition—that which exists by itself—does not demarcate substance from its accidents, e.g., "the soul from its perceptions" (p. 233). On this definition, the accidents of our soul turn out to be substances themselves. Using some of the principles already established in the *Treatise*, Hume offered an argument to support this claim. (1) "Whatever is clearly conceiv'd may exist; and whatever is clearly conceiv'd after any manner, may exist after the same manner." (2) Whatever is different is distinguishable, "and every thing which is distinguishable, is separable by the imagination." Therefore, since "all our perceptions are different from each other, and from every thing else in the universe, they are also distinct and separable, and may be consider'd as separately existent, and may exist separately, and have no need of any thing else to support their existence." Thus our perceptions are substances.[1]

49

Hume thinks we should abandon the dispute over the materiality and immateriality of the soul because that dispute assumes an idea of substance which we do not have. But instead of abandoning the dispute, Hume turns his attention to the details of the arguments, especially those invoked by the immaterialists. He cites the argument commonly used in the century (by Clarke and others) that matter is extended, has parts, and is divisible; thoughts are indivisible; thus, if thought is joined to, or is a property of body, where is it located? Various answers were given to this question: thought is in all the parts, only in some of the parts (e.g., the particles of the brain), or in the whole unit of body and soul. All these answers use the argument that thought would have to be extended and divisible. But thought is not divisible. Thus thought and extension cannot belong to one substance. Hume offers his own example to help this conclusion: what sense would it make to talk of "a passion of a yard in length, a foot in breadth, and an inch in thickness?" (p. 234) Or, "wou'd the indivisible thought exist on the left or on the right hand of this extended divisible body? On the surface or in the middle? On the back or foreside of it?" (p. 234)[2]

Hume calls this argument 'remarkable', but he points out that it does not relate to the *nature* of the soul, only to "its *local conjunction* with matter" (p. 235). He suggests that to assess this argument, it may be helpful to "consider in general what objects are, or are not susceptible of a local conjunction," that is, spatial location. The argument which Hume now proceeds to construct, as a way of explicating what can and cannot be locally conjoined to matter, is somewhat strange, some of the concepts difficult to understand. He starts off clearly enough: "The first notion of space and extension is deriv'd solely from the senses of sight and feeling." Secondly, only "what is colour'd or tangible . . . has parts dispos'd after such a manner, as to convey" the idea of space and extension. He then takes a different example, one from taste experience: when we diminish or increase a relish we do so differently from when we diminish or increase "any visible object." I suppose that tastes are increased by eating more food or drinking more wine; or perhaps he has in mind just adding more ingredients to the food. We speak of strong and weak tastes, but of more or less of a taste? We increase a visible object—make it larger?— by moving closer to it, that is by traversing some space.

Another example Hume gives of ways in which we locate objects spatially is that of several sounds striking our ears ("our hearing," he says) at once. We form an idea of the "degrees of the distance and contiguity of those bodies, from which they are deriv'd." This idea arises from "custom and reflection alone," not from any impression or movement. The objects from which the sounds are derived have a location, a place which (he seems to say) has an extension.[3] The next step in Hume's argument is easy: "What is extended must have a particular figure, as square, round, triangular" (p. 235). Whether these shapes are meant to be predicates of the place of the sounding bodies, or just of the bodies, is not clear, but the point of this example is to show that these shapes do not apply "to a desire, or indeed to any impression or idea," *except* the impressions or ideas of two senses, sight and feeling (touch), those senses from which we derive the first notions of space and extension. He appears to be saying, then, that the impressions and ideas of sight and feeling are themselves extended. Earlier, in the section on space and time, Hume had said that the idea of space "is convey'd to the mind by two senses, sight and touch." He there went on to say "That compound impression, which represents extension, consists of several lesser impressions, that are indivisible to the eye or feeling" (p. 38). Is an impression that is made up of other impressions itself extended? Spatially extended, located in a place? I suspect the answer to these questions is tied up with Hume's earlier remark that "my senses convey to me only the impressions of colour'd points, dispos'd in a certain manner" (p. 34). His objection to mathematical points as a way of analyzing extension is that they are not sensible: "If a point be not consider'd as colour'd or tangible, it can convey to us no idea; and consequently the idea of extension, which is compos'd of the ideas of these [mathematical] points, can never possibly exist" (p. 39). One of Hume's basic principles is that "Wherever ideas are adequate representations of objects, the relations, contradictions and agreements of the ideas are all applicable to the objects" (p. 29). This principle receives a more literal reading in I.IV.V, where the possibility of an idea of substance is rejected because there is no impression that *resembles* a substance (p. 233). In saying that the ideas of sight and touch are located in a place and have an extension, Hume seems to be working with a resemblance notion of those ideas.

That this *is* what he is saying is further supported by his next paragraph, where he rejects the oft-cited maxim, "that no thing can be or act where it is not." For Hume, *"an object may exist, and yet be no where"* (p. 235). 'Object' is being used widely, to cover whatever exists, especially ideas or perceptions. Far from this maxim being true, Hume says that "the greatest part of beings do and must exist" without existing in a place. He offers as an explication of his assertion the following: "An object may be said to be no where, when its parts are not so situated with respect to each other, as to form any figure or quantity; nor the whole with respect to other bodies so as to answer to our notions of contiguity or distance" (pp. 245-46). He says again that this description fits "all our perceptions and objects, except those of sight and feeling." He supplies us with several examples of objects or perceptions that do not exist any*where*, e.g., passions, smells, sounds, but he does not explicate those perceptions of sight and touch that do exist somewhere, in a place.

Having established to his satisfaction that only some perceptions and objects are located in a place, Hume now proceeds to explain how we come to apply "local conjunction" where it is inappropriate. He takes as an example an ordinary object—a fig or an olive—but he obviously has his eye upon the metaphysical debate between materialist and immaterialist. We tend to think of the taste of the fig or the olive as being *in* the fig or olive, and hence as being located in the place on the table where they are (p. 236). This notion is corrected by reflection, which tells us that the notion of a taste being where the object is is "altogether unintelligible and contradictory" (p. 238). One test for its unintelligibility is to ask (a question exactly similar to the question about thought and body) whether the taste is located "in the circumference of the body, is in every part of it or in one only." No satisfactory answer can be given to these alternatives. We have here, Hume assures us, the typical conflict between our *inclination* to put the taste in the object and our *reason*, which shows that this is not possible. The result of this conflict is that we try to take one alternative but doctor it up a bit. For example, we say (and again, the parallel with the moves made by those grappling with thought's relation to body are clear and must be intentional) that the taste exists in the object but in such a way that "it fills the whole without extension, and exists entire in every part without separation." We might take this way by invoking the scholastic maxim: the whole is in all and the whole is in every part (*totum in toto et totum in qualibet parte*). But this is no more than to say "a thing is in a certain place, and yet is not there" (p. 238).[4]

Some of the immaterialists *did* talk this way, because they accepted the maxim that everything is in some place. Others, such as Clarke, even wanted to hang on to the notion that the mind or soul was extended. The result was often very much as Hume satirizes it here. There were valiant attempts made to explicate a concept of 'place' that would fit mind without being too literal.[5] Hume shows the obvious solution, which the immaterialists might have taken, when he points out that coexistence of perceptions need not be *spatial* coexistence.[6] Thus the taste of the fig coexists with the shape, but is not

locally conjoined with the shape. We should, Hume remarks, not try
to give a place to that which is "utterly incapable of it." Our choice
is clear: "either to suppose that some beings exist without any place;
or that they are figur'd and extended" (p. 239). The third alternative
is to invoke that scholastic maxim about wholes and parts. Since the
second and third alternatives are absurd, the first is the one we must
take. The consequence of taking this first alternative affects materialists and immaterialists alike. The materialists "who conjoin all thought
with extension" must be condemned because *all* thought is not figured
or located in a place in the way body is. Equally we must blame those
who "conjoin all thought with a simple and indivisible substance,"
because *some* thoughts or perceptions are shaped and figured and
hence located.[7]

In this section of his *Treatise*, Hume is clearly interested in satiriz-
ing both positions. Thus it is not easy to know when he speaks in his
own voice. The assumption at work so far is, as we have seen, that
"to say the idea of extension agrees to anything, is to say it is extended" (p. 240). He now goes one step further. Objects, Hume says
everyone agrees, are not known by the mind immediately; only perceptions are. "That table, which just now appears to me, is only a
perception, and all its qualities are qualities of perceptions." Hume is
here repeating a point he has made previously, that all that is ever
really present to me are my own perceptions (e.g., *Treatise*, I.II.VI;
I.IV.II). He had also earlier characterized the ordinary point of view
as the belief that our perceptions *are* the objects we see. " 'Tis certain,
that almost all mankind, and even philosophers themselves, for the
greatest part of their lives, take their perceptions to be their only objects, and suppose, that the very being, which is intimately present to
the mind, is the real body or material existence" (p. 212). This remark can take us in either of two directions. One direction leads us
to direct realism, where perceptions are not intermediaries between
our awareness and external objects. The other direction leads us into
some kind of idealism or strong representative realism, where our perceptions or ideas become things which may or may not represent
other things not present to us. On this alternative, we appear to substitute a world of ideas for the world of things, the qualities we normally ascribe to external objects now become properties of our ideas.
In the section we are now examining, Hume clearly takes this alternative. Whether it is an alternative he himself is happy to accept, I am
not sure.[8] What is certain (as we shall see in a moment) is that he
pushes this alternative to the extreme in order to satirize a position
of one of the immaterialists whom Hume has in mind, Malebranche.

What Hume says at this point is that the visual and tangible perceptions of the table are themselves extended and have parts (p. 239).

Hume then remarks that the materialists (he says 'free thinkers', which meant the same thing for most eighteenth-century readers) may seize on those extended perceptions and ask the immaterialist how these are compatible with his simple indivisible spirit. The materialist can ask such questions of the immaterialist as, 'is the spirit or immaterial substance on the left or the right hand of the extended perception?'; 'is it in this part or another part of that perception?'; 'is it in one part or in the whole?'. No answer can be given to these questions that is not absurd. Having shown to his satisfaction that neither the materialist nor the immaterialist can fit his respective doctrine to the phenomena of perception, Hume goes on to suggest that "the immateriality, simplicity, and indivisibility of a thinking substance is a true atheism," similar to what Spinoza has been charged with, justifying "all those sentiments, for which *Spinoza* is so universally infamous" (p. 240). While all those who feared the mechanism of the materialists, who saw determinism and atheism in the denial of an immaterial soul, defended their doctrine as the only grounds for immortality and for morality, Hume turns the table on them. What he now goes on to do in the rest of this section is to show that the properties claimed by the immaterialist for mind or soul are precisely the ones ascribed by Spinoza to his one substance, and that the same difficulties confront Spinoza as confront the immaterialist. Hume has produced a startling and clever *tour de force*: immaterialism is an atheism! Such satire does not seem to have caught the eyes of his contemporaries, however. It did not affect the course of the debate. It is nevertheless of interest in our examination of the development of materialism in Britain.[9]

Spinoza's doctrine, Hume reminds us, is that the universe is simple. The substance in which thought and extension inhere is a unity; it is simple and indivisible, and it "exists every where, without any local presence" (p. 240). These were precisely the predicates used by the immaterialists in talking about soul or spirit and its relations with the body. For Spinoza, as Hume interprets him, feelings, perceptions, passions, configurations of matter all inhere in the same substance. "The same *substratum*, if I may so speak, supports the most different modifications, without any difference in itself" (p. 241). None of the modifications of substance—time, place, diversity—disturbs the simplicity of that one substance.

Hume then explicitly says that he will show that "this hideous hypothesis is almost the same with that of the immateriality of the soul, which has become so popular." He next reminds us of what he claimed to have shown in an earlier section, that since ideas are derived from preceding perceptions, it is impossible that "our idea of a perception, and that of an object or external existence can ever represent what are specifically different from each other." That is, if external existences differ from our perceptions, we cannot learn this from our perceptions. We thus have only two choices: (1) we can conceive of the external object as a relation without a relative (which is an empty if not absurd conception), or (2) we can "make it the very same with a perception or impression" (p. 241). His conclusion from the above principle is that we cannot with certainty transfer the connection or repugnance of impressions to objects, but we can transfer conclusions about the relation of objects with certainty to impressions. The latter is so because, even though an object is different from an impression, the quality of the object which I think of (and which will be transferred) is thought of or conceived of by the mind. But no quality of an object can be thought unless it is shared by an impression, since all our ideas are derived from impressions. Hence his conclusion that we can never discover "a connexion or repugnance betwixt objects, which extends not to impressions" (p. 242).

That his reasoning here is somewhat contorted, Hume recognized. He says it may "at first sight, appear a mere sophism" (p. 241). What is important for us to note is that his reasoning is a further attempt to push the second of the above interpretations of the ordinary view, that my perceptions *are* the objects I cognize. He needs this strong interpretation in order to make his next point. The materialists, Hume says, talk of the system of objects; the immaterialists talk of the system of thoughts and ideas. Spinoza tells us that all the objects I observe—the sun, moon, stars, earth, seas, plants, men, ships, houses—are not really objects (i.e., substances) but only modes or modifications of a substance, a substance in which all these modes inhere, which is simple, uncompounded and indivisible. The other system, the system of thoughts, is a "system of beings, *viz.* the universe of thought, or my impressions and ideas" (p. 242). The slide from impressions and ideas to *beings* is now complete. We begin to appreciate those earlier maneuvers to ontologize perceptions, to characterize some perceptions as extended, located in a place. We also see now what use he is making of the interpretation of the ordinary view that objects are the same as perceptions. When Hume examines this other system of beings, what does he find? "There I observe another sun, moon, and stars; an earth, and seas, cover'd and inhabited by plants and animals; towns, houses, mountains, rivers; and in short every thing I can discover or conceive in the first system" (p. 242).

When we discount a bit from Hume's satirical characterization of this system of beings, it becomes clear that it is Malebranche whom he has in mind. Malebranche accepted the maxim that the mind cannot know what is distant from the mind — that it can know only what is intimately united to the mind. He argues thus: it is indubitable that our minds do not fill spaces as vast as those between us and the fixed stars; when we know the stars, it is not reasonable to believe that our mind is in the sky. It is not even reasonable to think that our mind leaves our body when it knows the house down the road.

Our soul, then, must see stars and houses where they are not, since the soul does not leave the body where it is located, and yet sees them outside it. Now given that the stars immediately joined to the soul (which are the only stars it can see) are not in the heavens, it follows that everyone who sees the stars in the heavens and who then voluntarily judges they are there performs two false judgments.[10]

There are in fact "two kinds of beings": those which our mind sees immediately, and others which the mind knows only by means of the first sort. Malebranche's doctrine is considerably more subtle than these passages suggest, but Hume was not alone in finding in this doctrine a duplication in the system of thoughts (what Malebranche called 'intelligible objects') of the world of ordinary objects. In his *Examination of P. Malebranche's Opinion*, Locke had questioned the same point, charging Malebranche with scepticism, with not being able to say there is a sun or stars in the sky. Arnauld (*Des Vraies et des Fausses Idées*, 1683, and in a series of subsequent exchanges with Malebranche) anticipated Hume's reading. Arnauld said that Malebranche's philosophy of ideas transports us into an unknown country "where men no longer have true knowledge of each other, nor of their own bodies, or of the sun and stars created by God," a country where instead of men, we see only "intelligible men"; instead of our own body, we see only an "intelligible body"; and instead of the sun and stars in the sky, we see "intelligible sun and stars" (pp. 227-28).

There are not many immaterialists in Britain who took this extreme position, although Hume might have had Berkeley in mind, and Watts was a close follower of Malebranche.[11] In his *Philosophical Essays*, Watts cites Malebranche's doctrine of intelligible sun, moon, stars (p. 73). He has his own version of the idea that we see things in the mind of God. Watts was on the side of the immaterialists. Thus Hume may have had him in mind as well. But Hume's critique applies to many of those who were trying to defend the immaterialist thesis, even though not all of them fit exactly the model Hume is here constructing. What they all agreed on was that thoughts, ideas and perceptions are modifications of one simple, uncompounded, and indivisible substance—an exact parallel, Hume wants us to note, with Spinoza's account of modes and one substance. These identical accounts, Hume remarks, have not been accorded the same reception. Spinoza's account is treated with "detestation and scorn, and the second [that of the immaterialists] with applause and veneration" (p. 243). Both accounts or hypotheses are, Hume insists, equally unintelligible; most of the absurdities that were supposed to pertain to Spinoza's system apply as well to that of the immaterialists.[12] Hume rounds out his examination of these absurdities with a quick look at some of them.

He mentions three main points. (1) Some people invoke the scholastic notion that a mode is not distinct from its substance, but is in fact the same as the substance. Thus these people urge against Spinoza that the extension of the universe is the same as the universe. Hence substance—which is supposed to be indivisible—must be extended and must expand and contract to fit the different extensions. Hume thinks this argument has weight, as far as he can understand it, but when the terms are changed it holds as well against the soul and our extended perceptions. (2) Others say that the idea of substance is applicable to every part of matter. (Compare: thought is applicable to every part of the body.) Hence matter is not a mode of substance. Spinoza is wrong again, the critics say. But Hume has already shown that the definition of substance fits our perceptions and every distinct part of them. Thus they are substances also, not modes of one substance. The theologians (the immaterialists) are equally wrong. (3) Against Spinoza it has been said that because he makes his one substance the subject of all properties, it will have incompatible properties at the same time, e.g., round and square. But if impressions are modes of the soul, the same will be true of the soul.[13] Thus Hume thinks he has shown that the difficulties confronting materialists are the same as those confronting immaterialists. If anyone can succeed in establishing "the simplicity and immateriality of the soul," he will be, Hume argues, "preparing the way for a dangerous and irrecoverable atheism" (p. 244).

In this clever, well-informed critique, Hume is not saying that immaterialism reduces to, or is the same as, Spinozistic materialism. The comparison is directed against the structure and the language used by immaterialists and by Spinoza. Hume was not content to dismiss the whole debate because of what he took to be the obscurity or even unintelligibility of the concept of substance. To take that way would not have enabled him to comment on the internal logic of both sides in the debate. The talk of part and whole, of modes related to substance, of thought being not in every part of the body but nevertheless being in the whole—these were difficulties and absurdities that Hume wanted to expose. Whether he was more inclined to side with the materialists may not be entirely clear. Some of the remarks he makes about the main question in the debate, "whether matter and motion could think or be the cause of thought," appear designed to guard himself against an affirmative answer. He cites as from the Schools (though it was in fact often used by many writers in the debate) the notion that "matter and motion . . . are still matter and motion, and produce only a difference in the position and situation of objects" (p. 246).[14] From matter and motion, you will only get figure, relation of parts, change of place, etc. One kind of motion could not produce only motion in a circle, while another kind, an ellipse, produces "a passion or moral reflexion." From such considerations as these, Hume correctly reports it was commonly concluded that it was impossible "that thought can ever be caus'd by matter" (p. 247).

But Hume has his own easy refutation of this conclusion. Since he has earlier shown that "we are never sensible of any connexion betwixt causes and effects," and that it is only by constant conjunction that we establish what we take to be causal relations, it follows that for all we know a priori, "any thing may produce any thing" (p. 247). Although there appears to be no connection between motion and thought, "the case is the same with all other causes and effects." Hence, if the immaterialists want to prove a priori (that is, by arguing from their definitions and concepts of substance, matter, and thought) that "such a position of bodies can never cause thought; because turn which way you will, 'tis nothing but a position of bodies," they may just as well conclude that position of bodies "can never produce motion" either. In neither case is there any discernible connection between the supposed cause and the effect. We believe nevertheless that bodies do cause motion, because we find constant conjunctions in our experience of bodies followed by change of position of other bodies. Similarly, Hume remarks, we have experience of constant conjunction between "the different dispositions of our body and our thoughts and feelings" (p. 248). By comparing our ideas, we find that thought and motion are different from each other, but by experience we find "that they are constantly united." Thus the condition necessary for assigning cause with respect to matter and motion is also met with motion and thought.

Hume thinks we are left with a dilemma: either we say there are no causes save where we are able to perceive a connection by examining our ideas, or we must say that all constantly conjoined objects are causally related. To take the first horn of our dilemma means that we will have to say there are no causes in the universe, not even God himself, because "for ought we can determine by the mere ideas" there are no such connections. Even if we accepted the deity and made him "the great and efficacious principle," we would be led into other absurdities. For example, we might be led to say that God "is the author of all our volitions and perceptions," since there is no apparent connection between our volitions and perceptions, or our volitions and our bodily movements, or of both to "the suppos'd but unknown substance of our soul" (p. 249). Hume knew of course that this latter 'absurdity' was just what Malebranche claimed. He footnotes Malebranche at this point. He very likely knew also that Watts held the same doctrine. There were others as well in the century.[15] If our thought or volition is so inactive as to "make us have recourse to a deity," God then becomes "the real cause of all our actions, bad as well as good."

If we take the second horn of the dilemma, "that all objects, which are found to be constantly conjoin'd, are upon that account only to be regarded as causes and effects," it follows that, so far as we can tell from our ideas alone, "any thing may be the cause or effect of any thing" (pp. 249-50). This result gives the advantage, Hume says, to the materialists. In fact, while neither horn of the dilemma gives us an acceptable conclusion, the immaterialist horn—that God is the only real cause—comes out worse. In his summary of his discussion of this controversy, Hume lists three points that have emerged. (1) The "question concerning the substance of the soul is absolutely unintelligible." (2) "All our perceptions are not susceptible of a local union, either with what is extended or unextended; there being some of them of the one kind, and some of the other." (3) As "the constant conjunction of objects constitutes the very essence of cause and effect, matter and motion may often be regarded as the causes of thought, as far as we have any notion of that relation" (p. 250). It is only the third point cited by Hume in this concluding passage of the section on immateriality which he mentions as his basis for questioning the immateriality of the soul, in his A Letter from a Gentleman (p. 30). This point appears again in his essay "On the Immortality of the Soul." There he reaffirms his claim that "experience, being the only source of our judgments of this nature [of cause and effect], we cannot know from any other principle, whether matter, by its structure or arrangement, may not be the cause of thought."[16]

Hume is not far from Locke's suggestion that it is not inconsistent, as far as we know the nature of substance, for God to add to matter a power of thinking. Hume says, as far as we know about causal relation, matter and motion can be regarded as the causes of thought. If anything, Hume's conclusion is much closer to the materialists', since God is not part of his conclusion. But just as Locke saw no danger in his supposition for religion or morality (even for immortality), so Hume asserts that what he has said in this section (and presumably in this conclusion) "takes nothing from" the arguments for religion: "everything remains precisely as before" (p. 251).

In the previous section of the *Treatise*, Hume had argued that all of the accounts of external objects and of matter suffered from difficulties and contradictions. Modern philosophers, with their distinction between primary and secondary qualities, are particularly vulnerable, Hume thinks, because by making colors, sounds, tastes, etc., impressions in the mind, they are incapable of giving a coherent account of external objects. Difficulties in this account of matter were linked with difficulties in the account of mind. Hume sought a way around these problems by rejecting some of the standard concepts. Other eighteenth-century writers struggled to find a solution within the traditional concepts of matter and mind. But the fears of many over the growth of materialism became justified as the debate continued. There were some writers who, even on the corpuscular account of matter, advanced the view that thought was a property of the complex organization of the brain. As the concept of corpuscular matter gave way to matter as force and power, this claim became more attractive.

Notes

1. Watts advances a somewhat similar conclusion. He thinks grammar has led us to think of extension and thought as properties, but he sees no reason for not saying these are "the very substances themselves" (*Philosophical Essays*, p. 53). He thinks that "learned and *logical* Forms of speaking" have led us to look beyond extension and thought, but he is against multiplying Beings without necessity. "Why may not these very Ideas of solid Extension and a Thinking Power be supposed to be the *Substrata* or Substance themselves?" (p. 54)

2. This sort of example was not Hume's invention. Watts had said that if souls or spirits were in a place, "they must be extended, they must be long, Broad, and Deep and then they must be of some Shape or Figure" (*Philosophical Essays*, pp. 147-48). Watts and Hume may have borrowed this example from Malebranche or from Cudworth. In his *Recherche*, Malebranche had said that a thought is neither round nor square. Thought is not divisible. "A straight line can be used to cut a square into two triangles, two parallelograms, or two trapeziums; but by what line could a pleasure, a pain, or a desire conceivably be cut, and what figure would result from this division." (*De la recherche de la vérité*, 1674–75. The English translation is from the recent edition of Thomas M. Lennon and Paul J. Olscamp, Ohio State

University Press, 1980, p. 274. The standard French edition is that of Geneviève Rodis-Lewis, Vrin, 1974. The remark cited here is found in volume II, p. 24 of this edition.) Cudworth writes: "We cannot Conceive a *Thought*, to be of such a certain *Length*, *Breadth*, and *Thickness*, *Measurable* by *Inches* and *Feet*, and by *Solid Measures*. We cannot Conceive *Half*, or a *Third Part*, or a *Twentieth Part* of a *Thought*, much less of the *Thought* of an *Indivisible Thing*; neither can we Conceive every *Thought* to be of some certain Determinate *Figure*, either *Round* or *Angular*; Spherical, Cubical, or Cylindrical, or the like" (*The True Intellectual System*, p. 282).

3. Hume suggests another alternative, that the place is a mathematical point, "without parts or composition." This reference to some of the contemporary debates about space is not elucidated, but it is not I think important for the point he goes on to make.

4. Cudworth cites this maxim in his summary of the materialist-immaterialist debate among the ancients. It is, he tells us, objected against the unextended nature of incorporeal substances that they involve "an *Absolute Contradiction* and *Impossibility*", because "they are said to be *All in the Whole*, and *all in every Part* of that Body, which they are united to, or Act Upon" (*The True Intellectual System*, p. 782; cf. p. 831). Similarly, Gassendi used the principle in his Objections to Descartes on the Sixth *Meditation*: "Will you say that you are therefore unextended, because you are a whole in a whole, and are wholly in every part?" (p. 198 in the Haldane and Ross translation). Gassendi went on to question the intelligibility of this principle. "Can a single thing thus be at the same time wholly in several parts? Faith assures us of this in the case of the sacred mystery (of the Eucharist). But the question here is relative to you, a natural object, and is indeed one relative to our natural light. Can we grasp how there can be a plurality of places without there being a plurality of objects located in them. . . . Likewise, if a thing is wholly in one place, can it be in others, unless it is itself outside itself, as place is outside place."

5. This route was not unique to the eighteenth century. Cudworth tells us that there were older "Asserters of *Incorporeal Substance*" who accepted the materialist's principle that "*whatsoever Is*, is *Extended*; and what is *Unextended* is *Nothing*; but then denying that other of theirs, That *whatsoever* is *Extended* is *Body*: They asserting, Another *Extension*, *Specifically* Different from that of Bodies" (p. 833).

6. It is tempting to think that here, too, Hume learned from Cudworth. In one of his many remarks against the ancient materialists, Cudworth says that, among other things, the materialists would have to maintain "that no Substance can Co-exist with any other *Substance* (as Soul with Body) otherwise than by *Juxta-Position* only" (p. 833).

7. In writing of the materialists — those men who "allowed no existence to anything that had not extension" — Locke notes that they claim to be unable to "Imagine any sensible quality of any body without extension." As a corrective, Locke suggests that they might have "reflected on their *ideas* of tastes and smells as much as on those of sight and touch," or even had they reflected on their ideas of hunger and thirst, "they would have found that they included in them no *idea* of extension at all" (*Essay*, 2.13.25).

8. The details of Hume's analysis of our knowledge of the external world, and of the idea-object distinction, are examined in the companion volume, *Perceptual Acquaintance from Descartes to Reid*.

9. Apparently there was one reaction to this section, but the author completely misses the satire in Hume's account. See *A Letter from a Gentleman to His Friend in Edinburgh* (1745), edited and reprinted by E. C. Mossner and John V. Price, 1967. This *Letter* describes and summarizes a pamphlet attack on Hume. Judging from that summary, the author of that pamphlet takes Hume seriously and fails to understand the issues presented by Hume. David Berman has recently argued that there is in Anthony Collins's writing a related inversion to Hume's argument that immaterialism is an atheism. Collins argued that it was important for

Clarke to be able to explain the creation of matter *ex nihilo*, for without such an explanation there would be no reason to reject the doctrine of two unrelated substances, God and
matter (*Answer to Mr. Clarke's Third Defence*). Berman suggests satire in Collins's use of
'Christian' to characterize himself, in commenting to Clarke that if matter once be allowed
"to be a self-existent Being, we Christians who believe but in one self-exisiting Being, are
obliged by our own Reasoning to allow Matter all possible Perfections" (p. 387, in the 1731
edition of the Clarke-Collins exchange). In this passage, Collins professes to agree with Clarke
in replying to the atheists, but Berman believes Collins was implying that "the theist's logic
leads — once matter is allowed to be a substance — to pantheistic materialism." (David Berman,
"Anthony Collins and the Question of Atheism in the Early Part of the Eighteenth Century,"
Proceedings of the Royal Irish Academy 75, Section C, Number 5, 1975, pp. 85-102)

10. *Recherche*, I.XIV.I, p. 156 in the Rodis-Lewis edition, pp. 67-68 in the Lennon-
Olscamp edition.

11. The talk of two sorts of objects is also found in Berkeley, although for him the two
sorts are visible and tangible objects. In section 44 of the *New Theory of Vision* (1709), he
distinguishes two moons: the visible moon, which is "a small round, luminous flat" disk,
and the moon that I judge to be so many diameters of the earth distant from me. The same
duality holds for more ordinary objects also: a man, a tree, a tower. Section 50 says "there
are two sorts of objects apprehended by the eye, the one primarily and immediately, the
other secondarily and by intervention of the former." The *New Theory* appears to make visible objects properties of spiritual substance but not tangible objects. Thus Hume could have
had this duality of objects in mind.

12. It is at this point that Hume gives a footnote reference to Bayle's article on Spinoza.
John Laird (*Hume's Philosophy of Human Nature*, 1932) has pointed out that most of the
arguments used or criticized by Hume in this section of the *Treatise* are found in various
comments by Bayle, e.g., Remark E in the article on Leucippe; Remark C in Dicéarque; and
Remark F in Simonide. Laird thinks Hume's knowledge of Spinoza was probably based almost entirely on Bayle's remarks in his article on Spinoza. It would be very unlikely, however, that Hume was unacquainted with the long debates in Great Britain over these issues,
especially with the debate between Clarke and Collins (reprinted as late as 1731), Watts's
Essays, and of course Locke's *Essay*.

13. Cf. Locke, *Examination of P. Malebranche's Opinion*, *Works*, 1823, vol. IX, p. 234-
45: "The mind or soul that perceives is one immaterial indivisible substance. Now I see the
white and black on this paper, I hear one singing in the next room, I feel the warmth of the
fire I sit by, and I taste an apple I am eating, and all this at the same time. Now I ask, take
'modification' for what you please, can the same unextended indivisible substance have different, nay inconsistent and opposite (as these of white and black must be) modifications
at the same time?"

14. Cf. Locke, *Essay* 4.10.16: "For unthinking particles of matter, however put together,
can have nothing thereby added to them but a new relation of position, which it is impossible should give thought and knowledge to them."

15. In *A Letter from a Gentleman*, Hume credits the doctrine of occasional causes to
both Descartes and Malebranche. He says this doctrine "never gained great Credit, especially
in *England*" (p. 28). It is true that "*Cudworth, Locke* and *Clarke* make little or no mention
of it." That is, this is true for Locke in his *Essay*. His *Examination of P. Malebranche's Opinion* is a detailed discussion of that doctrine. There were others in England who, in varying
degrees, followed Malebranche, in particular on the point Hume mentioned about God being
the cause of our actions. Malebranche's influence in Britain was rather more extensive than
we usually believe.

16. In *Essays, Moral, Political and Literary* (1741–42; reprinted Oxford, 1963), p. 597.

However, in a long note in Book III, Part II, Section III of the *Treatise*, Hume characterizes as an error "the conjunction of thought and matter" (p. 504). This error results from the inclination we have to add relations as a way of completing an association or union. With an obvious reference to the section on immateriality, Hume writes: "Many of our impressions are incapable of place or local position; and yet those very impressions we suppose to have a local conjunction with the impressions of sight and touch, merely because they are con-join'd by causation, and are already united in the imagination." He says this inclination leads us to feign "a new relation, and even an absurd one."

Chapter IV

Space and Extension

Hume's replacement of conjunction by coexistence in his account of our conception of objects was based upon two claims. First, not all the qualities of objects *are* spatially located, nor (to use his alternate language) are all the perceptions present to us extended. The second claim on which Hume's resolution of the materialist-immaterialist controversy rests is the denial of the dictum, 'no thing can be or act where it is not'. This dictum had wide currency in both centuries. We saw Cudworth referring to those writers who urged that everything that exists must be extended. Locke also refers to this doctrine (2.13.25). It was applied to cognition as well as to the action of bodies: no action, including cognitive action, at a distance.[1] As the concept of matter changed from corpuscularity to that of force and powers, the need for interpreting this dictum as requiring spatial location was dissipated. But the notion of space itself was frequently linked with that of extension, albeit not always the same kind of extension as with bodies. Hume's remark that the perceptions of sight and feeling *are* extended is, I believe, part of that mode of thinking, where 'extension' was divorced from matter. Hume does not discuss this part of his first claim, so we cannot be certain how he understood the extension of perceptions. But discussion of space found in Locke and Newton may help to shed some light on Hume's claim (as well as light on that difficult Part II of Book I of his *Treatise*). These discussions of space are also important in the context of the changing concept of matter in the eighteenth century. Changes in that concept aided and altered the materialism developing in Britain. Locke's suggestion was rendered more plausible with a *force* concept of matter, than with a *corpuscular* concept.

Locke: Extension and Expansion

In his discussion of the idea of solidity (the idea "most intimately connected with and essential to body"), Locke distinguishes solidity from *pure space*: the latter is not capable of any resistance or motion. We can get the idea of pure space, he tells us, by thinking of one body alone moving, while all others are at rest. Then "the place it deserted gives us the *idea* of pure space" (2.4.3). Another body could move into this deserted place without encountering any resistance. But both body and space have *extension*, although of different sorts. The extension of body is "the cohesion or continuity of solid, separable, moveable parts" (2.3.5). The extension of space is "the continuity of unsolid, inseparable, and immoveable parts." The notion of unsolid and inseparable *parts* is the distinguishing feature of the extension of space. Locke offers as an example of pure space, "a concave superficies" (i.e., surface), where we think of the distance between its opposite parts without any body being there. The domed sky might be an illustration.

In 2.13, Locke elaborates on this notion of parts and extension applied to space. In 2.13.3, *distance* is characterized as space "considered barely in length between any two beings," the space between any two objects. Distance is a mode of space; the ideas of distances (an inch, a foot, mile) are modes of the idea of space. The idea of immensity is acquired by our repeating and adding distinctions: we discover that there is no end to that process (2.13.4). *Capacity* is space "considered in length, breadth, and thickness." The idea of extension, Locke adds, is applied to both distance and capacity. In 2.13.5, the extension of space is said to be 'circumscribed space'. He speaks of the "parts of the termination of extension or circumscribed space." Circumscribed space gives us the idea of *figure*. This idea is also acquired from the sight and touch of bodies. But what is interesting is that Locke claims we can acquire this idea as well from space: by considering the angles made in all the "parts of the extremities of any body or space." The figures that actually exist in "the coherent masses of matter" are augmented by "the stock that the mind has in its power, by varying the *idea* of space." Figures can be multiplied ad infinitum.

This account of the idea of figure is interesting in its derivation from our *thinking* about *space*, as well as from *sensing body*. Also of interest is the role that lines and angles play: they *define* figure but they are also thought of as being *present in* space. Locke's meaning is that we think of portions of space being *divided by* lines and angles, not *filled with* bodies. Space is enclosed by lines and angles.

For the mind having a power to repeat the *idea* of any length directly stretched out, and join it to another in the same direction, which is to double the length of that straight line or else join it to another with what inclination it thinks fit and so make what sort of angle it pleases: and being able also to shorten any line it imagines by taking from it one-half or one-fourth or what part it pleases, without being able to come to an end of any such divisions, it can make an angle of any bigness. So also the lines that are its sides, of what length it pleases, which joining again to other lines of different lengths and at different angles till it has wholly enclosed any space, it is evident that it can multiply *figures* both in their shape and capacity in *infinitum*; all which are but so many different *simple modes of space*. (2.13.6)

Space has points as well as lines and angles. The idea of *place* has a two-fold derivation: from considering "the relation of distance betwixt anything and any two or more points, which are considered as keeping the same distance one with another, and so considered at rest" (2.13.7). Change of place is noticed by distance from fixed points in space. Locke admits that "vulgarly speaking, in the common notion of *place*, we do not always exactly observe the distance from precise points, but from larger portions of sensible objects." He goes on to give examples of objects in relation with other objects: chessmen in a cabin on board ship, the ship in relation to the land and not in relation to the earth (2.13.8). Whether we follow the more common and useful way of comparing one object with another, or a more precise way in relation to fixed points of space, the idea of place is that of a relative position. Hence Locke remarks (anticipating an issue between Leibniz and Clarke) that "we can have no *idea* of the place of the universe, though we can of all the parts of it" (2.13.10).

In denying that we can form an idea of the place of the universe — because beyond the universe "we have no *idea* of any fixed, distinct, particular beings in reference to which we can imagine it to have any relation of distance" — Locke should not be taken to mean that the universe is not in space. There is a difference between saying "the world is somewhere" (which just means 'it does exist') and saying it occupies space. The universe *takes up* space without being *located in* space. "All beyond" the universe "it is one uniform space or expansion, wherein the mind finds no variety, no marks" (2.13.10). He refers to the space beyond the universe as "the undistinguishable *inane* of infinite space." Any body (and the universe is for Locke a body) takes up space. Does infinite space beyond the universe not have parts: lines, angles, and points? Not even by taking thought, can the mind discern parts and points? Locke does not explain how we can think of pure space having parts and forming figures but not infinite space. Is it because the notion of space having parts and forming figures is dependent upon its ability to receive bodies? Are spatial divisions after all dependent upon space-filling?

Locke insists that the ideas of space and solidity are two distinct ideas; body and extension are not, *pace* Descartes, the same (2.13.11). Solidity cannot exist without extension, but the two properties, as the two ideas, are different. The idea of extension "includes no solidity, nor resistance to the motion of body," as the idea of body does (2.13.12). Furthermore, "The parts of pure space are inseparable one from the other." The continuity of space cannot even be separated mentally. Were we able mentally to divide the parts of space, we would be able to "make in the mind two superficies, where before there was a continuity, and consider them as removed one from the other; which can only be done in things considered by the mind as capable of being separated and, by separation, of acquiring new distinct superficies, which they then have not, but are capable of" (2.13.13). An additional difference between the parts of body and space is that those of pure space are immovable (2.13.14).

Locke cites an argument sometimes used to support the claim that space and body are the same: "either this *space* is something or nothing; if nothing be between two bodies, they must necessarily touch; if it be allowed to be something, they ask: Whether it be body or spirit?" His answer is rather striking, for it shows Locke questioning the traditional categories: "To which I answer by another question: Who told them that there was, or could be, nothing but solid beings which could not think, and thinking beings that were not extended?" (2.13.16). His reply would seem to suggest that space might have an ontological status as a substance, as a being, but not belong to either of the standard two substances. Locke even casts doubt on our ability to identify space in terms of substance and accident: is space void of body a substance or an accident? Locke confesses not to know, suggesting that the answer is unimportant, especially since no one has "a clear distinct *idea* of *substance*" (2.13.17) nor any clear idea of accident (2.13.19, 20).[2]

That there can be space devoid of body is shown, Locke thinks, by supposing God were to place one of us "at the extremity of corporeal beings." Such a person would still be able to stretch out his arm beyond his body. Thus "he would put his arm where there was before *space* without body; and if there he spread his fingers, there would still be *space* between them without body" (2.13.21).[3] Locke presents this supposition while still attacking those who struggle to find a metaphysical category for space. The important point for Locke is to see that there is something "which is, or may be between two bodies at a distance, that is not body, has no solidity." Other writers had asserted "the impossibility of *space* existing without *matter*." To do so, Locke suggests, is to make body infinite, as well as to deny God the power "to annihilate any part of matter" (2.13.22). Locke then offers another conjecture about God's power:

> No one, I suppose, will deny that God can put an end to all motion that is in matter, and fix all the bodies of the universe in a perfect quiet and rest and continue them so long as he pleases. Whoever then will allow that God can, during such a general rest, annihilate either this book or the body of him that reads it, must necessarily admit the possibility of a *vacuum*; for it is evident that the space that was filled by the parts of the annihilated body will still remain and be a space without body. For the circumambient bodies being in perfect rest are a wall of adamant and in that state make it a perfect impossibility for any other body to get into that space.

By way of reinforcing the point, Locke concludes this example by remarking that "there is no necessary connexion between *space* and *solidity*," since we can conceive the one without the other.

The two theological suppositions Locke makes use of to convince his reader of the possibility of space without body are not necessary: any ordinary moving body should convince. Divide any body so that the parts can move "up and down freely every way within the bounds of that superficies" (2.13.23). Void space is needed for that motion. Locke conjectures that one reason some writers deny void space is that "the *idea* of *extension* joins itself so inseparably with all visible and most tangible qualities that it suffers us to see no one, or feel very few external objects, without taking in impressions of extension too" (2.13.25). This fact, he suggests, has led some writers to make extension the whole essence of body. Such men have only to switch their attention to sense qualities of other modalities, e.g., taste and smell, in order to discover nonextended qualities.

Locke's conclusion to this chapter on the simple modes of space shows him skirting the question of absolute or relative space. The answer to this question is left to each reader. His subsequent treatment of space would seem to make it absolute: at least, the space taken up by the universe is part of that infinite inane which contains all things. What Locke insists upon in this chapter is the distinctness of the ideas of space and body. We can apply the idea of space to "the distance of its [any body's] coherent solid parts"; or to what lies "between the extremities of any body in its several dimensions"; or to what lies "between any two bodies or positive beings, without any consideration whether there be any matter or no between" (2.13.27). As a further clarification, Locke suggests that the term 'extension' be restricted to matter, "or the distance of the extremities of particular bodies," while the term 'expansion' be applied to space in general, "with or without solid matter possessing it." Space is expanded, body is extended.

In a later chapter, Locke says that he prefers "the word *expansion* to *space*, because *space* is often applied to distance of fleeting successive parts, which never exist together" (2.15.1). The common idea for both expansion and duration is *continued lengths*. We continue adding ideas of lengths of space without end, but we "easily in our thought come to the end of solid extension: the extremity and bounds of all body we have no difficulty to arrive at" (2.15.2). If we were to say that the bounds of space are limited, "that beyond the bounds of body there is nothing at all," this would confine God "within the limits of matter." Not even the heavens can contain God: God fills all expansion. Thus God is specially linked with space, not with matter. God's omnipresence cannot be material. God fills eternity also (2.15.3).

That Locke probably had the Cartesians in mind (at least Descartes) in distinguishing the expansion of space from the extension of body is suggested when we recall Descartes's comments to Arnauld on the impossibility of a vacuum. Descartes insists that "there is true extension in the space we call void." From this, he concludes that space has "all the properties necessary for the nature of body."[4] Similarly, whereas Locke could conceive of a limit to the universe but not to God, Descartes claims that "no limit to the world can be conceived, without my conceiving extension outside it," but to conceive extension outside of the world is to extend the world. Thus a plenum results. But draw the distinction between the extension of body and the expansion of space, and the plenum disappears. Space now becomes limitless.

Space and time (not matter) are the more pervasive, even the more fundamental, concepts. Finite, real beings have a position with respect to one another in "those uniform infinite oceans of duration and space" (2.15.5). Duration and space are uniform and boundless. Without fixed points to locate objects, those objects would be lost in time and space, they would "lie jumbled in an incurable confusion." Usually Locke distinguishes portions of duration and space from duration and space: time and place are portions of infinite duration and space, "determinate distinguishable portions of those infinite abysses of space and duration" (2.15.6). There are two ways in which we mark out such portions. First, time is that portion of infinite duration "as is measured out by and co-existent with the existence and motion of the great bodies of the universe, as far as we know of them." In the same way, place is that portion of infinite space "which is possessed by and comprehended within the material world." Thus time and place are the measures of particular times and places of corporeal bodies. The second way we mark out portions of infinite duration and space is where we apply time "to parts of that infinite duration" without reference to bodies. Similarly for place: we think of portions of it which could receive body but which do not now have any (ibid., section 7). The extension "of any body is so much of that infinite space as the bulk of that body takes up" (section 8). Space defines body. Similarly for the duration of an object: it is a portion of infinite time.

In this combined chapter on space and duration, Locke confirms that space has parts, just as duration does. "Every part of duration is duration too, and every part of extension [expansion] is extension, both of them capable of addition or division *in infinitum*" (section 9). But the parts of expansion and duration are not separable, not even in thought. In this they are unlike the parts of bodies which are separable, both really and in thought (section 10). There is a difference with respect to parts, between duration and expansion: duration is uni-dimensional, "as it were the length of a straight line," while expansion is multi-dimensional and has figure, breadth, thickness. But in this passage, time gains the priority: duration is the "measure of all existence" (section 11). Space is less easily seen as applying to all existence—he cites angels and spirits—but Locke does not exclude this possibility. Duration is *perishing distance*, no two parts exist together, they follow each other in succession. Expansion is *lasting distance*, all its parts exist together (section 12). We can, however, conceive "the eternal duration of the Almighty," lasting distance. God comprehends in his knowledge all past and future things: omniscience *is* God's omnipresence. Locke concludes this chapter on a somewhat cryptic note, in an attempt to show duration and expansion equal: "every part of space" is "in every part of duration"—time is the measure of all existence—and "every part of duration" is "in every part of expansion." Does this latter clause mean that there is no part of duration which is not coincident with space—that time (that is, duration) is the measure of *all* existence, including space? If God is in all space, or fills all space, then in that sense duration might be in space.

Newton: Substance or Property

Locke's remarks on space and time provide a good framework for Newton's (and for Clarke's) account of these two notions. Motion is more prominent in Newton's account than in Locke's, but the distinction between the infinite reaches of duration and space *and* particular, finite portions of them is captured by Newton's distinctions between absolute and relative time and space. Absolute time of itself flows equally without relation to anything else. This is duration. (*Principia*, Scholium to Def. VIII) Relative, apparent common time is an external, sensible measure of duration by means of motion. Absolute space is continuous and immovable; relative space is some movable dimension or measure of absolute space.[5] Place, as it was for Locke, "is a part of space" filled by body. It too can be either absolute or relative. Position is a property of place. Any body is in some part of immovable space. A ship, for example, is in or moves in or is at rest in this space. The earth also moves through or in absolute space, that immovable space.

The order of the parts of time, like the order of the parts of space, is immutable. To move these parts out of their places would be to move them out of themselves: "times and spaces are, as it were, the places as well of themselves" as of all other things. Here again, we hear an echo of Locke's 2.15 passage. There are two different orders, one of succession, the other of situation. Time and space are the primary places of things. It is accordingly absurd to think these places could be moved. Absolute places are immovable. Immovable space is also characterized as those places which retain their position to each other "from infinity to infinity."

At the root of the difference between Clarke and Leibniz over space and time (and hence between Newton and Leibniz) is this notion of an absolute space that has parts, a notion shared by Locke and Newton. Leibniz saw in this way of talking a view of space as substance. He accepted the notion that the order of coexistence is space and the order of succession is time, but the disagreement Leibniz has with Newton is that Newton used this language of the order of parts for *space* and *time*, not for *objects* constituting space and time. Leibniz's argument against Newton's concept of absolute space as a substance is that one point of such a space would not differ from any other, in the absence of objects in that space. But what would count as being different? If these points are, as Newton and Clarke insisted, the *primary* place of objects, and if the parts of that space are related to each other and keep their relations eternally, there would seem to *be* a difference between one point and another, although not a *discernible* difference. It is just this lack of a discernible difference that led Leibniz to suspect the notion of an absolute space with parts. Difference of detectable places can only be found through difference of relations, and the relation of parts of space is by itself insufficient for even the different location of those parts. But of course, Newton's claim is just that the notion of those parts having a location is unintelligible. A primary place is a location for some object. The locution, 'time and places are, as it were, the places . . . of themselves', is obscure, but I think it cannot mean to treat the points of space as if they were objects with a location *in* space. To distinguish (even in thought) one point of that space from another, we may, as Locke seemed to suggest, have to think of those points being filled by objects. Then the relative distance between one object and another shows us the difference in the points of space.

Space for Leibniz is a property of objects, in the sense of the result of order relations between objects. To his charge that Newton turned space itself into a substance, Clarke denies that space is a *being*, a substance. Instead, it is a property, in the sense of a *consequence* of God's existence. Just as the nature of coexisting and successive *objects* constitutes for Leibniz space and time, so in a closely similar way, the nature of God constitutes space and duration. Leibniz misses this similarity, claiming that there are only two possibilities for Newton: either space (he says 'finite space', which in part accounts for his misunderstanding Newton: Newton's absolute space is infinite) is extended and hence is a property of something extended (implying a material God), or space is a relation, meaning a relation of a particular kind, i.e., coexistence and succession.[6] Leibniz's first alternative is met by Locke's distinction between extension and expansion, although this is not a distinction used by Clarke.[7] With this distinction, the materialism of space with bodily parts is avoided. Leibniz's other alternative does not exhaust the possibilities: it probably does not even capture his own doctrine, for the reason I have suggested, namely, that space and time *result from* objects rather than being a relation between or a property of them.[8]

Leibniz's second alternative may not be fully intelligible, but it is clearly this that Newton was trying to articulate in that famous General Scholium. Clarke puts the point to Leibniz succinctly: "For space and duration are not *hors de Dieu*, but are caused by, and are immediate and necessary consequences of his existence."[9] Newton tries to distinguish *being* eternal and infinite from eternity and infinity. Similarly, he sees a difference between duration or space and that which endures or is present. God "endures forever, and is everywhere present." It is from this aspect of his nature—that he exists "always and everywhere"—that God "constitutes duration and space." In one of his replies to letters from Bishop Butler, Clarke draws an important distinction between space as a property of God and space as that *in which* all other substances exist. 'Being a property of' involves belonging to a substratum: the self-existent substance is "it self (if I may so speak) the *Substratum* of *Space*, the *Ground* of the Existence of *Space* and *Duration* it self."[10] Butler responded by saying he found those locutions about space and God difficult to understand (pp. 23-24). Clarke admits in his reply that these *were* difficult expressions, but he tried an explication: "The Idea of *Space*, (as also of *Time* or *Duration*,) is an *Abstract* or *Partial Idea*; An Idea of a certain *Quality* or *Relation*, which we evidently see to be *necessarily-existing*; and yet which (not being itself a *Substance*,) at the same time necessarily *praesupposes* a *Substance*, without which it could exist; . . ." (pp. 27-28).

Clarke's explication is not very helpful. In his fourth letter, Butler had suggested that, while he agreed that space is necessary for *all* beings, he did not really have a clear idea of what it means to say spirit exists in space, if it does not mean that "such a particular quantity of Space terminates the *Capacity of acting* in finite Spirits *at one and the same time*; so that they cannot act beyond that determined Quantity" (p. 24). What acts of spirits did Butler have in mind? It may be cognitive acts. In some comments on God's ubiquity, Newton talks of God's perceiving and understanding all things. Clarke explains this to Leibniz in several places. For example, "God perceives everything not by means of any organ, but by being himself actually present everywhere."[11] The point was made in Clarke's very first reply to Leibniz's criticism of the notion that space is the sensorium of God. God, Clarke says, does not need a medium "whereby to perceive things"; for he, "being omnipresent, perceives all things by his immediate presence to them, in all space wherever they are."[12] Thus the suggestion seems to be that space as a property of God is linked with God's omnipresence, and that his omnipresence is cognitive. God is present to all things because he knows and perceives them. Clarke seems to reject the suggestion out of hand in his answer to Butler's sixth letter: "The *Ubi* of *Spirits*, being their *Perception* only; and the *Omnipresence* of God, being his *infinite*, *Knowledge* only; are mere

Words, without *any Sense* at all" (p. 42). It may be that Clarke only rejects the claim that God's omnipresence is *only* his knowledge, for it seems clear that one instance of God's ubiquity *is* his cognitive presence to all things.

Colliber, John Clarke, and Edmund Law: Space as Distinct from Matter

Samuel Colliber (*An Impartial Enquiry into the Existence and Nature of God*, 1718) identifies the cognitive reading of God's omnipresence as a view taken by some of the Schoolmen and by some of the new Cartesians (among the latter, he cites Poiret and Roel). "From the Opinion of the Deity's being absolutely Unextended our New Cartesians have infer'd that he is nothing else but *Cogitation* . . . i:e: they assert that he is for no other Reason Every where than because he Think's and is Conscious Every where" (p. 190).[13] Colliber only reports this view; he gives no indication that he accepts it. This view does surface occasionally in Britain. Berkeley gives such an analysis, both for God's presence to all things and for the presence of objects to us.[14] Isaac Watts later says: "When we say that God, the infinite Spirit, is *every where*, in a strict philosophical sense, we mean that he has an immediate and unlimited consciousness of, and agency upon all things, and that his knowledge and power reach also to all possible, as well as to all actual being."[15] In his notes to his translation of King's *De Origine Mali*, Edmund Law remarks: "Thus the unlimited exercise of God's *Knowledge* and *Power* demonstrates him *Omnipresent*."[16] Colliber is more concerned with space than with cognition, with the link between space and God. Space is characterized as "an Immaterial Expansion," an expansion "which pervade's and replenishe's the Material Universe" (p. 217). In the same way, God as immaterial expansion penetrates matter (pp. 217-19). Colliber follows Locke in distinguishing the extension of matter from the extension of space, the latter being indicated by the term 'expansion' (p. 212).[17] He cites Newton, Locke, and Bentley as writers who have demonstrated the reality of "a Space Specifically distinct from Matter"; but he points out an easy proof, one we can all use. Calling attention to the "Spaces between the Heavenly Bodys," he remarks: "That those Wide Spaces contain but a very Inconsiderable Portion of Matter (and That without any Vortical Motion as *Des Cartes* dreamt) may be concluded from the Free Passage which they give to the Tails of Comets" (p. 215).

Another demonstration of a space distinct from bodies is taken from the nature of gravitation:

If there is no Portion of Matter either Absolutely Light or Less Heavy in it's Own Nature (as the *Aristotelians* and Others have without sufficient Reason suppos'd) but Every Particle gravitate's in a just Proportion to it's Real Bulk (as is now generally agree'd); then it follow's that Every Greater Portion of Matter must gravitate in a just proportion to the Number and Size of the Particles which compose it. From which Principles it's manifest that no sufficient Reason can be giv'n why any Two Bodies of Equal Superficies should gravitate differently but only This, viz, That the One ha's either More or Greater Pores and contain's Less Matter than the Other. (pp. 216-17)

The space between the particles or the pores in extended bodies, this immaterial expansion which pervades and penetrates the parts of matter, is associated with God. Colliber seems to work with the same notion of space as a property of or a result of God as did Clarke and Newton. He does not identify God with space; he only means to say both God and space are immaterially extended, i.e., expanded. Finite spirits do not seem to have an affinity with space. At least, Colliber is not as firm as he might be about which kind of extension belongs to finite spirits. Cogitation, he says, "can't be without some sort of Extension or Expansion as it's Immediate Subject. Besides, having no other Notion of Cogitation than as by Ideas, it appear's to me impossible that any Being should either form or receive Ideas or Images of Extended Things in case it's Own Nature admit's of nothing like Extension" (p. 222). Being like extension (i.e., being expanded) is not the same as being extended. Colliber was not alone in the century in keeping the ambiguity around the nature of finite spirits. Since he agrees with Locke that cogitation is not incompatible with matter, we cannot say that in requiring finite spirits to be extended in some way if they are to receive ideas of body, he is trying to avoid a materialism of finite spirits. What is clear, though, is that there are at least two ingredients in Colliber's metaphysic that are immaterial: God and space.

That space was separate from body, but with its own kind of extension, was the prevailing doctrine; but it did not go unattacked. Edmund Law for one, in his extensive notes to his translation of William King's book on the origin of evil, read Locke's abstract ideas as *entia rationis*, and then argued that "Duration, Space, Number, etc., which evidently are such, can have no real Existence in Nature, no proper *Ideatum* or *Objective Reality*" (*An Essay concerning the Origin of Evil* (London: W. Thurlbourn, 1731), p. 7, n.3). King was in that tradition which distinguished place or space from matter. "*Place* therefore seems to be something beyond, beside and distinct from, the

Matter which it receives" (p. 8). Were matter annihilated, King argued, "whatsoever still remains will all belong to the nature of *Space*" (p. 9). Distinguishing the properties of space from those of matter, King characterized space as "something extended, immoveable, capable of *receiving* or *containing* Matter, and penetrable by it." Law charges King with overlooking the fact that space is either a mere negation or absence of matter or it is "the extension of *Body* consider'd *abstractly*." In neither case is space a positive substance or quality (p. 9, n. 5; cf. p. 25, n. 11).

In his extended attack against Law's notes in King, John Clarke (*A Defence of Dr. Clarke's Demonstration of the Being and Attributes of God*, 1732) speaks of space *containing* body, but he insists that space is not a substance: he takes what Law identifies as Gassendi's middle way for space. John Clarke says that nobody now contends that space is a substance, but nevertheless it is an ontic ingredient (p. 33). Space is, he argues, a mode, a mode of the infinite substance. John Clarke follows Samuel Clarke (and many other writers) in saying that "we cannot suppose any Being without Space" (p. 35), including spirits. Just as spirits are extended but not in the same way that matter is extended, so space has an extension. The extension of space is not divisible or separable: this is one way in which its "extension differs from that of body" (p. 42; cf. p. 49).

Hume: The Points of Space

Like most of his predecessors, Hume distinguishes space from body, and he gives parts and extension to both. Unlike Newton and Locke, he denies that we can have an idea of space without reference to objects *in* space; but since his objects are perceptions, it is seen space and perceived parts on which his analysis of space rests. The fact that Part II of Book I of the *Treatise* opens with a section rejecting infinite divisibility shows that, in that controversy, Hume was with Berkeley in working from and testing that claim by means of phenomenological examples. The ink-spot example (and others later in that part) demonstrates that there are minima, perceived minima. Hume's repeated remarks throughout this part that what is perceived, at least what his senses convey, "are only colour'd points, dispos'd in a certain manner" (p. 34; cf. pp. 39, 40, 62, 112) and his claim that these colored points are not infinitely divisible, simply follow upon Berkeley's account of visual and tangible perception. That account is rooted in the tradition of optical treatises. Although Berkeley rejects the geometrical explanation of distance perception, he retains the use of points in his analysis, insisting only that the points are visible and tangible. He speaks of our seeing visible points when we look at the wall of our room, or when we scan the scene outside.[18] In his *Philosophical Commentaries*, Berkeley talks of visible and tangible extension being a continuity of visible and tangible points (Entries 78a and 287). These extensions of course are separate, the points in each cannot "make one sum," hence "these extensions are heterogenous" (Entry 295).

Addressing himself to the debate over infinite divisibility of finite extension, Berkeley insists that "Every particular finite extension, which may possibly be the object of our thought, is an *idea* existing only in the mind, and consequently each part thereof must be perceived" (*Principles*, section 124). Since I do not perceive innumerable parts in any finite extension, that extension does not contain such parts. Berkeley has his own special reasons for restricting extension to *perceived* points, for he traces the materialism he was combatting (i.e., corpuscularianism) to the notion that there is another extension which exists independent of us and which is claimed to be infinitely divisible. Correspondingly, he has reasons for denying extension of God too:

The great danger of making extension exist without the mind. in y^t if it does it must be acknowledg'd infinite immutable eternal etc. W^{ch} will be to make either God extended (wch I think dangerous) or an eternal, immutable, infinite, increate being beside God. (*Philosophical Commentaries*, entry 290)

Berkeley seems to have assumed in this note that the extension claimed by some writers for God was material extension. He even appears to ascribe that notion to Locke, More, and Raphson, who, he says, "seem to make God extended. 'tis nevertheless of great use to religion to take extension out of our idea of God and put a power in its place. it seems dangerous to suppose extension wch is manifestly inert in God" (Entry 298).

If the only idea of extension is our visual and tangible perceptions, it is not clear what Berkeley could understand to be God's extension. In that note entry, he is probably speaking to those views which he rejected: God (like all spirits) is activity, not passivity. The charge Berkeley makes against the notion that God is extended may have been directed at Spinoza, but we have seen that most writers who ascribe extension to God meant the extension of space.[19] Just as points and lines were used to characterize our perception of space, so they are parts of the account of the nature of space in other writers. When we think of space being divided, we think, Locke tells us, in terms of points, lines, and angles. Arnold Koslow has called to our attention the fact that in some of his early writings, Newton also talks of "the extension of points, lines, and surfaces in space."[20] Koslow cites this passage from Newton's "De Gravitatione et Aequipondio Fluidorum":

In all directions space can be distinguished into parts with common limits we usually call surfaces and these surfaces can be distinguished in all directions into parts whose common limits we usually call lines and again these lines can be distinguished in all directions into parts which we call points. And hence these surfaces do not have depth nor lines breadth nor points dimension unless you say that coterminous spaces penetrate each other as far as the depth of the surface between them.[21]

If points can interpenetrate, they can hardly be dimensionless. Koslow also remarks that in another early work, Newton "developed the idea that there are least parts of space, time, and a least motion."[22]

The two geometries—the geometry of optics and the geometry of space—come together in Hume's section on our ideas of space and time. From the fact (as he took it) that our senses give us colored points ordered in a pattern, Hume argues to the conclusion that extension is not infinitely divisible. The extension he talks about is both that of bodies and that of space. He seems to have thought of bodies, i.e., this table, as being composed of colored and tangible points (just as Berkeley did); but, like Locke and Newton, he also thought of space as being composed of points. Hume differs from Locke and Newton in limiting the space we have ideas of to the *perceived* space, just as bodies for him are *perceived* bodies. While the parts of space (and time) become "at last indivisible," Hume insists that "these indivisible parts, being nothing in themselves, are inconceivable when not fill'd with something real and existent" (p. 39).

One objection to his claim against infinite divisibility is worth noting. "It has often been maintain'd in the schools, that extension must be divisible, *in infinitum*, because the system of mathematical points is absurd; and that system is absurd, because a mathematical point is a non-entity, and consequently can never by its conjunction with others form a real existence" (p. 40). Hume's reply points out that there is a third alternative—what he refers to as a 'medium'—to the "infinite divisibility of matter, and the non-entity of mathematical points." That alternative is to give a color or solidity to these points. A fourth alternative—"the system of *physical* points"—is said to be too absurd to require refutation. Hume does go on to discuss other issues in these debates—the question of penetration, of the boundaries or terminations of points, lines, and surfaces—but his reply to this first objection indicates the way in which he follows Berkeley in phenomenalizing space and time. Preserved in his account is the distinction between space and the body that fills it, between the extension of space and the extension of body. Whether this is a distinction Hume can maintain (especially since he does not claim a separation), his discussion in this part of the *Treatise* is about space and its extension, not about body.

There are many explicit passages in this part that link and equate the idea of extension with the idea of space. The title of the whole part is "Of the Ideas of Space and Time," and each of the first three sections carries a similar title, involving either the *ideas* of space and time or just space and time. Section III gives us an account of how we come by the idea of space:

> Upon opening my eyes, and turning them to the surrounding objects, I perceive many visible bodies; and upon shutting them again, and considering the distance betwixt these bodies, I acquire the idea of extension. (p. 33)

He goes on to identify the impression from which the idea of space in this example is derived: visual impressions of colored points (p. 34). Presumably it is by considering the order of those points that I acquire the idea of space. The same linkage between extension and space is found later in this section (p. 39). Such a linkage is important, in the light of the debates between Cartesians and Locke and Newton (and others). The question was: is extension restricted to body? In applying extension to space, Locke and other writers insisted it was not corporeal. Thus Hume seems to be assuming this distinction: expansion or a noncorporeal extension. At least in the example he gives in section III, the idea of space concerns the order-relation of the points.

Section IV presents a quick summary of "our system of space and time," and section V refers to the second part of that system, namely, *"that the idea of space or extension is nothing but the idea of visible or tangible points distributed in a certain order"* (p. 53). Hume has argued earlier that the ideas of space and time unfilled with objects is not possible: we need those objects (he usually speaks of 'points') in relation. Section V now argues against a vacuum, i.e., an unfilled space, space without matter. Hume takes some of the examples that have been used to support the claim of such a space, and of how we obtain the ideas of such a space. These are examples used by Locke. The main example—the suggestion Locke made of conceiving of all motion in the world to cease, and conceiving of one part of the world being annihilated—is combined by Hume with the standard example of the air-chamber (what happens to the walls of the chamber when the air is extracted). The details of Hume's response to these arguments for empty space need not concern us, but what is of interest is the fact that he picks up the negative features of these examples.

Edmund Law, in his notes to his translation of William King's *An Essay concerning the Origin of Evil*, had said of the idea of space that it was "the mere *negation* or *absence* of *Matter*" (p. 9, n. 5). He went on to suggest that those who argued for space as something real (not a nonentity) were misled by the fact that we can have positive ideas of privative qualities, e.g., of silence or darkness.

But to argue from such an Idea of Space, that Space itself is something external, and has a real existence, seems altogether as good Sense as to say, that because we have a different Idea of *Darkness* from that of *Light*; of *silence* from that of *sound*; of the *absence* of anything, from that of its *Presence*; therefore Darkness, etc. must be something positive and different from Light, etc. and have as real an Existence as Light has.

John Clarke, in his rebuttal to Law's remarks, takes the example of two walls, insisting (this was the standard argument) that there must be something keeping the walls apart (*A Defence*, p. 2). To Law's specific example of negative terms, John Clarke, while calling attention to some differences between silence or darkness and empty space, is content to seize on the property space has of "the *Capacity* of receiving all Body" (p. 4).

Hume notes that in those examples cited by Locke, he appeals to rest and annihilation. Hume responds with some remarks on negative ideas:

'Tis evident the idea of darkness is no positive idea, but merely the negation of light, or more properly speaking, of colour'd and visible objects. A man, who enjoys his sight, receives no other perception from turning his eyes on every side, when entirely depriv'd of light, than what is common to him with one born blind; and 'tis certain such-a-one has no idea either of light or darkness. The consequence of this is, that 'tis not from the mere removal of visible objects we receive the impression of extension without matter; and that the idea of utter darkness can never be the same with that of vacuum. (p. 56)

Hume is concerned to account for our idea of space. That idea requires more than negation. There must be a pattern of impressions before we can acquire the idea of space. Even uninterrupted motion cannot give rise to that idea: "Suppose again a man supported in the air, and to be softly convey'd along by some invisible power; 'tis evident he is sensible of nothing, and never receives the idea of extension, nor indeed any idea, from this invariable motion." Some of Hume's most fascinating examples follow; for, having established that "darkness and motion, with the utter removal of every thing visible and tangible, can never give us the idea of extension without matter, or of a vacuum; the next question is, whether they can convey this idea, when mix'd with something visible and tangible?'' (p. 56) Hume's examples now seek to answer the question, can sight or touch convey the idea of a vacuum if what is seen or touched is perceived as disconnected from its environment, in isolation? Suppose that, "amidst an entire darkness, there are luminous bodies presented to us, whose light discovers only these bodies themselves, without giving us any impression of the surrounding objects." Similarly for touch or feeling: "allow something to be perceiv'd by the feeling; and after an interval and motion of the hand or other organ of sensation, another object of the touch to be met with; and upon leaving that, another; and so on, as often as we please" (p. 57). The question for both examples is, can the dark areas in the vision case and the intervals between feeling objects in the other case give us "the idea of extension without body?" Hume's answer is 'no'.

He then offers his own explanation of why people have been led to believe they do have the idea of a vacuum or of space without objects in relation. He first points out some similarities between the motion of the hand touching objects, and the luminous objects seen in the dark, *and* "a real extension, or composition of visible and tangible objects" (p. 58). First, the sensation of motion is the same in the touching example and in those cases in which we are feeling a compound object with parts. Similarly, the visible luminous objects in the dark affect the eyes in the same way as the eye is affected when the distance is filled by visible objects (pp. 58-59). The objects sensed are also sensed in the same way in unfilled as in filled space, in the visible or tangible as in the invisible or intangible distances. Third, another similarity between the two kinds of distance—visible and invisible—is that they have "nearly the same effects on every natural phenomenon." Hume seems to mean that the fact that the distance is visible or tangible does not alter the fact that qualities, e.g., heat, light, attraction, diminish with distance. That is, "The distant objects affect the senses in the same manner, whether separated by the one distance or the other" (p. 59). As with Locke, so with Hume, distance is the space between points. The idea of space, however, requires both the space and the points to be ordered. It is because of these various similarities of the two kinds of distance that people imagine they gain the idea of space from either, that we "have an idea of extension without the idea of any object either of the sight or feeling" (p. 60). But to think that the idea of distance alone, without being visible or tangible, can give us the idea of extension is an error (p. 62).

Hume even speaks to the claim advanced by John Clarke, that the capacity to receive body is evidence that there is real space apart from body. Might it not be the case, Hume asks, that the invisible and intangible distance has a "capacity of receiving body, or of becoming visible and tangible?" (p. 63) His answer to this seems to be that we cannot experience that capacity, we can only work from observable properties. Furthermore, to call this capacity a vacuum is to make extension and matter the same: a clear indication again that the debate with the Cartesians is at the front of Hume's mind and that he sides with Locke and Newton in distinguishing extension from matter. In applying extension to space, Hume does not follow Locke or Newton in talking of space devoid of body, the absolute space, the infinite abysses of space. But it is still the extension of space that he discusses. The space he discusses is the experience we have of visible and tangible points in relation. Space, we might say, is experienced, perceived sequences of perceptions. Could we go so far as to say that Hume's space is *cognitive* space?

A direct answer to this question may not be easy. Viewing Hume in the context of eighteenth-century discussions of the concepts of space and extension shows him to combine different aspects and to reflect different positions taken in those discussions. Although some writers accepted the principle that what is present to mind is its own perceptions *because* the mind must be present to what it knows (and the mind is not extended),[23] Hume rejects the principle 'no thing can be or act where it is not' but accepts the dictum that *perceptions* are what is present to mind. Having rejected the claim that everything that exists is in a place, Hume nevertheless claims that some perceptions *are* extended, meaning, it seems, that they have a shape. That is, he then—seemingly recognizing that cognitive presence is not spatial presence—appears to give a spatial location to perceptions of sight and touch. He also says that perceptions have parts, and he applies the language of body to them.

We need to ask, however, whether we should take his comments about the extension of sight and touch perceptions as saying that their extension was bodily or material extension. If the discussion of space and time in Part II is applying extension to space, and if this is in clear opposition to the Cartesians and their identification of extension with body, then it may be that 'extended perception' is not equivalent to 'material perception'. As we have seen, space for Locke and others has parts, as well as points and lines. Are the parts of Hume's extended perceptions these sorts of parts, nonmaterial parts? Part of the difficulty with reading Hume in this way is that, in his discussion of the immateriality of the soul, he is citing arguments advanced by other writers. Samuel Clarke certainly denied, as most writers did, that the soul has parts. But in his discussion, Clarke uses the body sense of *parts*, and the body sense of *extension*, to defend his claim that the soul is immaterial. Clarke did not follow Locke's lead in talking of space as extended, but others did. It was a commonplace to speak of space as being extended but immaterial. If, in the section on immateriality, Hume is speaking to that controversy, then we may have to say that he is using the body sense of 'extension' when he talks of some perceptions being extended.[24] He speaks of 'local conjunction', contrasting that with nonlocal conjunction.

On the other hand, if what is present to me are my own perceptions, not bodies, then the extended nature of visual and tangible perceptions may just mean visual and tangible shapes. If we press this phenomenalist or cognitive reading of Hume on perceptions, then local conjunction means 'space-filling' in the sensible, perceptible sense. Is this the intention behind his talk of colored points? Does he mean it is not bodies that our senses reveal, but seen shapes? If this table just is a group of perceptions (p. 239), then the table that is talked about cannot be the material table, and the extension of the perceptions that is the table cannot be material. In the same way, the parts of these perceptions cannot be material parts.

Unravelling Hume on these questions is fraught with difficulties, in large part because of his style of exposition in the *Treatise*. Just as there are uncertainties as to Hume's voice in his *Dialogues*, because of his skill in making the participants express overlapping views, so Hume's dialectical and sometimes satirical style in the *Treatise* frequently hides his own beliefs. We shall not attempt to resolve the ambiguities in that work over the concept of extension, but it is important for us to hear the echoes in Part II of the common view that space is extended in a nonmaterial way. When these echoes are combined with Hume's evident stress upon a phenomenological account of our perceptions, we may see an indication that he was not materializing any perceptions.

Conclusion

One dominant claim throughout this period was that 'no thing can be or act where it is not'. That dictum was applied to perception and knowledge as well as to physical action: no cognitive action at a distance. Minds, it follows, must be where the objects that are perceived or known are located. The question then was, are minds located in the way in which bodies are located? There were writers who ascribed extension to minds, including writers who attacked what they viewed as a growing tendency towards materialism. The materialism they feared was identified with the extension of body, with material extension. Those who attacked such materialism but who still spoke of the mind as being extended and having a location (not being able to operate at a distance) did not think they were ascribing an extension or a location for mind that was the same as the extension and location of body. The extension of body is a function of parts: *partes extra partes* was a common formula. Such parts are hard and impenetrable. The mind was said to be indivisible and not possessed of parts. 'Extension', then, would seem to have two meanings: one for hard, impenetrable parts, another for a whole which had no parts and to which primary qualities do not apply.

Space was also said by many writers to be extended. Some of those who talked this way about space suggested using another term for the extension of space: 'expansion'. Was the expansion of space considered to be like the extension of mind? For those, like Locke, who talked of the expansion of space, space was said to have parts, but the parts of space were not particles. One of the reasons for distinguishing space from body was to show that space is not material. The parts of space are defined in terms of points and line, not in terms of hard, impenetrable particles. There were four different items to which extension was ascribed:

(a) material bodies with divisible parts;
(b) immaterial, finite minds which have no parts;
(c) space which has nonmaterial, perhaps geometrical, parts; and
(d) the immaterial, infinite mind or spirit, God, who has no parts but who is present to all things.

The Cartesian identification of extension with body seems not to have surfaced in discussions ascribing extension or place to finite minds, but it almost invariably surfaced in discussions about how God is linked with space or about God's omnipresence. We discovered an interpretation of God's omnipresence in cognitive terms: omnipresence was his omniscience. We did not find anyone who defended this interpretation outright, but several writers referred to it. There were other writers (e.g., Arnauld and Locke) who, in their use of the term 'idea', interpreted the perceptual talk of objects being present to mind in cognitive terms: 'understood' or 'known'. If to be in a place requires extension, and if the way in which God is said to be in every place is by *knowing* all things, and if being present to a finite mind is being known by that mind, 'extension' in senses (b) and (d) is clearly distinguished from extension in sense (a). It is tempting to suggest that (b) and (d) type extension is a way of referring to the ability of spirits (both finite and infinite) to *know* objects with (a) type extension.

Hume, rejecting the dictum that 'no thing can be or act where it is not' by calling attention to the fact that not all conjunctions require *local* (spatial) conjunction (coexisting in time is a nonspatial conjunction and can hold between a spatial and a nonspatial item), went on to say that some ideas and perceptions *are* located in a place and are extended. The perception of a table consists of parts which give us a notion of distance and contiguity, of length, breadth, and thickness: "the very idea of extension is copied from nothing but an impression, and consequently must perfectly agree to it. To say the idea of extension agrees to any thing, is to say it is extended" (pp. 239-40). Does Hume mean that the idea of extension is itself extended in sense (a)? Is the impression from which the idea is derived extended in that sense? One interpretation of Hume is that both the idea and the impression of extension are extended, are in fact brain impressions. One could modify this interpretation by saying the impression is extended in the brain but the idea is not. This modified interpretation picks up the echoes from Descartes's account of the psychophysiology of perception. But the agreement of the idea of extension with the impression of extension, in the context of this passage from the *Treatise*, does not easily lend itself to a (b) type extension.

The account Hume gives of our idea of space may shed some light on his talk of extended ideas. In the first place, Hume applies extension to space and to time. The idea of space he says, is composed of the impressions of colored and tangible points ordered in a certain way. It may be that what this account does is to identify space (or perceived, experienced space) with that perceived sequence. Space on Hume's account may be more like Leibniz's relational space than like Locke's or Newton's absolute space. But the extension which is the order of perceived points is not the extension of Cartesian body. We still seem to have two senses of 'extension': (a) type extension and the extension of perceived or experienced sequences. This second type of extension may be classed as (a_1), the extension of perceptions which have parts. Only two kinds of perceptions have the sorts of parts that constitute extension, visual and tangible perceptions. The parts of such perceptions are no more like the parts of matter for Locke, Newton, or Samuel Clarke than are the parts of space for Locke, Newton, or Clarke. Thus, however we read Hume's talk of extended perceptions or extended ideas, the extension is not (a) type extension. Nor is the extension of space for Hume the same as (c) type extension.

The question of how to interpret Hume's statements that the perceptions of sight and touch are extended, has parallels with the question of how to interpret the statements by other writers that the mind or soul acts from a place. Unless we give such discussions a cognitive reading, so that talk of the mind being located in the whole and in every part of the body just means that there are cognitive connections throughout our body that enable us to be aware of the sensations on its surface and in the insides, we shall fall into an impossible literalist meaning. Similarly, with those who talk of the mind being where the objects are of which it is aware, there can be any one of three possible meanings: either (1) the mind is literally next to the objects in space, as a few writers claimed; or (2) we do not know objects directly, only our perceptions, which are 'next to the mind' (the spatial phrase here was usually given an analogical reading); or (3) the application of spatial terms to the mind can also be treated as a metaphor, where the intended meaning is cognitive and epistemic.

These various interpretations were responses to questions about the nature of sense perception, of our perceptual awareness of physical objects. The problem was how to understand our knowledge of body, to explain how what is immaterial can come into contact with material objects. That the 'contact' in this instance is perceptual and conscious did not dissuade many writers from using the language of body for describing perceptual acquaintance. The misleading nature of that language was one of the facets in what many saw as a developing materialism. The concepts of space and extension were at the root of the ambiguity: the space within which perceptual awareness can occur, and the space within which mind or soul was related to the world and to its own body. Bodily presence was not always clearly distinguished from cognitive presence.

Similar problems of interpretation arose on the level of our perception of God—how to understand his presence, his omnipresence to the world. How can God affect the material world if he is not present to that world? There was a long tradition of ascribing a special relation between God and the space of the world, God's work-space. The *sensorium Dei* invoked by Newton had its roots in much older metaphysics. A recent writer (Jean Zafiropulo) traces it back to Boethius. In Porphory's translations and commentaries on Aristotle, "the world 'sensorium' appears for the first time, in the sense of the seat or place of physical sensation. But under the pen of Boethius this sensorium assumes an enlarged meaning and ends by becoming 'the *sensorium Dei*'; that is, for Boethius the word becomes the materialization of the thought of God."[25] It is the *sensorium Dei* "in which the creator has awareness, creates and acts at the same time."[26] Human cognition is the reverse of God's, the immaterialization of the material world. While God's creation and knowledge take place, as it were, in the space of the world (His space), man's awareness takes place in the space of his brain. But the brain is material, its space is of the body sort, the capacity to be filled by body. If all space is of this sort, the *sensorium Dei* may lead to a corporeal God. Thus the need was at hand to immaterialize that space. God is in space in a way very different from the way in which planets are in space. Two senses of 'extension' help us, it was thought, to avoid the materialization of mind and awareness, both in our own case and in God's.

But the elaborate workings of the mechanism of the body in perceptual awareness were not easily ignored. The temptation to think of ideas, or only some ideas, as being extended and having parts could not be resisted by some writers. In the same way, it seems obvious, too, that thought is closely tied with the brain, perhaps as property to substance. Once these last two moves are made, however, it is not clear just what is meant by an extended idea or perception, or what is meant by saying that thought is a predicate of the brain.

Notes

1. I detail some examples of the cognitive application of this dictum in my *Perceptual Acquaintance from Descartes to Reid*, chapters III and IV (forthcoming).

2. In this remark about the nature of space, Locke's challenge to the traditional categories was picked up by one of his defenders, Mrs. Catherine Cockburn. In an added section, *Some Cursory Thoughts on the Controversies concerning Necessary Existence, the Reality and Infinity of Space, the Existence and Place of Spirits* (in her *Remarks upon Some Writers in the Controversy concerning the Foundation of Moral Virtue and Moral Obligation*, 1743), she says that those who "maintain the real existence of space, seem to me to have given advantage to their adversaries, by calling it *extension*," since their adversaries take 'extension' to be an abstract idea. Thus to say space is extended means for them that it has no existence outside the mind (p. 389). Space is needed for motion; bodies move; therefore, there is space. She admits that we do not know how to class it, what category of being it belongs to. She thinks that Watts denies space just because he "cannot find out what kind of being it is" (p. 390). She cites Locke's remark questioning the adequacy of the categories of two substances for characterizing all that there is. Space, she suggests, may be a being between those two substances, located on the scale of being between them. It may be *"an immaterial unintelligent substance, the place of bodies, and of spirits, having some of the properties of both"* (p. 319).

3. In his *Elémens de la philosophie de Neuton* (1744; first ed., 1738), Voltaire refers to this supposition as "cet Ancien Argument" (p. 15).

4. See letter to Arnauld, 29 July 1648, pp. 236-37 in *Descartes: Philosophical Letters*, translated and edited by A. J. P. Kenny (Oxford: Clarendon Press, 1970). See also p. 251.

5. One important difference between Locke and Newton is that for Newton, absolute space as a measure of relative space can be plural: the dimension of a subterranean, an aerial,

or celestial space determined in relation to the earth. Voltaire expresses the absolute and separate nature of space and time by saying "Newton regards space and duration as two beings" (*Elémens*, p. 12). While to say they were substances is too strong—since they are properties—nevertheless as properties of God they are more, have more being perhaps, than ordinary properties.

6. Whether these relations can be understood without a prior notion of time is doubtful. That is, coexistence and succession would seem to be temporal relations, not relations in terms of which time can be defined. If this is right, then time becomes for Leibniz (as it did for Kant) the more fundamental concept.

7. In his *A Defence of Dr. Clarke's Demonstration* (1732), John Clarke says that *"Space is the Extension or Expansion of that infinite Being"* (p. 49).

8. Arnold Koslow has made a similar suggestion about Leibniz's theory of space: it is not so much relational as it is "about individual substances and the simple, non-relational attributes they must necessarily possess." ("Ontological and Ideological Issues of the Classical Theory of Space and Time," in *Motion and Time, Space and Matter: Interrelations in the History of Philosophy and Science*, ed. by Peter K. Machamer and Robert G. Turnbull (Columbus: Ohio State University Press, 1976), p. 225.)

9. *A Collection of Papers, Which passed between the late Learned Mr. Leibnitz, and Dr. Clarke, In the Years 1715 and 1716. Relating to the Principles of Natural Philosophy and Religion* (1717). The text of both writers is given in French and English on opposite pages. The above quotation is on p. 47 of the reprint of this exchange edited by H. G. Alexander (Manchester University Press, 1956). This is the edition I have used for all references.

10. The exchange between Clarke and Butler is found in *Several Letters to the Reverend Dr. Clarke, From a Gentleman in Glocestershire* (1716). Butler was raising questions about Clarke's Boyle lectures. The remark quoted here is from Clarke's answer to Butler's third letter, p. 21. The references which follow from this exchange are given in the text, as page references only. Butler's letters are very brief, two or three pages only. Clarke's replies are somewhat longer.

11. The Leibniz-Clarke exchange, p. 109.

12. Ibid., p. 13.

13. Colliber notes that St. Thomas rejects this reading for the location of Angels. See *Summa Theol.*, Pt. I, Q. 54, 55.

14. For the details on the cognitive reading of presence to mind, see my *Perceptual Acquaintance from Descartes to Reid*.

15. *Philosophical Essays on Various Subjects* (1733), p. 167. Later in the century, Priestley cites this passage. See his *Disquisitions Relating to Matter and Spirit* (1777), pp. 221-22.

16. *Essay concerning the Origin of Evil* (1731), pp. 46-47n.

17. Pages 212-30 in Colliber's book constitute an Appendix: "Two Discourses concerning the Nature of Space and Duration."

18. *An Essay towards a New Theory of Vision* (1709), section 80-85.

19. Edmund Law calls attention to Cudworth's discussion of the possible location of spirits. The language of points is used there. "That If the Soul be an *Extended Substance*, then it must of necessity be either a *Physical Point* or *Minimum*, the Least *Extension* that can possibly be, (if there be any such Least, and Body or Extension be not *Infinitely Divisible*) or else it must consist of more such *Physical Points* joyned together. As for the former of these, it hath been already declared to be Impossible, that one Single *Atom*, or *Smallest Point* of *Extension*, should be able distinctly to perceive all the variety of things: to which might be added, That to suppose every Soul to be but one *Physical Minimum* or *Smallest Extensum*, is to imply such an Essential Difference in Matter or Extension, as that some of the *Points* thereof, should be *Naturally* devoid of all *Life*, *Sense*, and *Understanding*, and

others again Naturally *Sensitive* and *Rational"* (*The True Intellectual System of the Universe*, 1678, p. 825).

20. "Ontological and Ideological Issues," p. 245.

21. Ibid. This work of Newton is reprinted and translated in *Unpublished Scientific Papers of Isaac Newton*, edited by A. R. Hall and M. B. Hall (Cambridge: Cambridge University Press, 1962).

22. Ibid., p. 246.

23. For example, William Porterfield, *A Treatise on the Eye* (1759).

24. I have dealt with this question at more length in my study, *Perceptual Acquaintance from Descartes to Reid*. There I place the talk of extended perceptions in the wider context of an inventory of Hume's use of the term 'idea', and of his talk of the faculties of the mind. My suggestion in this chapter that Hume be placed in the tradition of two kinds of extension is reinforced by the analysis of that companion study.

25. *Sensorium Dei dans l'hermétisme et la science*, Jean Zafiropulo et Cathérine Monod (1976), pp. 12-13.

26. Ibid., p. 15.

Chapter V

Matter: Inert or Active

Opposition to Locke's suggestion that God might be able to give to matter the power of thinking arose not only because this suggestion carried the rider that immateriality of the soul was not necessary for immortality. It arose as well, as we saw in Chapter III, from the fear that this suggestion would lead to a conception of man as a machine or automaton. An equally important source of opposition was the corpuscular concept of matter: to ascribe thought to such matter, however complex its organization might be, would be to ascribe activity to that which is dead and inert. The insistence on this concept of matter by the immaterialists became more strident as that concept began to give way to a different view. Once matter was allowed to be active in any way, the possibility that matter might have the power of thinking was more difficult to reject. It became important to decide whether gravitation, repulsion, and attraction were powers inherent in matter, or forces imposed from without. If the latter, it would of course have to be an immaterial substance that did the imposing. God as first cause became for many the constant intervenor in nature, the model of knowledge and action for finite minds. If God and finite minds do intervene in nature to move bodies, how is such action possible, unless God and finite minds are, in some sense, in space? The notion of God's omnipresence in the world was one Newton invoked. Many other writers struggled to protect the cognitive application of the principle of no action at a distance. Even when the eighteenth-century Newtonians began to make explicit a changed concept of matter, one that was compatible with the idea of action at a distance, many writers continued to work with the older notion.

Newton and the Concepts of Matter

Several recent historians of science have tried different ways of characterizing the various concepts of matter present in the eighteenth century. Robert Schofield has identified two concepts of matter in the century. One concept is that of what he calls 'materialism': "All matter is extended, solid, figured, and entirely passive or dead."[1] He is here characterizing one of the Hutchinsonians, Samuel Pike, one of a small group who actively opposed the second, Newtonian concept, which Schofield describes as 'dynamic corpuscularity' or 'mechanism'. Schofield's materialists did not always go so close to the corpuscular constitution of matter as Pike did, but they always insisted that matter acts only by contact and that it is not self-active. To the undifferentiated, homogeneous, indivisible corpuscles, the dynamic corpuscularian added "certain immaterial, central forces of attraction and repulsion under whose influence the primary particles acted upon bodies, at a distance."[2] Most of Schofield's 'materialists' accepted the existence of a subtle matter or fluid present in all bodies. In physiology, the fluid was an alternative to animal spirits. Some Newtonians also appealed to this subtle fluid, which, in the form in which it was described in the third edition of Newton's *Principia* (the General Scholium at the end of Book III), hovered ambiguously between being material and being immaterial. The main contrast in the views of matter distinguished by Schofield is between the 'materialists', who insisted upon matter's inertness, and the 'dynamic corpuscularian', who added forces to matter.

Schofield's label 'materialism' should not be confused with those writers I have cited who were attacked as being materialists. Schofield uses this label to characterize the view that matter possesses forces. The peculiarity about his label is that the view of matter identified by that label is precisely the one defended by the traditional, orthodox writers who were called 'immaterialists'. An immaterialist is a person who defends the view of matter Schofield describes as 'materialism'. As well, Schofield's 'dynamic corpuscularian' label also fits the immaterialist, so long as those forces are not inherent in matter itself. Schofield's dynamic corpuscularian walks a thin line, for the forces added to matter can replace the corpuscularity and passivity of matter in importance. The 'materiality' of matter recedes as matter becomes active. Thus Schofield's labels catch some of the important features about the concept of matter in the century, but they are confusing labels for identifying the traditional immaterialists, who defended a passive concept of matter, and for distinguishing them from the new materialists, who made matter active.

Two other recent historians of science, Heimann and McGuire,[3] find Schofield's classification misleading also. The contrast they think important is that between those who "viewed powers as being non-inherent in matter; that is, 'powers' are not ascribable to bodies in and of themselves," and those who conceived of powers "as being substantively present in entities, thus defining the entities' essence in terms of inherent activity" (pp. 235-36). It is this contrast between forces and powers as external to or as intrinsic to matter that is useful here. It was in this same form that Locke's suggestion was debated; could thought be an intrinsic or natural property of matter?

Forces were always part of Newton's account of the world as he expounded it in the *Principia*, although he claimed to treat them not as physical qualities: "For I here design only to give a mathematical notion of those forces, without considering their physical causes and seats."[4] Newton's language was of motive force as "an endeavour and propensity of the whole toward a centre, arising from the propensities of the several parts taken together"; or of accelerative force "as a certain power or energy diffused from the centre to all places around to move the bodies that are in them"; and in general, of "particles endued with attractive power." Despite Newton's denials that he meant in these passages to talk of force as real (physical or spiritual), Schofield points out that many of his readers and followers in the eighteenth century took him to mean real forces.[5] Ernan McMullin remarks that it is difficult to take words such as 'attraction', 'pulling', 'acting upon' in a nonontological way, "as figures of speech, connoting nothing whatever in the way of agency, either active or passive, on the part of the bodies involved. Not only were his critics unpersuaded, but Newton, in his incessant drafting and redrafting, was just as prone as they to take such terms as 'attraction' to mean what they say."[6]

On the question whether forces could be inherent in matter, Newton often emphatically rejected this. Schofield cites a letter of 1693 from Newton to Bentley (not published until 1756) in which Newton denies action at a distance and affirms a strict materialist doctrine of matter.

It is inconceivable, that inanimate brute Matter should, without the Mediation of something else, which is not material, operate upon and affect other Matter without mutual Contact. . . . That Gravity should be innate, inherent and essential to Matter, so that one Body may act upon another at a Distance thro' a *Vacuum*, without the Mediation of any thing else, by and through which their Action and Force may be conveyed from one another, is to me so great an Absurdity, that I believe no Man who has in philosophical matters a competent Faculty of thinking, can ever fall into it.[7]

Schofield thinks Newton was trying to avoid having his 'forces' read as 'occult qualities', not that he was denying real forces. In any event, Newton was more outspoken on this point in the *Opticks*; in the second edition of 1713 he added 'Queries' in which he made explicit, as Schofield says, "the particulate nature of matter within a frame of force."[8] The fact that these additional remarks were presented as 'Queries' gave Newton greater freedom to speak more openly. Whether tentative suggestion or not, Query 31 opened boldly:

Have not the small particles of bodies certain powers, virtues or forces, by which they act at a distance, not only upon the rays of light for reflecting, refracting, and inflecting them, but also upon one another for producing a great part of the phenomena of nature? For it's well known that bodies act one upon another by the attractions of gravity, magnetism, and electricity; and these instances show the tenor and course of nature, and make it not improbable but that there may be more attractive powers than these.

Our understanding of Newton's concept of matter is further complicated by his introduction, in the General Scholium to Book III, of the aether hypothesis. This was the notion, as Schofield says, that "the apparent forces of attraction between bodies might be caused by impulse of the medium in which they are placed."[9] In that Scholium, Newton said that "Hitherto we have explained the phaenomena of the heavens and of our sea by the power of gravity, but have not yet assigned the cause of this power."[10] The final paragraph appears to offer a suggestion: "a certain most subtle Spirit which pervades and lies hid in all gross bodies; by the force and action of which Spirit the particles of bodies mutually attract one another at near distances, and cohere, if contiguous." Much else is ascribed to this subtle spirit. The *Principia* does not expand on this suggestion, because, as Newton says in the final sentence of this Scholium, "these are things that cannot be explained in few words, nor are we furnished with that sufficiency of experiments which is required to an accurate determination and demonstration of the laws by which this electric and elastic Spirit operates." Query 21 of the *Opticks* does offer some account of how this elastic force could impel bodies "from the denser parts of the medium towards the rarer, with all that power we call gravity." But it was for other writers in the century to elaborate on this suggestion, just as it was Newtonians, not Newton, who extended the dynamic corpuscular account of matter. The echoes of the debates over these issues among eighteenth-century Newtonians and anti-Newtonians are found in some of the more directly theological writings as well. The parallel movement in eighteenth-century science and eighteenth-century philosophy of mind are revealed in this literature.

God as External Cause of Motion

Just as the discussion of Locke's suggestion was framed around the question of whether properties of matter are natural and intrinsic, so the understanding of gravitation and motion centered on what matter was thought to be capable of on its own. For Colliber (*An Impartial Enquiry*, 1718), self-activity ("a Natural Independent Vital Principle of Action," p. 28) was a property only of God. Matter for Colliber was *"a Multitude of Solid, Movable, and Divisible Extensions having an Aptitude to Communicate Motion by Impulse"* (p. 31). Motion is "neither Absolutely Uncaus'd nor yet the Effect of any Internal Universal Active Principle Essential to Matter" (p. 38). The "Atheistical Materialists" (he mentions Spinoza and Hobbes) have been no more successful in accounting for motion on the basis of matter only, than they have in giving to matter the property of intelligence (p. 33). The attempt to account for motion by making gravity a property of every atom or particle of matter similarly fails (pp. 34-35). Gravity is "a Merely Accidental Effect entirely Dependent on Somewhat External," that is, on "the Immediate Agency of the Eternal *Immaterial Being*" (p. 36; see also p. 161).

In a detailed account of how fluids rise in a tube by attraction, Humphrey Ditton (*The New Law of Fluids*, 1714) reaches the same conclusion about the cause of gravity and attraction. He says that the philosophical part of mankind know that "matter is not under its own Laws, nor mov'd by *meer fatal Mechanical Necessity*, but at the Will and Pleasure of *a Supreme Governing Mind*, who created, and continually presides over *the whole Corporeal Universe*. . . ." (pp. 53-54). In this sense, "every thing we see is *Supernatural*; that is, above the pure Energy and Laws of Matter" (p. 54). Ditton distinguishes *natural* effects from *supernatural* ones, the latter being the result of *"some Power or Vertue more immediately impress'd on them* [bodies] *by the Will of the Creator, without the Intervention of any Subordinate Material Cause"* (p. 55). Attraction is not explicable *"in Any pure Mechanical way"* (p. 56). It is *"a Law impress'd on Matter by his*

[God's] *Divine Will and Power and not resulting from any deriv'd inferior Causality or Agency, of Matter upon Matter"* (pp. 56-57). In short, attraction is *"a Power extrinsic to the Essence of Matter as such*, and superadded to or *impress'd thereon"* (p. 60).

One of the most detailed discussions on the passivity of matter is found in Andrew Baxter's *An Enquiry into the Nature of the Human Soul* (1733). Baxter was a strong spokesman for immaterialism, insisting that matter is a solid, extended substance (p. 10).[11] Matter has the property of resistance, but resistance is only reaction. Every change in matter requires an immaterial cause, as does also the very existence of matter. Matter is inactive. The resistance of matter is in fact inconsistent with any power or force belonging to matter (p. 22). Matter cannot both be resistant and self-active (p. 127). Thus physical theory must be changed. Instead of talking of gravity, attraction, elasticity, repulsion as natural powers in matter, we must talk of impulses or forces impressed upon matter *ab extra* (pp. 22-23). Action at a distance is rejected, for nothing can act where it is not. The "force of moving bodies to act on other bodies . . . proceeds solely from their resistance to a change of their state" (p. 52). The consequence of powers not being *in* matter is that all the effects ascribed to such inherent powers *"are immediately produced by the power of an immaterial Being"* (p. 79). Thus his account of matter protects us against atheism. Baxter ascribes to the action of such an immaterial being the phenomena of attraction, repulsion, cohesion, the heaviness of matter (pp. 94-95). Only God or created intelligent beings can act. God's action is continuous: unless *"an immaterial Power* continually re-excited motion in the material universe, all motion would stop in it, in a very short time, perhaps in less than half an hour" (p. 86, n.d). The forces impressed by God are constantly impressed. Strictly, then, those forces are not "the action of matter upon matter, but the vertue and power of an immaterial cause, or being, constantly impressed upon it" (p. 33, n.k). Nor should we be searching for the cause of these forces other than in God's will. Baxter cited Derham's remark that

This attractive or Gravitating Power, I take to be congenial to Matter, and imprinted on all the Matter of the Universe by the Creator's *Fiat* at the Creation. What the *Cause* of it is, the *Newtonian Philosophy* doth not pretend to determine for want of Phaenomena, upon which Foundation it is that that Philosophy is grounded.[12]

To look for other causes for these forces would be to search among second causes in nature, and no such causes for Baxter have the ability to act.

Mechanical motion is defined by Baxter as *"motion excited in matter, by other matter in motion, by means of the necessary resistance it makes to be brought to rest"* (p. 128). A machine is said to be *"a system of matter so disposed, that the fixed or immoveable parts of it may direct the motion impressed (by the power) on the moveable parts, that it may be by them communicated, to the weight, or thing designed to be moved. . . ."* (pp. 130-31). To inject or initiate motion in such a system requires the action of a being outside that system and different in kind. Baxter recognizes the dangers of making God an occult quality, to explain what we do not understand (p. 141). But he is firm nevertheless on God's constant intervention in nature, even as we shall see in a later chapter, in human action. The workings of our physiology (even the circulation of the blood) are due to God's action. To search for a mechanical cause of the circulation of the blood, in the sense of powers implanted in matter, is wrong: it requires *"the intervention or efficiency of any cause immaterial"* (p. 134). Thus Baxter is another example of those immaterialists who took that horn of Hume's dilemma which leads to making God the only real efficacious cause.

In *An Appendix to the First Part of the Enquiry into the Nature of the Human Soul* (1750), Baxter reaffirmed his belief that matter is inactive, impenetrable, and resistant to change. It has no active powers. Its resistance to change is due to its inertia, a property usually called *vis inertiae*, which is equal in all parts of matter. He quotes from MacLaurin's *An Account of Sir Isaac Newton's Philosophical Discoveries* (1748), where it is suggested that some kinds of matter may have less inertia than others. The inertia is due to solidity. Baxter does not think there can be any degrees of inertia, but the important point for him is that matter does resist change: "As long as matter is allowed to make any resistance at all to a change of its state, 'tho ever so little, it could never become a self-moving substance" (p. 8). And of course, if matter had no (or very little) resistance, it could not stop or impel matter. The appeal to a subtle elastic fluid to explain gravity, as Newton suggested in the General Scholium, and as MacLaurin, Pemberton and others were trying to develop, is wrong and useless since this fluid is supposed to be unresisting, yet a form of matter.[13] Baxter argues that if there are different degrees of resistance, Newton's laws of motion will be wrong or in need of revision. To speak of a chain of causes, as some writers do, is to speak uncritically. Such a chain cannot be of *material* causes only, if it really is to explain change, for "a material cause, is a cause without *power*, as well as without *knowledge*" (pp. 19-20). For Baxter, it is just as absurd to talk of second causes in the material world as it is to "suppose free agents *mechanical instruments in the moral world*" (p. 20). Material causes lead to "fatal necessity." His conclusion is always the same: "where there is motion, where before there was none, there must be a *principle* of *beginning the motion*, different from matter" (p. 51).

In his strong denial of action to second causes, Baxter may be showing the influence of Malebranche, although, unlike Malebranche, he did attempt to give man some active role in human action. Baxter was fairly typical of a number of other writers in the century. John Clarke, in his notes to the English translation of Rohault's *System of Natural Philosophy* (1723), talks of active principles impressed upon matter by God. Clarke was another immaterialist. Similarly, Thomas Morgan (*Physico-Theology: Or, A Philosophical-Moral Disquisition concerning Human Nature, Free Agency, Moral Government, and Divine Providence*, 1741), announces in his Preface that he has set himself "to study Nature, and the general Laws which are settled and established among the several Gradations, Ranks and Classes of Beings, so far as they are connected with intelligent, moral Agency" (p. iv). He speaks of "the mechanical Powers and Properties of Bodies" as being "purely passive." Bodies are "incessantly acted upon by some universal, intelligent, designing Cause" (p. v). Morgan followed the standard definition of matter as "extended, solid, or impenetrable and moveable." It is also infinitely divisible. His main point is that bodies are not self-activating; they require an extrinsic active power or energy. What we call "Mechanism and the necessary Laws of Nature, is the free Agency and continued Energy of the Author and Director of Nature" (p. 59). To make matter active, Morgan insists, is an atheism (p. 61).

Robert Clayton (*An Essay on Spirit*, 1750) agreed that matter is inert and not self-active, but he brings the active forces into very close contact with matter. Accepting the Lockean claim that we do not know the essence of either spirit or matter, Clayton insisted that we discover by experience that "the one has the Power of Motion in itself; whereas the other can neither put itself into Motion, nor put a Stop to its own Motions, when once begun" (p. 8). Since matter is incapable of producing any kind of motion, Clayton argues we may conclude, "whenever we see any thing moved," that it is Spirit or God who causes that motion (p. 10). The original cause of all motion is Spirit. Clayton speaks of the 'attractive force' or power of Spirit, a force needed just as much to begin as to stop motion (p. 11). From the fact that all motion is in a specific direction, Clayton argues that the being capable of moving itself or another must "also be endowed

with an *Intellect* or Understanding, capable of directing that Motion"
(p. 12). Clayton does not allow material second causes, but he does
introduce other immaterial causes which carry out God's design. Since
"*Nothing can act where it is not*," not even God, other spirits are
needed as concomitants of matter (p. 10). The number of such spirits
must be great: "because every, even the least Particle, of active, or attractive Matter, must be *directed* in it's Motions by some Spirit, united
to that Matter, which may have just such a Quantity of Intellect communicated to it by its Creator, as will enable it to perform those Functions, which are assigned it by its Creator, in order to carry on the
general Oeconomy of this Universe" (pp. 12-13). The conclusion of
this line of thought is that "All Nature, therefore, seems to be animated, or alive; and this whole World to be replete with *Spirits*" (p. 14).

William Porterfield (*A Treatise on the Eye*, 1759) also said that
gravitation, cohesion, attraction are only possible by means of the action of some active, intelligent cause, although Porterfield seems to
go rather the route of occasional causes, where God's intervention
occurs at the beginning. God, for example, has so arranged things that
my volitions do not move my body but serve as the occasion for the
movement (pp. 144-45).[14] Porterfield is not always so occasionalist.
He does allow other possible candidates for immaterial principles at
work in nature: "the Soul of the animal [in reproduction], or of
some other subordinate Being, some vital Principle, plastic Power, or
Archaeus" (p. 29). He thinks it wrong to "reduce all to mere Mechanism." The motions of the body "do not depend on Mechanism alone,
but on Mechanism joined with certain active Powers or Forces imprinted by the Author of Nature upon all Bodies of this Universe."
He cites as such powers or forces those of attraction and repulsion.

The view of matter as inactive is also found in an anonymous pamphlet, *An Essay Towards Demonstrating the Immateriality and Free
Agency of the Soul* (1760), written against Collins and in response to
another anonymous tract. Matter, this writer says, is "absolutely inactive" (p. 170). The parts of matter "must be actuated by some
spirit or other" (p. 46). He is concerned to argue that spirit and matter are essentially different: spirit is not extended and matter is not
active or perceptive (p. 72). Of the cohesion, attraction, and repulsion of matter, this writer says they are *accidental* qualities of matter;
it is the continuous influence of some spiritual being which imposes
the qualities on matter. How spirit acts on matter is left obscure (pp.
76-78). The force of gravity is the work of some spirit acting either
mediately or immediately (p. 86). This view of matter even appears in
a sermon by Richard Price published in 1766, *The Nature and Dignity*

of the Human Soul. Even after the Newtonians had moved the concept of matter much closer to that of dynamic corpuscularity, Price was still saying matter is inactive; it is also discerptible, i.e., can be divided into a multitude of parts. Like Clarke, Price insisted that there is no way that these parts can be compounded to get anything other than figure and motion. To suppose that consciousness and thought might be modes of figure and motion "is to run into the most senseless jargon."[15]

In a tract directed against Baxter, John Jackson (*A Dissertation on Matter and Spirit*, 1735) accepts the passivity of matter but modifies the immaterialist view of mind. Spirit or mind is initially inactive, is located and extended, always acting from a place, although Jackson argued that the soul moves without contact. His notion of extension and place applied to mind is not quite the same as the traditional view of those properties of matter. But for him, both matter and spirit are indivisible. Thus the indivisibility of matter is no hindrance to its acquiring the property of thought. If matter could become conscious, it would depend not upon its extension "but on a particular *Connection* or *Union*, and particular *Impulses*, and *Impressions* altogether unknown to us" (p. 8). Before the soul has any ideas, it is an inactive substance, as well as unconscious. These properties of action and consciousness have to be infused into the soul. Jackson maintains that the argument from inactivity does not prove that matter cannot acquire consciousness. The soul "without Ideas must be allow'd to be as *dead, inert*, or *unactive* as the Body is without *vital motion*" (p. 14). The soul is changed from inactive to active by the action of matter and animal spirits on it, and thus ideas are produced. He does recognize an "internal self-motive Power or Agency" as a positive property of the soul, but this power has to be activated. He also remarks that there are in matter inconsistent properties: gravitation, but also cohesion. And he points out that, if contact or *vis inertiae* is, as Baxter had argued, necessary to move matter, then no unresisting substance, such as mind or spirit, can move matter (p. 20). Another critic of Baxter, Joseph Wimpey (*Remarks on a Book intitled, An Enquiry into the Nature of the Human Soul*, 1741), rejected the claim that *vis inertiae* is essential to matter, arguing that it "arises from and is always proportional to the force of gravity in all bodies" (p. 14). Since *vis inertiae* depends on gravity, and since gravity is not (on Baxter's theory) inherent in matter, the *vis inertiae* cannot be inherent either (p. 18).

Hume also commented on this *vis inertiae*, "which is so much talked of in the new philosophy, and which is ascribed to matter" (*An Enquiry concerning Human Understanding*, 1748, Section VII, Part II,

Note; p. 73 in Selby-Bigge edition). This term, Hume insisted, only denotes the facts about body: that a body at rest or in motion continues forever in its present state, till put into some new state. Similarly, talk of gravity is a way of referring to observed effects. Hume claims that "It was never the meaning of Sir Isaac Newton to rob second causes of all forces or energy; though some of his followers have endeavoured to establish that theory upon his Authority." Hume supports his claim about Newton by remarking that "that great philosopher had recourse to an etherial active fluid to explain his universal attraction." Hume also comments that Malebranche's doctrine of the "universal and sole efficacy of the Deity" has had no authority in England: "Locke, Clarke, and Cudworth, never so much as take notice of it." Those writers supposed all along "that matter has a real, though subordinate and derived power." He wonders, then, how it is that Malebranche's doctrine has "become so prevalent among our modern metaphysicians."

Those 'modern metaphysicians' would include Baxter, Berkeley, Watts, and of course Malebranche. In characterizing such writers, Hume says they hold that "those objects which are commonly denominated *causes*, are in reality nothing but *occasions*" (p. 70). God's volition is the true power and force at work in nature:

Instead of saying that one billiard-ball moves another by a force which it has derived from the author of nature, it is the Deity himself, they say, who, by a particular volition, moves the second ball, being determined to this operation by the impulse of the first ball; in consequence of those general laws which he has laid down to himself in the government of the universe. (p. 70).

Hume thinks this occasionalist account "of the universal energy and operation of the Supreme Being is too bold to carry conviction"; it gets "into fairy land, long ere we have reached the last steps of our theory" (p. 72). Hume does not think we have any more of an idea of God's power (how it works) than we have of the power of bodies. If ignorance were a good reason for rejecting anything, we would have to deny God's power as well as the power of matter (pp. 72-73; cf. *Treatise*, pp. 159-60).

Natural Causes and Powers in Matter

Hume does contrast "brute unconscious matter" with "a rational intelligent being" as possible causes (*Enquiry*, p. 136), but it is clear from many comments in that work that he did hold the view that matter does have powers. While his epistemic claim is that "all operations of bodies without exception, are known only by experience" (p. 29), he talks frequently of forces and powers producing effects: we simply do not know the forces. We reduce and simplify by resolving "the many particular effects into a few general causes, by means of reasonings from analogy, experience, and observation" (p. 30). The causes of these general causes are characterized as "these ultimate springs and principles." He suggests what such ultimate causes might be: elasticity, gravity, cohesion of parts, communication of motion by impulse. He also talks of the law of motion as dealing with the force it takes to move a body (p. 31). Nature keeps her secrets from us: "she conceals from us those powers and principles on which the influence of those objects entirely depends." We see bodies move, but of the "wonderful force or power, which would carry on a moving body for ever" we can form no conception. We are ignorant of such "natural powers," but we assume that like sensible effects have like secret powers (p. 33). There is no *known* connection between "the sensible qualities and the secret powers" (p. 42; cf. pp. 54, 55). There is "no part of matter, that does ever, by its sensible qualities, discover any power or energy"; the power or "force which actuates the whole machine" of the universe "is entirely concealed from us" (p. 63). Though concealed, it is clear that Hume believed in and accepted the standard Newtonian forces. His opposition to those modern metaphysicians who sought an external source of these forces and powers strongly suggests that Hume's own metaphysic located these powers in matter. Whether he thought of them as inherent in matter, or only placed there by God, we cannot say.

There were other writers in the century who left no doubt about action being inherent in matter. When in 1704 John Toland (*Letters to Serena*) said, *"action is essential to Matter,"* and that it, not just motion, exists in "the most heavy and hard Body," (p. 160) William Wotton (*A Letter to Eusebia*, 1704) objected that this gets rid of God in the causation of the world (p. 48). Toland carefully distinguished *local motion* (change of place) from the moving force of action (p. 161). He referred to the self-action of matter as 'autokinesy', echoing Cudworth in the use of this term.[16] Toland also says that the notion that levity and gravity are inherent in matter "is now by every body exploded" (p. 184). Presumably he had in mind Newton's rejection of gravity as a primary property of matter. For Toland, autokinesy would seem to be an essential property, although he does not give us any details on what it is or how it operates. His use of this notion may, however, be an indication of some awareness on his part of the doctrine of forces in Newton's account. Since Toland was considered to be a threat to religion because of his earlier book, *Christianity Not Mysterious* (1697), his appeal to autokinesy probably confirmed this judgment in the eyes of the immaterialists, even though Toland's account of matter occurs in the letter in which he discusses and rejects as false Spinoza's system (p. 135). Significantly for the direction which matter theory was to take in the eighteenth century, Spinoza's system was false for Toland because it failed to ascribe self-action to matter.

The defenders of religion were not always immaterialists, Robert Greene is an interesting figure because he is an early example of a writer (a divine in fact) who attempted to articulate a force concept of matter. He was also writing strictly to defend religion against atheists, deists, Socinians, and Arians. As early as 1712, in his *The Principles of Natural Philosophy*, Greene modestly claimed to show "the insufficiency of the Present Systems." He argued that neither extension nor solidity is the essence of matter. Extension and solidity are, in fact, only ideas formed by the mind, not real properties. More sweepingly, the notion of matter as divisible, figured, extended, capable of motion is nothing more than an abstracted idea (p. 123).[17] He finds it odd that someone, such as Locke, says we cannot know the essence of matter but yet makes so much of figure, motion, and extension. Greene even suggests that, on the view of matter accepted by Locke, matter cannot be seen or felt. Even the solidity which Locke ascribes to matter is felt as resistance, "whereas Solidity or Impenetrability is the not entering of one Dimension of Space or Matter into another," and this solidity is not felt but conceived (pp. 127-28). Moreover, the corpuscular theory is incapable of explaining the experienced qualities (e.g., color) by reducing it to "small and figur'd Corpuscles, acted by a certain and determin'd Motion," unless we can tell what the nature of the corpuscles is (p. 130). Without that knowledge of the motion of corpuscles, such an explanation would be like explaining the mechanism of a clock by resolving it into the figure and motion of the wheels "without knowing the intimate Springs, by which the regular Circuitry, they make are caus'd and produc'd."

Greene's book is long and prolix. It is not always easy to see what his own doctrines are. In a later book, *The Principles of the Philosophy of the Expansive and Contractive Forces* (1727), he identifies his main conclusions of the earlier book as follows: there is no vacuum;[18] matter is not similar and homogeneous; light is homogeneous; the qualities of matter that occasion the sensations of taste, smell, feeling, hearing, and seeing "are not derived from different Modifications of" matter but from "certain innate Forces which are inherent" in matter (his anti-corpuscularianism). Greene now claims to show how all the phenomena can be explained by his expansive and contractive forces. Action or force, "which is divided into an Expansive and Contractive one," is the very essence of matter (p. 123). He explains that he does not mean matter is the support or seat of such forces; it *is* that force:

The Substratum or Essence of Matter therefore I take, and Think I may Affirm, to be Action or Force, and if I can Produce those Actions and Forces, which will not only solve all the Phaenomena of Matter, which we are acquainted with by our Sensations from it, but even those, which may possibly arise to other Animals of a Distinct Nature and Species from us, I hope I shall have Given a full account not only of the Essence of Matter, but its Real and Essential Properties (p. 286).[19]

Thackray thinks Greene's writings deserve our attention, "if only for the way they attacked Newtonian belief in homogeneous matter and a vacuum, seeking rather to explain the observable world in terms of heterogeneous matter and 'expansive and contractive forces'."[20] Thackray also points out that "Greene was among the first to realize that force could provide a more basic concept than solidity or extension when describing matter" (pp. 133-34). But Schofield's more cautious judgment is that Greene only succeeded in replacing the homogeneous matter of the corpuscularians by "an infinity of material substances." Schofield, that is, thinks Greene's forces "turn into qualities" (*Mechanism and Materialism*, p. 121). Again, Greene's text is so confusing that it is difficult to know precisely what his appeal to force and activity is. Schofield is firm in his conviction that Greene has "merely renamed Newton's attractive and repulsive forces," and that he did not dissolve "the corpuscular cores into Boscovich-like Points." Schofield bases these remarks on Greene's profusion of applications of his principles. Perhaps Greene's conception was better than his application. He clearly had in mind a concept of matter which, instead of corpuscles, took forces as the nature of matter.

The development of force theories of matter was carried further by at least two other writers in the eighteenth century before Boscovich's work appeared, a work to which Priestley appealed in his version of materialism. Before we examine these theories along with Priestley's, we should note one attempt to bring some order into the controversy over thinking matter. This work, published in mid-century, is anonymous. It would appear to have been written by a nonscientist but a person who was well acquainted with the thinking-matter debate and fairly well informed about some of the more recent scientific work. The author of this work (*An Enquiry into the Nature of the Human Soul*) points out that modern writers represent the soul and body as incompatible and incapable of any communication. The author claims

that experience shows us that a system of matter, when properly organized (e.g., as in our own body), is a great use and instrument of
the soul. He does not believe we can distinguish the work of the body
from the work of the soul in their joint operations. Recent discoveries
concerning gravity, electricity, magnetism show that matter is more
than just particles in motion. Hence matter of a certain sort may have
a principle of sensation. He is properly cautious about what we know
and don't know about matter and mind, but he attempts to show
"that a System of Matter, rightly constructed in the human Fabrick,
is necessary to preserve and regulate Thought as well as Health, as
long as Mind and Body remain united" (p. 12). He cites some obvious
correlations with illness and bodily disorders, and suggests that for
this correlation to be effective, the matter of the body has to be more
than particles with solidity and motion. Also, to do all the things that
we do with our minds—e.g., contemplate God, apprehend the beauty
of the universe, seek happiness—particles of matter hardly seem sufficient as aids (p. 14).

Against Baxter's claim that matter is incapable of self-motion, this
author asks: what kind of matter is it that Baxter has in mind? Is it
solid particles in motion? If so, he would agree that self-motion is not
possible for such matter. But, "as I believe, there is no such Matter in
being, so defective and inert, as these Gentlemen make it; and if we
take along with us all the Properties of Matter before recited, or whatever other Powers there may be assembled in it, I imagine, there are
many Reasons to conclude the Contrary, and to persuade us, that
there are probably in it Principles and Springs of spontaneous Motion,
as we find it revealing itself to us in the Works of Creation" (pp. 15-
16). It is the attraction and repulsion of particles that he thinks indicate in matter more than solidity. He views it as extravagant to say
that all of these activities are carried by the agency of spirit (p. 17).
He cites in addition many observations from electricity, biology, and
other sciences to support the claim that matter and living bodies are
very active, generative, and powerful.

Notes

1. *Mechanism and Materialism: British Natural Philosophy in An Age of Reason* (Princeton: Princeton University Press, 1970), p. 125.

2. Ibid., p. 95.

3. "Newtonian Forces and Lockean Powers: Concepts of Matter in Eighteenth-Century
Thought," in *Historical Studies in the Physical Sciences*, volume 3, 1971.

4. Bk. I, Definition VIII. See also Bk. I, Section XI, Scholium. The edition of the *Principia* that I have used is the 1819 edition of Motte's translation, revised and corrected by
William Davis (3 volumes).

5. Schofield, *Mechanism and Materialism*, pp. 8-9.

6. *Newton on Matter and Activity*, (Notre Dame, Ind.: University of Notre Dame Press, 1978), p. 71. McMullin argues that Newton was trying "to reshape the entire conception of matter" (p. 43). The passivity of matter was altered, McMullin thinks, in three ways, corresponding to the *vis insita* (a conserving agency), the *vis inertiae* (which McMullin sees as an 'endeavor to act'), and Newton's appeal to resistance (the response which a body makes "to any attempt to disturb its motion"). McMullin points out that all three of these forces "are taken to be rooted somehow in the matter-constituent of things, in matter's tendency to conserve whatever motion it has and to impose motion by way of reaction in consequence of this resistance" (pp. 41-42).

7. Schofield, *Mechanism and Materialism*, p. 9.

8. Ibid., p. 11.

9. Ibid., p. 13.

10. *Principia*, volume II, p. 313.

11. Baxter is careful to say that what exists is contingent. In the light of Hume's later remark that the contrary of any matter of fact is always possible, the following statement by Baxter is interesting: "Any *being* (this stone for instance) as existing this minute, hath no necessary connexion with itself, as existing the next." This is what is meant by a contingent being. "If the existence of a *being* this minute inferred its existence the next, it would be a physical contradiction that any thing had ever once existed, should ever cease to exist" (pp. 225-26). A second edition of Baxter's work appeared in 1737, a third in 1745. My references are to the second edition.

12. W. Derham, *Physico-Theology: Or, A Demonstration of the Being and Attributes of God* (1713), p. 31n. in third edition of 1714.

13. Baxter devotes a long note in his *Enquiry* (sect. I, note k) to a discussion of Newton's elastic, subtle fluid, citing both the *Principia* and the Queries to the *Opticks*. He raises a number of difficulties with this notion which deserve careful attention by historians of science.

14. Porterfield characterizes Leibniz's pre-established harmony system as saying mind and matter are distinct from each other, the one acting by final causes, the other by mechanism. They only "agree like two Clocks" which go alike but influence not each other. In this way, "God, foreseeing the Volitions and Inclinations of every man's soul, did from the Beginning so contrive and regulate the Machine of his Body, that, by the mere necessary Laws of Mechanism, such Motions should be excited in the Body, as might agree and correspond with the volitions of the Mind" (p. 145).

15. Porterfield uses the general principle invoked in the thinking-matter controversy to make the same point: "no Effect can have any Perfection or Excellency, which was not either actually in the Cause, or at least in a higher Degree" (p. 217). He uses this to argue that figure can only produce other figures, motion only other motions. There can be no cross-category causation (pp. 217-18).

16. Cudworth distinguished the same two species of action: local motion, which is "*Heterochinesie*," and "*autochinesie* or *Self-Activity*" (*The True Intellectual System*, p. 844). John Witty, while rejecting the notion, refers to the notion of self-action in matter by the same word (*The First Principles of Modern Deism*, 1707, p. 263).

17. By an 'abstracted idea', Greene means a false idea or one that does not stand for anything real. Toland (in *Letters to Serena*) had used the same phrase about space: the idea of space only designates "the Relations that any thing has to other Beings at a distance from it" (p. 180). Toland viewed Newton's absolute space as "a real space distinct from Matter" and hence as an abstracted—i.e., false—idea. The true idea of space is of a relation. Toland claimed also that levity and gravity are qualities which result from the "World in actual Being," meaning, I think, that they depend upon the whole fabric of the universe and are relative, not inherent in matter. Edmund Law's way of making a similar point (in *An Enquiry into*

the Ideas of Space, Time, Immensity and Eternity, 1734) is to say space is an idea of reason, a mere idea of the relations of things. Cheyne also (in *An Essay on Regimen*, 1740) said space, time, motion, and velocity were abstracted ideas.

18. Again, modestly, Greene suggests that Newton was influenced by Greene's 1712 book, which Greene sent him, because Newton now accepts the idea of a plenum. Commenting on this claim, Thackray says: "If this latter claim seems folly, we may at least note that Greene, unlike many later British writers, was acutely aware that Newton's ideas changed over time" (p. 128).

19. Greene also attempted to apply the concepts of the two forces to the mind, promising to produce a *psycheometria* with these forces. "Thus Memory, Recollection, Wit, and a Quickness of Thought and Apprehension is deriv'd from the Expansive Force of the Mind, as Perception, Judgment, Reasoning, and Solidity is owing to the Contractive Force of it; for in the first we may observe a kind of Elasticity in the Production of our Ideas, and a Volatility as well as Incoherence of them, and in the second a Contraction by their Closeness, Connexion, and Gravity" (p. 127). His promised 'psycheometria' does not materialize. The attempt is rather artificial and not helpful.

20. Thackray, *Atoms and Powers*, p. 127.

Chapter VI

Priestley's Materialism

Our survey of the differing views on the nature of matter has shown that those writers who were against materialism sought to explain material changes in terms of immaterial principles. So convinced were they of the passivity and inertness of matter that it became necessary for them to go outside the system of matter to account for the actions of matter. For those who found real causation only in God, the result was that God was active in the world, either at the beginning or continuously. Clayton's Leibnizian plurality of immaterial spirits, reminiscent of some of the earlier alchemical and magical notions of a world alive with forces and powers, does not seem to have been a route anyone else took in eighteenth-century Britain. That the Newtonian recognition of forces existing in matter had, by mid-century, gained some acceptance among cautious thinkers is suggested by Hume's apparent adoption of the idea of springs and forces in matter. Hume was undoubtedly right to wonder how Malebranche's alternative—that God is the ultimate cause of activity—had managed to take root in Britain. The reason seems to have been the many concerns, shown mainly by traditional religious writers, that matter not share properties with mind or spirit. A world of matter alive with spirits is one thing, but a world of matter alive is quite another! Self-activity belongs to conscious, intentional, moral agents such as men who, in these ways, mirror God's properties. Once allow that matter might be made to think, even by God, the next step would be to make matter self-active.

But the prevailing concept of matter did change, as these controversies developed through the century. The main change was the incorporation of force in the very definition of matter. Some versions of this view almost replaced matter by force. A sort of silent partner in this movement towards this extreme view—silent because it never attained great prominence, and hardly ever figured in the debates, but was frequently cited—was the claim that the amount of hard, impenetrable corpuscular matter in the world is very small, much smaller than the amount of empty space, even within matter itself. In commenting upon Newton's subtle fluid, Baxter points out that behind that suggestion of a fluid as the cause of gravity there is the assumption that all bodies "are exceedingly porous and rare: and this notion is carried so extravagantly high, as to suppose *that all the matter in the known universe might not take up one cubical inch of space*."[1] In support of this view, Baxter cites what is said "concerning a progression of pores by *Sir Isaac Newton* himself, at the end of his Opticks," as well as Pemberton's discussion in his *A View of Sir Isaac Newton's Philosophy* (1728). Pemberton was explaining how bodies could have more pores than hard matter, a condition necessary if bodies were to transmit light. His explanation of how this is possible, while still leaving bodies hard, ends with the following remark:

Which shews that this whole globe of earth, nay all the known bodies in the universe together, as far as we know, may be compounded of no greater a portion of solid matter, than might be reduced into a globe of one inch only in diameter, or even less.[2]

References to this notion of the great porosity of matter can be found in a variety of books both before and after Pemberton's account. For example, John Clarke's *A Defence of Dr. Clarke's Demonstration* (1732, pp. 6, 9), or George Cheyne's *The Natural Method of Cureing the Diseases of the Body and the Disorders of the Mind* (1742, p. 9). McMullin remarks that John Keill "had already inferred that the quantity of matter in a piece of glass might have no greater proportion to the bulk of the glass than a grain of sand to the bulk of the earth."[3] It was, McMullin says, the insistence on "the tenuity thesis" by Pemberton, Desaguliers, and other Newtonians that led Voltaire to remark that "we are not certain 'there is a cubic inch of solid matter in the universe, so far are we from conceiving what matter is.'"[4]

With the amount of corpuscular matter being so small, and with attention focused upon attractive and repulsive phenomena, the stage was set for Priestley's dramatic transformation of the thinking-matter controversy. Two writers were of particular importance for Priestley: David Hartley and Boscovich. Hartley's physiological explanation of thought, though couched within the older, corpuscular view of matter, suggested to Priestley that thought might be a property of the brain. Boscovich's force theory of matter provided Priestley with a new kind of materialism, in terms of which the idea of thinking matter was more acceptable.

In his survey of eighteenth-century Newtonians, Schofield presents a number of writers who moved closer to a natural philosophy of force than Schofield thinks Robert Greene did. He cites two in particular, Benjamin Worster (*A Compendious and Methodical Account of the Principles of Natural Philosophy*, 1722) and John Rowning (*A Compendious System of Natural Philosophy*, published in parts between 1734 and 1738). Rowning's book is of particular importance for us since it was used at the dissenting academy in Daventry, where Priestley studied.[5] Both men considered matter to be particulate but acting under force of attraction and repulsion, "immaterial principles or powers which are not occult but manifest in phenomena." (Schofield, *Mechanism and Materialism*, p. 36). Worster also made use of the aether. Rowning, Schofield says, "carried his speculations" on the action of repulsive and attractive forces, "further than any other person was to do until the appearance of" Boscovich's *Theoria* "some 20 years later" (p. 37). Rowning even suggested that the particles of matter do not come into contact, being prevented from approaching "nearer than a certain distance by a repelling power diffused around each single particle" (p. 39). There are, he suggests, several "concentric spheres of attraction and repulsion, surrounding the particles of bodies."[6]

Another writer, Gowin Knight (*An Attempt to Demonstrate, That All the Phaenomena in Nature May be Explained by Two Simple Active Principles, Attraction and Repulsion*, 1748), marks for Thackray a "further step along the road towards the 'immateriality of matter' and the haunting ideas of Boscovich" (*Atoms and Powers*, p. 142). According to Thackray's summary, Knight saw that "the traditional concept of atoms differing in shape and size was redundant in a world to which forces were admitted." He also said the particles of bodies do not touch each other. Bodies were more porous than solid, the surfaces of particles being surrounded by repellent particles. Other particles attract. The phenomena of nature are thus a play of these two kinds of force particles.

Boscovich's work (*Theoria Philosophiae Naturalis*, 1758; English translation in 1763 as *A Theory of Natural Philosophy*) has recently been rediscovered and re-evaluated.[7] It is a complex and technical work, which I would not presume to summarize. What is important for my purposes is (1) to consider Boscovich in the tradition of force concepts of matter in eighteenth-century Britain, and (2) to understand the nature of the appeal Priestley makes to Boscovich's doctrines. For the first, Schofield's brief summary of the main doctrines of matter in the *Theoria* will suffice.

To Boscovich, however, these particles are indivisible and non-extended geometrical points, possessing inertia as individuals, and, as pairs, a tendency to approach one another at some distances and recede from one another at others. . . . Rather than supposing these tendencies to result from a multitude of different forces — gravitational, cohesive, etc. — he declares that there exists, for each point with respect to any other, a single, continuous, action-at-a-distance curve of attractive and repulsive accelerations, a radially symmetric, single valued function of distance, asymptotic toward repulsive infinity at the center, crossing the zero-acceleration axis many times before sensible distances are attained, after which the curve approximates, within any measurable degree of accuracy, the attractive, inverse-square, gravitational curve of Newton. . . . (p. 236)

McMullin says that force for Boscovich "is no more than a propensity of matter-points to approach, or recede from one another" (p. 117). Moreover, McMullin says, Boscovich was "trying to avoid attributing agency directly to the matter-points." McMullin quotes an interesting passage from Boscovich indicating that he was aware of the various views about the status of forces, claiming that his theory fits any one of those views:

Whether this law of forces is an intrinsic property of indivisible points; whether it is something substantial or accidental superadded to them . . . ; whether it is an arbitrary law of the Author of Nature, who directs these motions by a law made according to His Will; this I do not seek to find, nor indeed can it be found from the phenomena, which are the same in all these theories.[8]

Boscovich's conception of matter in terms of centers of force instead of hard corpuscles gave Priestley a way of taking sides in the developing debate over thinking matter. In his 1772 work, *The History and Present State of Discoveries Relating to Vision, Light, and Colour*, Priestley cites Boscovich's notion that "light is endued with an insuperable impulsive force" (p. 384). Priestley says that the easiest solution to the objections of Euler on the materiality of light "is to adopt the hypothesis of Mr. Boscovich, who supposes that matter is not impenetrable . . . but that it consists of physical points only, endued with powers of attraction and repulsion, in the same manner as solid matter is generally supposed to be." Thus a body with sufficient momentum to overcome the powers of repulsion will be able to penetrate that body, "for nothing will interfere or penetrate one another, but *powers*" (p. 391). Boscovich even demonstrated that the body thus penetrated would not even be moved out of its place.

Priestley also refers to his friend John Michell, who, Priestley says, hit upon this theory independently of Boscovich.[9] Priestley's account of what led Michell to his theory is important for appreciating the relation between philosophy of mind and theories of matter in the century. Priestley says: "This scheme of the *immateriality of matter*, first occurred to Mr. Michell on reading *Baxter on the immateriality of the soul*" (p. 397). Priestley's own views on matter and spirit are best found in his *Disquisitions Relating to Matter and Spirit* (1777). In the preface to that work, he tells us that "I had always taken it for granted, that man had a soul distinct from his body." He says he had some difficulties with this belief, but on the whole he accepted it. But the work of David Hartley in physiology and psychology, and the new theory of matter of Father Boscovich and Mr. Michell led him to reject the two-substance view of man. Now, "I rather think that the whole man is of some *uniform composition*; and that the property of *perception*, as well as the other powers that are termed *mental* is the result of . . . such an organical structure as that of the brain" (pp. xiii-xiv). He identifies as the vulgar (and wrong) view of matter that it is solid, impenetrable, and possessed of *vis inertiae* (just the view held by Baxter and attacked by Greene).

On the two-substance view, Priestley says, the soul was considered to be "so intirely distinct from matter, as to have no property in common with it" (p. xi). Priestley himself had earlier accepted this doctrine, even though the connection between soul and body was "unknown and incomprehensible" (p. xii). He reminds us of all the features of this traditional view: matter "is said to be naturally destitute of all other powers," save the passive one of *vis inertiae*. Mind or spirit is immaterial, has no relation to space (a point on which, as we have seen, there was not always agreement), and has the powers of perception, intelligence, and self-motion (p. xxxviii). He notes that there were several different analyses of space in relation to mind or spirit. One view said that spirit is nowhere, "has a mode of existence that cannot be expressed by any phraseology appropriated to the mode in which matter exists" (p. 54). Another view tried to find a sense of place for mind in terms of mathematical points (p. 55).

In discussing Baxter, Priestley suggests that so much power is given to God in the action of matter that Baxter has almost eliminated matter. Baxter had said that even resistance "is the power of the immaterial cause, indefinitely impressed upon, and exerted in, every possible part of matter" (*Enquiry*, II, p. 322). In another passage, Baxter had said "the *constant action* of an immaterial Being constitutes the very solid extension of matter" (vol. II, p. 349n.). Priestley's comment seems just: "But asserting, as he does, that these powers are the immediate agency of the Deity himself, it necessarily follows that there is not in nature any such thing as *matter*, distinct from *the Deity*, and his operations" (p. 8). Priestley hears Berkeley's denial of matter in Baxter's account of God's activity: matter becomes superfluous (p. 65); Baxter has made "the Deity himself to *do*, and to *be* every thing" (p. 9).

Priestley claims to base his own account of matter on appearances, although he is forced to distinguish between real or natural appearances and superficial ones (p. 4). The familiar experience of pressing my hand on the table and finding that I cannot penetrate the table, or of the behaviour of billiard balls which stop moving only when impeded, may seem to lead to the conclusion that matter is in fact destitute of powers (pp. 3-4). But a proper consideration of these experiences will lead us, Priestley believes, to conclude that the resistance we feel "is never occasioned by *solid matter*, but by something of a very different nature, viz. *a power of repulsion* always acting at a real, and in general an assignable distance from what we call the body itself" (p. 4). His reference to "late observations" that have been made in support of this conclusion, are to Michell and Boscovich, but they could also be to Rowning and Knight (pp. 4, 8). The power of attraction is needed to hold bodies, even particles, together. Without attraction, solidity itself disappears, as well as shape (pp. 5-6).[10]

It is important for Priestley to reject impenetrability as a property of matter, since if matter is not impenetrable, the phenomenon of resistance can be ascribed to powers, even to powers acting at a distance. Priestley cites a variety of experiments which show (so he claims) that bodies do not really ever have actual contact with one another, but his ultimate support for his claim is that 'philosophers' know that, "notwithstanding their seeming contact, they are actually kept at a real distance from each other" (p. 12). His understanding of this claim is that the *ultimate particles* of bodies are prevented from coming into actual contact. He refers to his work on electricity, where he attempted to "ascertain the weight requisite to bring a number of pieces of money, lying upon one another, into seeming contact, or be near to one another only as the particles that compose the same continued piece of metal" (p. 13). The answer is "very considerable."[11]

Priestley reproduces a passage from his earlier *History and Present State of Discoveries Relating to Vision* (1772), where he characterizes Boscovich's hypothesis as follows:

[that] matter is not *impenetrable*, as before him it had been universally taken for granted; but that it consists of *physical points* only, endued with powers of attraction and repulsion, taking place at different distances, that is, surrounded with various spheres of attraction and repulsion. (p. 19)

With impenetrability rejected, with the great porosity of matter accepted, and with the powers of attraction and repulsion characterizing matter, Priestley drew the obvious conclusion to the thinking-matter debate:

Since the only reason why the principle of thought, or sensation, has been imagined to be incompatible with matter, goes upon the supposition of impenetrability being the essential property of it, and consequently that *solid extent* is the foundation of all the properties that it can possibly sustain, the whole argument for an immaterial thinking principle in man, on this new supposition, falls to the ground; matter, destitute of what has hitherto been called *solidity*, being no more incompatible with sensation and thought, than that substance, which, without knowing any thing farther about it, we have been used to call *immaterial*. (p. 18)

Since it was the old concept of matter that made it difficult to ascribe thought to matter, that difficulty is now eliminated (p. 18). If the phenomena and known properties of man can be accounted for with reference to this new concept of matter, then we need not retain the notion of two substances (p. 25). Priestley notes that the powers of sensation or perception and thought "have never been found but in conjunction with a certain *organized system of matter*" (p. 26). Thus we must conclude that thought in man "is a property of the *nervous system*, or rather of the *brain*" (p. 27). There is a close correlation between the working of the brain and thought.

In fact, there is just the same reason to conclude, that the powers of sensation and thought are the necessary result of a particular organization, as that sound is the necessary result of a particular concussion of the air. For in both cases equally the one constantly accompanies the other, and there is not in nature a stronger argument for a necessary connection of any cause and any effect. (p. 28)

In a later discussion with Richard Price (*A Free Discussion of the Doctrines of Materialism*, 1778, p. 61) he remarks: "In my opinion there is just the same reason to conclude that the brain *thinks*, as that it is *white* and *soft*."

Sometimes Priestley writes as if he only means to say thought is a property of the brain, correlated with other properties and activities of the brain; not that thought *is* brain activity. At other times, he tries to make features of thought material. For example, he says ideas are "produced by external objects, and must therefore correspond to them; and since many of the objects or archetypes of ideas are divisible, it necessarily follows, that the ideas themselves are divisible also" (p. 37). The idea of a man, e.g., consists of ideas of head, trunk, arms, etc. These are its parts. "If the archetypes of ideas have extension, the ideas which are expressive of them, and are actually produced by them, according to certain mechanical laws, must have extension likewise" (p. 38).[12]

Priestley's own view is not that all reduces to matter, but rather that the kind of matter on which the two-substance view is based does not exist. When the new concept of matter is put in place of the old one, the radical difference between matter and spirit disappears. Priestley's phrase 'the immateriality of matter' expresses what he considers the new concept of matter to have done. When this concept is put together with the view of man as a uniform composition, the result is a sophisticated system of centers of force interacting with each other, all organized into a whole.

With the altered concept of matter, the more traditional ways of posing the question of the nature of thought and of its relations to the brain do not fit. We have to think of a complex organized biological system with properties the traditional doctrine would have called mental *and* physical. Hume's subtle way with the immaterialists will not affect Priestley's concept of man either, primarily because Priestley has rejected the notion of substance, not just of two substances. But I may be making Priestley more sophisticated than he in fact was. One difficulty in the way of this attempted reading of his doctrine is that he linked his philosophy of mind with Hartley's physiology, as well as with the new force concept of matter. Hartley's notion of matter is more traditional, shows no influence on these force concepts. Priestley admired Hartley's explanations of all modes of thought in terms of vibrations of brain and nerves. There was no physiology of Boscovichian points which Priestley could use in his linking of thought and brain. What Hartley's physiology did which Priestley admired was to offer an account which showed, as Priestley said in response to Price, that thinking is explained by brain activity. But the Hartleian brain is composed, it would seem, of corpuscular, not of force, matter. Priestley is right to say, on this view of matter, that "It is a gross mistake of the system of materialism to suppose . . . that the vibrations of the brain are themselves the perceptions. For it is easy to form an idea of there being vibrations without any perceptions accompanying them"

(*Disquisitions*, p. 91). Besides these vibrating powers, the brain has percipient or sentient power added to it.

Attacks on Priestley

That above remark of Priestley's was made against one of his critics, the anonymous author of *Letters on Materialism and Hartley's Theory of the Human Mind* (1776).[13] This tract, well written and forcefully argued in detail, was one of several critical reactions to Priestley. The *Letters* came out before Priestley's *Disquisitions*; the latter contain some of Priestley's response to the tract. There are further discussions of this work in Priestley's *The Doctrine of Philosophical Necessity* (1777), written as an appendix to his *Disquisitions*. In 1778 John Whitehead published *Materialism Philosophically Examined*. The attacks on Priestley began in 1775, in the pages of *The London Review*.

This journal carried long excerpts as reviews of most of the important books, as they appeared in print. Priestley received much attention in the pages of this journal. For example, in the January 1775 issue, the first item is a review of his *An Examination of Dr. Reid's Inquiry*. The reviewer speaks of Priestley as an author to whom the public is indebted; he is praised as ingenious and industrious. The review and the quotations are continued in the February issue. By March 1775 the correspondence columns are receiving letters commenting on the review, objecting to Priestley's attack on James Beattie in particular. In a review in May of James Harris's *Philosophical Arrangements*, the reviewer reflects some of the recent views on the nature of matter: "Nothing is absolutely solid or impenetrable" (p. 335). The correspondence columns again carried in May a letter against Priestley's book on Reid. The June issue announces a review of his book on Hartley for their July issue, but in the June issue there is a review of a book by 'sGravesande that quotes Priestley's conception of man as a whole, not a union of two substances. This remark refers to the introductory essay from his book *Hartley's Theory of the Human Mind* (1775). The July review of that work praises Priestley for the Hartley volume, saying that Hartley has been held in high esteem by all those who are capable of comprehending him. The review continues in the August issue. The correspondence this time contains a letter objecting to Priestley's claim that (as the writer reads him) man is not naturally immortal. The whole man, this writer insists, must "survive the grave, if there be a God, on whom he depends" (p. 174). Wollaston's *The Religion of Nature Delineated* is cited in support.

In this August issue, the editors of *The London Review* say that they have received a long defense of Priestley, which they will include in the next issue. They remark that the author of this defense is "either the Doctor himself or some able friend" (p. 175).[14] The defense is the first item in the September issue (pp. 177-88). The controversy raised by Priestley is said to be on the "Mortality of the Soul." The writer casts doubt on the need for a spirit attached to matter, as a way of accounting for voluntary motion. Such a spirit, he says, is only a supposition. The writer proposes to build a "real theory on the substantial foundation of physical experiment" (p. 179). He refers to the question of whether matter is so insensitive and inactive as many claim. He also distinguishes between organized and unorganized matter. As evidence for the view that bodies are not completely inert and passive, the writer of this defense cites elasticity and ability to resist other bodies. He even suggests that bodies have "a mechanical species of perception," that they perceive each other, and that they are sensible of each other's presence.[15]

If animals were divested of every sense save touch, the writer claims, they would have the same sort of feeling of external bodies as he imputes to insensible matter. "The mere animation, therefore, of the matter, composing a living body, does not give it the power of feeling" (p. 179). When an animal sleeps or is in a paroxysm, it lives but is as "insensible of pain and inconscious of its own existence as a clock, watch, or any other mechanical automaton." Hobbes and other writers were not wrong in imputing "an *imperfect* sense or perception to particles of unorganized matter," although they went too far in calling it consciousness (p. 180). Consciousness "implies a species of self-knowledge." A *combination* of particles, then, may form "a conscious and intelligent compound." The writer then makes a broad statement on the nature of mind:

That thinking is nothing more than the sense, or perception, which our internal organs entertain, of the difference, or relation, between the different perceptions of the external organs, has nothing in it inconsistent or contradictory; and that, what we call *mind*, as Dr. Priestley justly observes, is nothing more than the system of our internal organs, is equally consistent. (p. 180)

Of the opposing view—that there is a separate spirit or soul—the author quotes J. B. Robinet,[16] who said that for some writers the soul "is a little complicated body, made of finer stuff than ordinary, whose component parts answer to those of our grosser flesh; a kind of Jack in the box, whose wooden doublet fits him so nicely that everybody thinks it alive" (p. 181).[17] The image of the clockwork man keeps appearing in this controversy.

The correspondence columns continued, in September and October 1775, to carry letters on this issue, mostly against Priestley. One writer in the October issue insists that the soul is simple and hence indestructible, and that "no organical system, however perfect, is capable of generating" such affections as sensations, perceptions, and ideas. These, he says, are mental operations (p. 342). He asks: "Where in the brain will you place that judgment, you form, in weighing the analogy, agreement and disagreement of ideas?" The editor of the journal notes that he has received more letters on this debate than he is able to print. In the November issue, the editors refer to attacks on Priestley in *The Monthly Review*, which carried more satire on Priestley and which seems to have taken an opposing position on the suggestions of Priestley. *The London Review* was charged with being favourable to Priestley.

The editor of *The London Review* responded to *The Monthly Review* with a defense of Priestley, but a defense that became a general survey of the controversy: Clarke, Collins, Buffon, and many other writers are mentioned. *The Monthly Review* had cited Clarke against Priestley. The editors of *The London Review* ask who Dr. Clarke is, that his views take precedence over those of Priestley: "Dr. Clarke was confessedly so merely a reasoning machine, that he would almost tempt one to think matter might think, and that he himself was a living proof of it" (p. 564). What is most important about this defense of Priestley is the editors' admonition that, before charging Dr. Priestley with the materialism of others, those who attack him should note that the brain for him is not solid, inert, unfeeling, unthinking matter. This is one of the few recognitions in this debate around Priestley of the radical difference in his concept of matter, thereby altering the nature of his materialism. The defense by the editors goes to the point of this difference: there is no evidence of "absolute solids," the resistance, the impenetrability, and compossibility of all bodies are relative. Their defense ends on a strong note:

On the whole, I look upon this charge, brought against Dr. Priestley, of maintaining the *materiality* of the Soul, in that sense, in which ancient and modern atheists (to use the term adopted by the Reviewers) [in *The Monthly Review*] have accepted it as being favourable to infidelity, to be as invidious and scandalous as it is false and in fact groundless. (p. 567)

The appendix to the volume for the first half of 1775 contains a letter from J. Seton, which makes all the traditional points against the materialists. Berington refers to this letter in his attack on Priestley: he viewed it as an important letter. Seton opens his letter by saying that Priestley's doctrine strikes at the heart of all morality and religion (p. 525). He refers to the quoted passage in the review of 'sGravesande above, about the whole man. He does not yet know Priestley's edition of Hartley, but he insists that the soul must be naturally immortal if resurrection is true. Seton thinks the editors of *The London Review* have been too supportive of Priestley.[18] Seton draws a distinction between *space* and *place*. Mathematical points are located in a place, but they occupy no space. Priestley had said that his mind is no more in his body than it is in the moon. Seton wants to say that the soul has a place in the body, but that it does not occupy any space. He asks: "Do you mean to insinuate that when the *mind* thinks of any distant place, the planet Jupiter for instance, it is actually transported thither?" Seton accepts the two-substance view, citing Baxter in support. He rejects the inference that even if thinking is a refined species of feeling, "*mental* influence and *material* impulse are one and the same" (pp. 528-29). Making good use of his distinction between space and place, he thinks he has dealt with the question of the relation between mind and body:

That the mind occupies no quantity of space, and so far has no relation to space in general, is most certain. It gives motion to the body and changes its place with the body, and yet is not moved by the body, as one body is by another, nor capable of changing its place without it. . . . Certain it is, it hath the power of giving motion to body, without being susceptible of motion, or capable of having motion communicated to it by body. (p. 529)

The attention given to Priestley in these two journals is some indication of the extent to which the thinking-matter controversy had reached a wide reading public, wider than in the days of its introduction by Locke, or even during the Clarke-Collins exchange. The debate could have been transformed had Priestley's readers understood the radical change in the concept of matter which he assumed. But *The London Review* editor's caution to take full note of the difference between Priestley's materialism and other varieties went almost unheeded.[19] Berington's critique of Priestley is, as I have said, carefully constructed; it is no idle tract. Serious and judicious, it nevertheless misses this important feature. Berington addresses his attention more to Hartley's vibratory materialism than to Priestley's immaterializing of matter. It was, then, 'this mechanical system' of Hartley (and, as he points out, of Bonnet's *Essai analytique sur les facultés de l'ame*) to which he reacted, especially to the rejection, which he believed was contained in that system, of liberty and 'free election' (p. 11). The consequence of Hartley's physiology was '*human mechanism*',

Berington was convinced (p. 113). He returns to this point in a satirical vein later in his *Letters*, referring to a Mr. Cox who might, with the help of Priestley, be able to "enrich his collection with two or three *men machines*, of his own construction, that might really operate in a *human* manner, might gradually advance to the summit of knowledge in all the arts and sciences, and perhaps present the public with their several discoveries in religion, philosophy, and politics" (p. 143).[20] The debate was never long free of this fear of mechanizing man.

Berington does distinguish between two different motives leading to the adoption of materialism. The doctrine of materialism

may be viewed either as the system of the libertine, or of the philosopher. The libertine adopts the notion of matter being the sole existing substance, that he may thence infer that he himself is nothing more than an organized machine, and therefore that the powers of death to him are infinite, whose sway reaches to every being of the creation. (p. 16)

For the philosopher who embraces materialism, he is "inclined to it from the reflection, that a being of infinite power might have endowed a mass of matter, such as the brain in man, with such exquisite powers, as should be sufficient to produce all the phenomena of *mind*, from the simplest sensation to the most complex and exalted and intellectual operation" (pp. 16-17). His harshest criticism is leveled at the materialism of the libertine:

Materialism is therefore of dangerous tendency, because it contributes to darken the prospects of futurity; because it unbinds the reins to vice, confirming the libertine and the unbeliever in their bad opinions and incredulity; it is therefore also inimical to virtue; finally it overturns the whole fabric of natural religion, because its injunctions can no longer be enforced, when the professors of it are told, that the same will be the ultimate fate of the virtuous and vicious — utter annihilation. (p. 25)

Berington did not accept the purely passive view of matter. He ascribes powers to it, he speaks of it as active; but he carefully distinguishes its activity from that of the soul. He rejects the Malebranchian notion of occasional causes (p. 75), but his matter is still corpuscular and particulate (p. 50). The activity to which he refers is that of the mutual action and reaction between body and soul, in ways that he does not specify. He is also careful to point out that spirit may be *present to* bodies, not as one body is spatially present to another, but by acting upon body. "I can act more immediately on the bodies in my chamber, than on those situated at the outside of my windows; to the first then I shall say, I am nearer placed, or more present. The most intimate presence is that of the Soul to its body" (p. 77). He claims that "we seem to act" on the brain "by an *immediate* exerting of force," but he gives no account of that force or how it operates.

In commenting upon Berington's account of the place of spirit and its interaction with the body, Priestley first asserts the reality of space over and above the reality of matter. Berington had sided with those who took space to be an ideal phenomenon, an abstracted idea; space for him was just the extensive order of the co-existing bodies. Priestley's second comment on the interaction of soul and body in Berington's account is that such interaction is unintelligible without some property common to both. He does not think it makes sense to say the soul acts on or with the body but yet is 'no where' and has 'no motion' (*Disquisitions*, p. 57). To think of soul and body interacting without having a common property is much more difficult to do, Priestley says, than to conceive "that the principle of sensation may possibly consist with matter" (p. 61). Priestley also suggests that the author of *Letters on Materialism* actually paves the way for materialism when he gives to matter some active power as the basis for the interaction (p. 71).

Priestley returns to this same point against Berington in an added section to his *The Doctrine of Philosophical Necessity* (1777). In his attempt to allow some power to matter, while giving some inferior qualities to spirit, Berington has virtually conceded Priestley's point about the commonality between matter and spirit (p. 177). Priestley asks Berington: "if one species of active power . . . may be imparted to matter," why may not "*another*, or *any other* specie of it" also be ascribed to matter? (p. 178). Since thought has "always been defined to be . . . a particular species of active power," the conclusion is clear.

John Whitehead (*Materialism Philosophically Examined; or, The Immateriality of the Soul Asserted and Proved*, 1778) says that "The principle object" of his remarks "is to prove, that *intelligence* and *thought* are not, cannot be, the result of any modification of matter." He seizes on Priestley's rejection of solidity and impenetrability, saying that these properties, together with *vis inertiae*, are the only properties essential to "the being or existence of matter" (p. v). Even if matter has the power of attraction and repulsion, it is impossible for those powers to produce sensation, reflection, and judgment. Thus, as far as Whitehead is concerned, the controversy comes down to the question, is matter possessed of any powers capable of sensation and thought? (p. vii)

Whitehead recalls Newton's three rules of philosophizing, as well as to Newton's reluctance to say gravitation is essential to matter.

Moreover, he thinks the idea of gravitation presupposes body, for it is bodies that are attracted and repelled. His conclusion is that "attraction and repulsion cannot be the *natural properties* of matter, but are owing to the agency of the Deity" (p. 14). He cites in support of *vis inertiae* the writings of Kepler, Keill, Wollaston, Baxter, Clarke, 'sGravesande, and Newton (pp. 16-17). He also rejects action at a distance since he accepts the popular dictum that no thing can be or act where it is not (p. 31). This dictum is, Whitehead says, "one of the first principles of science" (p. 32; cf. p. 136). To invoke the aether or other intervening media will not help, because we must then ask how that medium is moved (pp. 35-36).

We find in Whitehead's tract the familiar arguments against the idea that matter can think:

For it seems to me that if matter can think, thought must either be essential to its very nature, or it must be the necessary result of some composition of it; for otherwise, if something is to be *added* to matter, as the subject of thought, which is *not matter*, this would be the very thing we contend for, and which this writer [Priestley] elsewhere denies; if therefore, matter can think, thought and sense must be essential to its nature, or some composition of it. . . . (p. 38)

Nor does Whitehead see how a system of matter helps the case, for "organization is nothing more than an *apposition* of parts after a peculiar *mode* or form" (p. 42). No new properties can emerge from a composition of parts. This is the old saw: "If sensation and thought are the result of an organized system of matter, they must reside in all the parts of that system, i.e., every part must contain a piece of sensation, and a piece of a thought" (p. 43). Yet another oft-repeated objection is advanced by Whitehead: on the materialist's doctrine, "all our *sensations, ideas, reasoning,* and every other *power* deemed *mental,* can only be a certain mode or species of motion" (p. 51).

Three other writers reacted to Priestley, two of whom did speak to his changed concept of matter. Richard Shepherd (*Reflections on the Doctrine of Materialism*, 1779)[21] opens by remarking that "one sect of philosophers tell us, there is no such thing as matter," while "another as confidently assert, there exists nothing in nature but matter" (p. 1). He points out that Priestley replaces the common view of matter with a new one: "He considers matter, not as that inert substance, which it is commonly represented, but as possessing the powers of attraction and repulsion" (p. 3). Referring to Priestley's appeal to force and the cause of cohesion of particles of matter, Shepherd insists that what coheres "must be something solid" (p. 8). Aligning himself with the immaterialists, this author claims (with Clarke) that gravitation cannot be "the action of matter on matter," nor can the power required to move muscles be accounted for by anything less than "an immaterial cause" (pp. 10-11). Matter for him is "totally void" of activity. Even if it be granted that matter has the powers of attraction and repulsion, this will not help Priestley's argument that thought is a property of matter: "In attraction and repulsion, there is no advancement made towards thought" (p. 15). Shepherd quotes Locke's view that spirit has a place, but he says it has a place and acts in a place "in a manner as different from that, in which matter occupies it, as the respective natures of spirit and matter are from each other" (p. 23). Similarly, the powers of attraction and repulsion are as different from sensation, perception, and thought as the latter are from inert matter (p. 25).

Shepherd recognizes Priestley's use of Boscovich's ideas on powers and forces, but he fails to appreciate the significance of these ideas for Priestley's ascription of thought to matter. The Rev. Richard Gifford comes closer to such an appreciation. He opens his *Outlines of An Answer to Dr. Priestley's Disquisitions Relating to Matter and Spirit* (1781) by citing Cudworth's comment about those persons who were "possessed with a certain Kind of Madness, that may be called *Pneumatophobia*, that makes them have an irrational, but desperate abhorrence from Spirits or incorporeal Substance." This madness goes along with *Hylomania*, "whereby they madly dote upon Matter" (p. 1).[22] Gifford argues that, even with Priestley's repulsive power, there are particles of hard matter which do occupy space. So long as there is any hard matter, it is impenetrable. "Suppose, if you please, that all the solid Matter in the Solar System might be contained in a Nutshell, yet this Nutshell must necessarily be *impenetrable*" (p. 6). All the parts of the matter in the nutshell would also be impenetrable. Even if we recognize, as Gifford does, that "Upon the Doctor's System, there is not in Nature any such Thing as Matter, distinct from Attraction and Repulsion" (p. 21), Gifford believes that Priestley makes too much of powers, for it is "Matter in Motion, that Causes the Phaenomena of Attraction and Repulsion" (p. 30).

Gifford claims that in order to understand consciousness, we must look farther than to the material system. He cites Clarke's letter to Dodwell, and repeats some of Clarke's arguments against thinking matter (pp. 32-33). He also cites Cudworth in support of the principle that a whole cannot have more than the parts. Throughout there are many quotations and references to most of the standard authors in this controversy: Clarke, Locke, Baxter, Berkeley, Norris, Malebranche, Hutcheson, Reid, Law, Price, and Butler. Gifford says of Locke that he is "often quoted by Infidel Writers" (p. 36). He rejects Locke's suggestion that "an individual, percipient Power" could be "superadded to a material System" (p. 33). Gifford's work is rather carefully done, but he shows little recognition that by making matter force and power rather than hard particles, Priestley has changed the nature of the materialism. He sticks to the traditional concepts of matter, allowing attraction and repulsion, but only as produced by corpuscular matter in motion. His work is a good catalogue at the end of the century (just as Cudworth's *True Intellectual System* was earlier) of most of the objections to materialism.

A more sophisticated critique of Priestley's views is found in John Rotheram's *An Essay on the Distinction between the Soul and Body of Man* (1781). Echoing the ancient doctrines of separable and inseparable accidents, he distinguishes those properties of matter "that are fugitive and variable" from those that are "fixed and permanent" (p. 1). The latter are "the natural properties that belong to it as matter." Matter is naturally inactive. "Inert and devoid of all absolute and essential power, it became the more apt to receive the relative powers," e.g., attraction and repulsion (pp. 2-3). He speaks of the soul of plants, the power they have of living (p. 5). It is an *active* power but one dependent upon the matter of the plant. In speaking of the power to initiate motion—which we are conscious of in ourselves—Rotheram asks whether this is a "power superadded to that portion of matter of which our bodies are framed" (p. 9). Properties are not "given, removed, and exchanged in a new and arbitrary manner." He denies that this power can be a property of our bodies, for it is not evident in the matter of our bodies (pp. 11-13). Were matter to be given such a power, its constitution would have to be altered "to prepare it for the reception of this new power" (p. 14).

Like all those who oppose materialism, Rotheram insists that extension and figure are foreign to thought. With thought, he suggests, we have "arrived at a new creation, an ideal world, whose furniture and whose laws are totally different from the material" (p. 18). He contrasts the properties we discover by sense with those we discover by reflection and consciousness: the physical and the mental. We require two substances for these different qualities and properties (p. 23). Referring (though not by name) to the Hartley-Priestley theory of vibrations, he asks: "If an idea be a vibration, then it may be asked, wherein consists the idea of a vibration itself. Vibrations are supposed to represent every other object, [but] what is it that represents this universal representation? If a vibration, then it is a vibration of a vibration, and the idea is compounded with its object" (p. 31). The question is not "about the production of images or forms, but about the sense and perception of them" (p. 36). Meaning and sense, Rotheram saw, cannot be reduced to figure and motion. "If sense be said to be nothing more than matter figured and moving, then sense differs not from the world without us; and every external object, having all the requisites of sense, is itself sentient" (p. 37). Rotheram makes some excellent points about the way in which representation—cognitive representation—requires more than the theory of vibrations allows, for it is unable to explain how vibrations can have meaning, how they can represent for us the objects to which we want to refer.

Conclusion

The questions and issues surrounding the various forms of materialism in eighteenth-century Britain were the focus of considerable attention. *The London Review* and *The Monthly Review* were not the only more general publications in which the question of thinking matter is debated. MacLaurin's rather popular work, *An Account of Sir Isaac Newton's Philosophy* (1748), summarizes the main positions. Some writers, he says, settle for mechanism and matter only; others admit nothing but perceptions and spirits. MacLaurin thinks those who admitted only spirit and immaterial causes put a stop to inquiry into nature: immaterialism is antiscience (p. 95). The main positions are also noted in *The Annual Register* for 1763, a publication devoted to general information and reading in history, politics, and literature. The author of the article "Concerning the Perceptive Faculty" remarks:

That there are sensations arising in man no one I believe doubts, but what it is which is perceptive of them, is a question with some; whether it is man as a compound being of soul and body, or whether the living percipient is not a mind, or spirit alone, without a body, or else a quality only resulting from the construction of a body, without any distinct or separate spirit annexed thereto. (p. 182)

The author of this article thinks that we cannot demonstrate which of these views is correct, we can only reach probability.

Behind much of this controversy over thinking matter lurked the fear of materializing man. With knowledge and understanding of the human physiology increasing, the notion of the *mechanism* of the body was becoming familiar. For many, the one definitive safeguard against mechanizing the mind was the assurance that the mind is immaterial. The immateriality of the soul was important not only for immortality; it was needed as well to keep the materialism of the body from absorbing the mind. To suggest that thought might be a property of the brain, or to suggest that man is one, not two, substances, was for most people unacceptable not only because of the force of tradition, but also because of the fear of turning man into an automaton, albeit a clever and sophisticated one.

No one in Britain actually advanced such a concept of man. There was no British La Mettrie. Equally, no one applied the new concept of matter as centers of force to work out a detailed view of man as composed of a single substance. Priestley's fascinating suggestions were not taken up and extended; they were hardly even perceived as different from earlier versions of materialism. The issues raised by Locke's suggestion of thinking matter, by the commitment to the principle of cognitive contact (no perception at a distance); by the struggles with the notion of the place of mind (even, for some, with the mind's extension): all of these played themselves out through the century, but no one gave the emerging view of man as one substance — foreshadowed by Priestley — a systematic articulation.

Notes

1. Andrew Baxter, *An Enquiry into the Nature of the Human Soul; Wherein the Immateriality of the Soul is evinced from the Principles of Reason and Philosophy*, 1733; 3rd edition, 1745, vol I, sect. I, note k, p. 36.

2. Book 3, chapter 2, p. 356. This supposition of the porosity of matter is what came to be called the 'nut-shell theory'. For a discussion of it, see Thackray, *Atoms and Powers*, pp. 53-67. The term 'nut shell' appears in Priestley's *Disquisitions Relating to Matter and Spirit* (1777), p. 17. The paucity of hard matter in this view of matter led Priestley to "wonder that it did not occur to philosophers sooner, that perhaps there might be nothing for it to do at all, and that there might be no such thing in nature."

3. McMullin, *Newton on Matter and Activity*, p. 113.

4. Ibid. For Voltaire's remark, see his *Letters concerning the English Nation* (1733), p. 147. What I take to be a reference to this notion of the porosity of matter is also found in Berkeley's *Philosophical Commentaries*, Notebook B, entry 128: "Matter tho' allow'd to exist may be no greater than a pin's head." In his *Examination of P. Malebranche's Opinion* (*Works*, IX, p. 215), Locke makes a similar remark. Speaking of the difficulties of explaining how material bodies can cause perception, he says he thinks these difficulties are reduced when we "allow extreme smallness in the particles of light, and the exceeding swiftness in their motion; and the great porosity that must be granted in bodies."

5. Schofield tells us that Priestley did in fact read Rowning at the Daventry Academy in 1755 (*Mechanism and Materialism*, p. 39), but it is Boscovich and Michell whom Priestley cites later in the century for this concept of matter.

6. Although Rowning did seek to explain most phenomena in terms of three principles — the attraction of gravity, the attraction of cohesion, and the repulsion of bodies — he still thought of matter as inactive (pp. xvii and 7, eighth edition, 1779). Moreover, he thought, these active principles of attraction and repulsion are not essential to matter but are impressed upon it by God.

7. Besides the discussions in Schofield and Thackray, see L. L. Whyte, *R. J. Boscovich: Studies in His Life and Work* (London: Allen & Unwin, 1961).

8. McMullin, *Newton on Matter and Activity*, p. 117. The citation is from Boscovich, Child's edition, p. 183.

9. Michell's theories are found in *A Treatise of Artifical Magnets* (1750) and in several papers in *Philosophical Transactions* of the Royal Society for 1767 and 1784.

10. Priestley points out that Locke recognized the importance of cohesion, but not its explanation in terms of powers.

11. He also cites Melvill's "Observations on Light and Colours" (1756), where it has been shown that "a drop of water rolls upon a cabbage leaf without ever coming into actual contact with it; and indeed all the phenomena of *light* are most remarkably unfavourable to the hypothesis of the solidity or impenetrability of matter" (pp. 13-14).

12. Price had said, in reply to Priestley (*A Free Discussion of the Doctrine of Materialism*, 1778), that "A *connection* and *dependence* by no means proves *sameness*" (p. 49). Priestley responds by saying that "the business of thinking is wholly carried on *in* and *by* the brain itself, because all the effects from which we infer the faculty of thinking can be traced to the brain, and *no further*" (pp. 49-50).

13. The DNB identifies the author of this work as Joseph Berington, a liberal Catholic priest who later held discussions with Priestley.

14. Berington also suggested that since Priestley had not publicly responded to one of the letters against him (by a Mr. Seton), and since this defense is unsigned, that Priestley may be the author of it: "we are authorized to esteem it yours, or, which nearly amounts to the same, to conclude that it came forth under your tutelage and kind protection" (p. 7).

15. This suggestion hardly sounds like something Priestley would make. Berington scoffs at the suggestion, saying: "I defy the callous fibres of the most gloomy metaphysician not to dissolve in laughter," at this notion of a mechanical species of perception (p. 33). Priestley subsequently disowned this defense saying that he neither wrote it nor knows who did. (See his *The Doctrine of Philosophical Necessity*, 1777, p. 205.)

16. *Vue philosophique de la gradation naturelle des formes de l'etre, ou Les essais de la nature que apprend à faire l'homme* (1768).

17. Robinet's remark was cited in a review in the *Monthly Review* of Charles Bonnet, *Essai analytique sur les facultés de l'âme* (1760). See also his *Essai de psychologie* (1754).

18. The editors add a note here saying that Seton only partially quotes Priestley, but they then go on to dissociate themselves from the view that the soul dies at death.

19. James Meikle, in *Metaphysical Maxims: Or, Thoughts on the Nature of the Soul, Free Will, and the Divine Prescience* (1797) gives a passing recognition of the difference: "It is, indeed, a masterly stroke of the materialist, to deny a *vis inertiae* to matter; for, if granted, it must overthrow other doctrines. But it is equally absurd, to make matter both matter and spirit" (p. 12). Meikle does not name Priestley, but he writes against the materialists who identify the brain with the soul. What he says fits Priestley.

20. A more sober judgment of Hartley is given by Christopher Wordsworth (*Scholae Academicae*, 1877): "Towards the end of the last century, Hartley was considered a great light among philosophical minds at Cambridge. He was a contemporary of Hume and a fellow-follower of Locke. His system (which was based on physiology) gathered up the floating materialism current at Cambridge, and was for a time adopted by Coleridge while he was at the University, as well as by Priestley and other Necessitarians and Unitarians" (p. 123).

21. Shepherd's book was published under the pseudonym of Philalethes Rusticans. The DNB identifies him as the author.

22. The quotation is from p. 135 of Cudworth's *True Intellectual System*. Cudworth labels these men 'atheists'.

Chapter VII

The Concept of Action

Throughout the eighteenth century there was a rather wide-ranging debate over liberty and necessity. Along with that debate went a serious attempt to clarify the concept of action. It was important, for those who believed that man can and does act freely, to articulate a supporting concept of action; but even those who defended some version of necessitarianism felt the need to characterize human action. Some writers boldly denied that we do move our body or its limbs: mind can no more move or affect body than body can affect mind. Others said that to move my body (my arm or leg) I have to work the mechanism of nerves, muscles, and animal spirits. Some agreed that we do move the nerves and muscles and in that way move our body; others said that if we did move the nerves and muscles we would have to have a detailed knowledge of physiology. Some distinguished between acts and action, noted that we can only do what we know or have concepts for; and still others insisted that action is spontaneity, giving a new force to matter, originating something new.

As with so many of the topics discussed by eighteenth-century philosophers in Britain, Locke's statement of them frequently set the framework for their pursuit. His discussions of power, of liberty, of the person, and of action are echoed and cited. The continental influence is not lacking, however. That famous exchange between Leibniz and the Newtonian divine, Samuel Clarke, was a focus of much attention after 1717 in theory of action. Another continental figure whose views can be traced in Britain in this area is, of course, Malebranche. His statement of the conditions to be met if in fact man were capable of action set some of the themes for later discussion in this century.

Malebranche: I Will, But Do Not Cause, My Arm to Move

Malebranche's discussion of action should be considered in the wider context of his metaphysics. Only God is truly active; no second cause is efficacious. Malebranche criticizes all those who have appealed to special entities in nature — substantial forms, real qualities, virtues — as the causal powers of change. Explanations in terms of these supposed entities are explaining "natural effects through certain beings of which they have not one single particular idea."[1] Any appeal to powers inherent in nature is an appeal to something divine. To bring new action about is the act of a creator: "Everything that can act upon us as a true and real cause is necessarily above us" (p. 446). Both St. Augustine and reason tell us that this is so. It follows, then, that body is unable to act on mind. Hence there is nothing above the mind except God. God becomes the only cause of change in nature: "The motor force of bodies is therefore not in the bodies that are moved for this motor force is nothing other than the will of God" (p. 448). Malebranche offers an argument to support this conclusion. It is evident that bodies, no matter what their size, are not able to move themselves. We have only two kinds of ideas: ideas of minds and ideas of bodies. Since bodies lack self-motion, change can only be the result of minds. But when we examine the idea we have of finite minds, "we do not see any necessary connection between their will and the motion of any body whatsoever" (p. 448). It follows that no finite, created mind is able to move bodies. If we consider the idea of God — of a being infinitely perfect and all powerful — we discover that there is a necessary connection between God's will and the movement of bodies: "it is impossible to conceive that He wills a body to be moved and that this body not be moved." Bodies are only natural or occasional causes, not real causes; they have no force or action. All the apparent forces in nature are in reality the will of God: "There are therefore no forces, powers, or true causes in the material, sensible world" (p. 449).

Malebranche places great weight on the argument of necessary connection. He repeats it several times, even concerning the movement of our limbs: "it is clear that there is no necessary connection between our will to move our arms, for example, and the movement of our arms" (p. 449). There is in fact a contradiction in the notion that I can move my arm, for a true cause is one between which and its effect we can apprehend a necessary connection. He makes the same point in *Eclaircissement* XV, where he says that the main argument advanced by philosophers for the efficacy of second causes is taken from the will of man: man wills, determines himself, and hence is free. Moreover, how else to understand sin: we do not want to say God is the author of our sins. To this last point, Malebranche concedes that "man wills, and determines himself, but it is because God makes him will and moves him incessantly towards the good."[2] Malebranche even allows ideas and feelings as the motives behind action; but since God is the source of all our ideas and feelings, we are not really the cause of what we do. The theological pressures are met with some dubious distinctions. Our mind wills, acts, determines itself: Malebranche does not doubt that this is so.[3] But admitting that we determine ourselves by willing is not, for Malebranche, to say my "will is the true cause of the movement of my arm," for there is no connection (no necessary connection) between willing my arm to move and the fact that my arm moves.[4]

Malebranche advances another argument for this conclusion. What would I have to do in order to move my arm? I would have to send animal spirits through specific nerves towards particular muscles. The animal spirits would then inflate the muscles or muscle-fibres, and then the arm would move. But men who do not know anything at all of physiology appear to move their limbs, frequently more easily and quickly than those who have a knowledge of anatomy. The truth is that no one moves his limbs: there is no one who knows sufficient physiology to move even one finger. *Eclaircissement* IV links the necessary-connection argument with this argument about physiological knowledge:

I see very clearly that there cannot be any connection between the will I have to move my arms and the agitation of the animal spirits, that is of some small bodies whose movement and shape I know not; those bodies will choose certain channels from among a million channels that I do not know, so as to cause in me the movement I want through an infinity of movements that I do not want.[5]

Thus once again he concludes that "it's obvious that my arm will be moved, not by my will which is impotent in itself, but by God's will who can never fail in having his effect."[6]

Malebranche agrees in the *Eclaircissement* that under certain conditions, when he moves his arm, he has an internal feeling of the actual willing by which the arm has been moved or appears to have been moved, i.e., his own willing. He even has a feeling of effort, an effort he believes he has made. Moreover, he also has the feeling that his arm moves when he makes this effort. But this feeling of effort, which he says is given to us to make us aware of our weakness in this world (presumably by realizing how little that effort can accomplish), is not by itself capable of moving the animal spirits.[7] Even if we were able to move those spirits, there would be much other physiological information we would need but lack, e.g., information about which nerves to select for sending the animal spirits down.[8] We would need to have this sort of very specific knowledge each time we perform any movement. We would need to have that knowledge quickly so that we could move our arms and legs quickly:

The arm, for example, is only moved because the animal spirits inflate some of the muscles which compose it. Now in order for movement, which the soul impresses on the spirits which are in the brain, to be communicated to those spirits which are in the nerves and these to others which are in the arm's muscles, it would be necessary for the volitions of the soul to be multiplied or to change in proportion to the contacts and almost infinite shocks, which would be in the small bodies which make up the spirits, for bodies cannot of themselves move those bodies which they encounter, as I believe I have sufficiently demonstrated.[9]

The conclusion is clear: in order to move my arm, I must be able to determine the movement of the animal spirits in the brain.

In Book VI, Part II, chapter VIII of the *Recherche*, Malebranche considers the question of the natural and mechanical cause of the movements of our limbs. He distinguishes voluntary, natural, and convulsive movement.[10] Each of these has a different cause or different kind of mechanism. For voluntary action, he suggests it is useful to examine the composition of the arm, the muscles and tendons. He cannot doubt that the movement of the arm depends on the contraction of muscles. He tells us that the common opinion is that the contraction occurs by means of the animal spirits that fill the cavity of the muscle fibres. Thus the question of voluntary movement is "reduced to knowing how the small quantity of animal spirits contained in an arm can suddenly swell its muscles according to the orders of the will with sufficient force to lift a load of a hundred pounds and more."[11] It will not do to attempt a chemical explanation, analogous to the action of acids or alkaloids; for we are dealing in this case with voluntary movement, and chemical reactions are not voluntary, nor—Malebranche seems to be saying—are they capable of control by our will. In any event, the same objection would arise here as did earlier: it can't be that I move my muscles by some process of fermentation, since I lack the necessary knowledge of all the chemical reactions that would take place in my body when my arm moves.

Instead of chemical reactions, Malebranche offers a different model. Take a large balloon, and inflate it about half-way with air. Then, keeping the air in, place a large stone on the balloon, or place a plank over the balloon and have a man sit on the plank. If someone will then blow a bit of air into the balloon, that additional air will cause the stone or the man to rise. Thus a very little force is required to raise a large weight by means of air inflating a balloon. If we apply this model to the muscles and conceive of the muscles or of each of the fibres of the muscles as being able to receive animal spirits through a small opening, we will understand how "the motion of spirits that expand in the muscles can overcome the force of the heaviest loads we carry."[12]

Motives, Clocks, and Balances

The physiology of animal spirits was widely accepted and used in Britain during the eighteenth century. Many writers wanted to be sure, however, that the physiology did not run away with the agent, did not take over human action. The spontaneity of action and the distinction between physical causes and agent causes were two concepts frequently used to guard against this danger. In his Boyle lectures for 1717-18, John Leng,[13] with his eye on the thinking-matter controversy, remarked that if all was matter and motion—especially if all reasoning was the effect of matter and motion "causally working upon us"— there would be nothing voluntary, hence there would be no obligation (p. 8). According to Leng, free thinking and true liberty consist in acting according to the law of reason and concluding only on sound evidence (p. 14). The mind does have the power to move the body (p. 73). Those materialists who deny this power "think a Man is as necessarily moved to act, as a Clock to strike, though it may be by a longer Chain of Causes." Leng says that those who make this claim first say that all is matter differently modified. If they do not hold this view, then he suspects that they "confound a *moral* Motive, or rational Ground of a Man's acting, with a *physical* efficient Cause." Thus they are unable to distinguish "an abstracted Reason inducing, and a bodily Impulse forcing us to do this or that."[14]

John Broughton (in *Psychologia: Or, An Account of the Nature of the Rational Soul*, 1703) also insists on the self-moving power of the soul "exerting itself in all the Operations of Thought and Spontaneous Motion" (Preface). Spirit is the principle of life and sensation, while the body is the principle of mechanism and local motion. Broughton thinks we are conscious in ourselves of spontaneous motion, motion that cannot be initiated mechanically, as in a clock: "we think to move, and immediately upon that Thought we do move" (p. 38). Much later in this work, he admits that we do not know how the soul moves the body; but since matter is entirely passive, the body cannot move itself unaided (p. 399). Broughton might accept an account such as Malebranche's, but he insists it is the soul that initiates the activity of animal spirits in volition. "For if we suppose the Soul to act immediately, only upon the spirituous and Subtle Parts of the Body, we must grant it necessary, that these be duly qualify'd to communicate Motion to the grosser Parts, because they do that mechanically" (p. 402).

In his Boyle lectures of 1705, Samuel Clarke (*A Demonstration of the Being and Attributes of God*) insists that intelligence requires liberty: "Without liberty, nothing can in any tolerable Propriety of Speech, be said to be an Agent or Cause any thing. For to act necessarily, is really and properly not to Act at all, but only to be Acted upon" (pp. 127-28). We all have experience of self-motion, Clarke maintains (p. 175). Accepting the physiology of animal spirits, Clarke, unlike Malebranche, says that we do move our animal spirits; it is contrary to experience to say that "the Spirits by which a man moves the Members of his Body, and ranges the Thoughts of his Mind, are themselves moved wholly by air or Subtle Matter inspired into the Body" (pp. 176-77). He compares that account of action, according to which the animal spirits are moved only by air and subtle matter, to the movement of the wheels of a clock. We do have a power to determine the animal spirits in our nerves and muscles; our actions are not as "necessary as the Motions of a Clock" (p. 180).

Clarke's views on human action, especially his insistence on the difference between human action and the movement of mechanisms such as clocks and balances, are extended in his exchange with Leibniz. In his *Theodicy*, Leibniz had cited Bayle's comparison of a man's soul to a balance, where reasons and inclinations are put in place of weights. Reasons, passions, even ideas tip the balance of the will one way or other, or, when equal, the balance is unmoved. Leibniz suggested that a better approach is to think of the soul as a force "which has at one and the same time a tendency many ways, but acts on that part only where it finds the greatest ease, or the least resistance." In his second paper to Clarke, Leibniz referred to his *Theodicy* and to the example of the balance.

Clarke (in his fourth reply) picked up the balance example, insisting that it leads to universal necessity and fate if applied to man. There is an essential difference between a balance and man: the latter but not the former is an intelligent agent. When the weights in a balance are equal, "there is nothing to move it." Agents are not moved by motives as a balance is by weights: "they have active powers and do move themselves, sometimes upon the view of strong motives, sometimes upon weak ones, and sometimes when things are absolutely indifferent" (Leibniz-Clarke correspondence, p. 45). Clarke claimed that Leibniz's pre-established harmony is a perpetual miracle: it rules out the operations of the soul on body and makes body, by mere mechanical impulses of matter, conform to the will of the soul in all spontaneous motions of the body. In spontaneous motions—i.e., in actions—the soul gives to matter new motions or new forces. If, as Clarke thinks Leibniz would say, the giving of new forces to matter is supernatural, then "every action of man, is either supernatural or else man is as mere a machine as a clock" (p. 51). If the mechanism of the body is all that is involved in my moving my arm or in my arm moving, there is no action, only fate and necessity. When men act, something new is added to nature.[15]

Leibniz responds (in section 14 of his fifth paper) by saying that the principle of sufficient reason applies to balances as well as to agents. Properly speaking, he says, "motives do not act upon the mind, as weights do upon a balance; but 'tis rather the mind that acts by virtue of the motives, which are its dispositions to act." To say, as Clarke does, that the mind prefers weak or strong motives, or that it prefers that which is indifferent, is to treat motives as if they were external to the mind. Leibniz objects that the mind cannot act or have good reasons to act when it has no motives, when things are indifferent. "For if the mind has good reasons for taking the part it takes, then the things are not indifferent in the mind" (Sect. 16). To Clarke's view that complete fatalism is the only alternative to man's acting supernaturally, Leibniz responds that the dilemma is ill-grounded. A man does not act supernaturally; his body is a machine and can only act mechanically, yet his soul is a free cause (Sect. 95).

Leibniz had his own contorted account of free action. What is important in this exchange is the way in which Clarke saw the alternatives. The body is a machine and works by mechanism. If actions require the interference of mind in the machine of the body, how then can there be actions? Clarke's fifth reply repeats the difference between a balance and an agent: only the latter is active (p. 97). He distinguishes the mind's power of acting and the "impressions made upon the mind by the motives." In acting, there is the motive, the impression made on the mind, and the doing. Clarke insists that "every action is the giving of a new force to the thing acted upon" (p. 110). Communication of motion between body and body is not action. Action is spontaneity, the beginning of motion. He does not think the body mechanism is all that is involved when one acts.

But is it possible, that such kinds of motion, and of such variety, as those in human bodies are should be performed by mere mechanisms, without any influence of will and mind upon them? Or is it credible, that when a man has it in his power to resolve and know a month before-hand, what he will do upon such a particular day or hour to come; is it credible, I say, that his body shall by the mere power of mechanism, impressed originally upon the material universe at its creation, punctually conform itself to the resolutions of the man's mind at the time appointed? (p. 116)

Clarke expounds his concept of action further in two additional publications, responses to three short anonymous letters and his reply to Collins's *A Philosophical Enquiry concerning Human Liberty* (1717). The first of these, *Letters to Dr. Clarke concerning Liberty and Necessity; From a Gentleman of the University of Cambridge; With the Doctor's Answers to Them* (1717),[16] concerns Clarke's Boyle lectures. The author of these letters starts by saying that if, as some writers were saying, "the *Will* is no other but the *Last Judgment of the Understanding*," why is the will not necessitated? His point is that the judgment is not free in assenting to speculative propositions; it cannot but assent to truth. The same should be true for assent to practical propositions. Even God cannot but judge that to be good and just which is good and just (pp. 403-04). Clarke draws a distinction between judging and acting:

The Spring of *Action*, is not the *Understanding*: For a Being incapable of *Action* might nevertheless be capable of *Perception*: But the Spring of *Action*, is *The Self-Motive Power*, which is (in *All* Animals) *Spontaneity*, and (in *rational* ones) what we call *Liberty*. (p. 406)

The letter-writer then asks how a person can be self-moving if what he does is not connected with his judgment. An action that is only contingently related to judgment is not, he thinks, a self-caused action. He ends his second letter with a distinction between external necessity or blind impulse and necessity internal "which results from the very Being and Constitution of rational Nature" (p. 408).

Clarke's reply reaffirms the contingent connection between judgment and action (he says there is no connection at all between them). If they were physically connected, then both judging and acting would be passive. Then, "Neither *Man*, nor *Angel*, nor even *God himself*, would *act* in any other Sense, than a *Balance* determined on one side by an overplus of Weight," actions being impossible only where physical necessity holds.[17] The letter-writer then asks, if there is no connection between judging or perceiving and acting, "Will it not follow, that *unintelligent Substance* may be capable of *Self-Motion*, and *mere*

Matter be as absolutely *Free* as *Infinite Wisdom* itself? Nay, if in any Instance, Action or Self-Motion does not follow the last Perception or Judgment of the Understanding, the Agent must in that Instance be over-rul'd by a *blind Impulse*: There is no Medium" (p. 411). To this, Clarke replies that judging "is as distinct from the Actual Exertion of the Self-motive Power; as *seeing* the Way, is, from *Walking* in it" (p. 413). It is wrong to think that if "The Perception of the Understanding is denied to be the immediate efficient necessary Cause of the Exertion of the Self-motive Power, that therefore *unintelligent Matter* may be capable of Self-Motion." Unintelligent matter is not an agent: consciousness is required for action, but consciousness "which makes *Action* to be *Action*, is entirely a distinct Thing from That *Perception* or *Judgment*, by which a Man determines beforehand concerning the *Reasonableness* or Fitness of what he is about to act" (p. 413). I can refuse to open my eyes in order to see the way, but still try to walk. I can refuse to use my judgment but still act. Thus, when I do use my eyes to see and my understanding to judge, my walking and my acting cannot be identified with my seeing and judging.

Clarke's reply to Collins makes most of these same points. The perceptive and active faculties are different: "To be an *Agent*, signifies, to have a *Power of beginning Motion*: And *Motion* cannot begin *necessarily*; because *Necessity of Motion*, supposes an Efficiency Superiour to, and irresistible by, the thing moved" (p. 6). Collins, by linking willing with preferring, obscures this point. Collins, Clarke says, always supposes that "if a Man is not determined as *necessarily and irresistibly*, as a *Weight* determines the Motion of a *Balance*; then he can *in no Degree* be influenced by, nor can have *any Regard* to, any *Motives* or *Reasons of Action* whatsoever" (p. 12). The clock and balance examples appear frequently in these debates. Collins thinks, Clarke charges, that the only difference between a man and a clock is that the former has sensations and intelligence, the latter not, but sensation and intelligence are not the power of action (pp. 14-15). Perhaps the most important addition to the argument in his reply to Collins is in his remarks about motives. Motives are not the causes of action. "When we say, in *vulgar* Speech, that *Motives* or *Reasons* DETERMINE a Man; 'tis nothing but a mere *Figure* or *Metaphor*" (p. 11). If reasons or motives were causes, "then either *abstract Notions*, such as all *Reasons* and *Motives* are, have a *real Subsistence*, that is, are themselves *Substances*; or else *That which has it self no real Subsistence*, can *put* a Body into *Motion*" (p. 43). Moreover, to make reasons or motives causes, would be to suppose that they "make the same *necessary Impulse* upon *Intelligent* Subjects, as *Matter in Motion* does upon *unintelligent Subjects*" (p. 16). It is the man himself, the active substance, which is "the only proper, Physical, and immediate CAUSE of the Motion or Action" (p. 26).

Two books commenting upon these debates are worth a notice. The first is *An Impartial Enquiry into the Existence and Nature of God* (1718), by Samuel Colliber. He refers to some "Atheistical Materialists" (in particular, Spinoza and Hobbes) who have given intelligence to matter (p. 33). The concept of self-activity is said to be "a Principle of Beginning External Action," an idea we get from nothing else but "Cogitation" (pp. 38-39). Freedom or liberty requires a power of perceiving, judging, and choosing, as well as of determining actions consequent on judging, all these powers being free from bias. Depraved minds cannot be free; a poor judgment will not be able to discern real from apparent good, thereby curtailing freedom. In order to be free we also need to be able not to act as well as to act. 'Voluntary' is not a good and sufficient mark of liberty because what is done voluntarily may be necessitated by external force (p. 42). There are even cases in which free action comes from necessity, the necessity a good man is under to do what is good.[18]

> Our Notion of Humane Liberty is then only Complete, when it includes a Perception and Judgment determin'd only by the Real Nature and Circumstances of the Object, without the irresistable Influence either of External Force or Internal Defects; Perceived by an indetermin'd Ability of Considering and Deliberating, and Follow'd by a like Indetermin'd ability either of Approving or Not Approving, Choosing or Not Choosing, Acting or Not Acting Accordingly. (pp. 43-44)

The second book commenting on Clarke's various debates is by Samuel Strutt: *A Defence of the late Learned Dr. Clarke's Notion of Natural Liberty: In Answer to Three Letters wrote to Him by a Gentleman at the University of Cambridge* (1730). Strutt defined natural liberty as "a Power in the man, resulting from his Frame and Composition, to will, or not to will; act, or not to act; with, or without the last Judgment of the Understanding, or any Motive, Liking, or Inclination, whatsoever" (p. 5). He reads Clarke's insistence that motives are not causes as meaning we can act without motives. We all do actions for which we have no reason or motive (p. 6). We do these things simply because we will them. He offers as examples of such motiveless actions, a man striking the pavement with his cane as he walks along, or playing with his fingers on the table. These are actions done by the man without his even being sensible that he is doing them. These particular actions may not even have a volition, hence they may in fact be necessary but not, he insists, mechanical. He distinguishes mechanical motion (due to physical impulse and contact only) from animal motion (due to powers of the animal). This is the power of self-determination. If we can act without volitions, Strutt asks where is the absurdity "to suppose, we *can act, merely and solely, in consequence of Volition*" (pp. 7-8). He denies that such actions — with or without volitions — are examples of effects without causes, since (though he is not entirely clear about this) it is the man who is the agent of the action. Volition is "*Resolving or Determining to do, or not to do, some Action*" (p. 9).

As Clarke had stated against the letter-writer from Cambridge, so Strutt insists that a man may will an action after judgment, but judging and willing are different. Moreover, the will is under no necessity to will after or in accordance with judgment. Certainly there is no *physical* necessity to will. Assenting or dissenting to propositions does not determine a man to act (p. 11). Strutt's reason in support of this remark is that assent and dissent do not exist in the nature of things, they are only properties of the mind, affections. Only what exists can determine; assent, dissent, liking, resolving are all different powers of man "and have no other *relation* to each other, than as it is *convenient or inconvenient*, just or unjust, for him to act or not to act, in Conjunction with these several and distinct powers" (p. 11; cf. p. 30). Reference to nonexistent properties or powers is Strutt's way of making Clarke's point, that it is the man who acts, not some property of the man. And like Clarke, Strutt says that the last judgment and the action "have *no connection or relation* to each other" (p. 17). He also cites an article in *The London Journal* for 25 October 1730 in which the author has shown that motives are "no other than the *Mediums* by which we act, and not the *Causes* of *Action*" (p. 23). The spring of action is not in the understanding, but "is a *distinct independent Power*" (p. 30). Strutt should have seen that he is also close to Locke on this analysis, but he thinks Locke holds that our will is not free, when Locke says it is the man, not our will, that is free. Locke did speak of motives acting on the mind: Strutt says again that "*Motives* can no more *work* than *play*, since they do not *exist* in the nature of things" (p. 43). He remarks that it is odd indeed to say, as some writers seem to say, that a man is free when he cannot but act in accordance with the last judgment of his understanding, for this makes man like a machine moved by weights and balances (p. 45).

Action and the Body Mechanism

There were other writers throughout the century who boldly claimed that mind moves body, even though they offered no explanation as to how it does so. In *An Essay on the Origin of Evil* (1731; translation by Law of *De Origine Mali*), William King had said that we have in ourselves a self-conscious thinking principle "whose actions are to will, refuse, doubt, reason, etc." (p. 51) We can also move matter "and shake the Limbs of our Body by thought only, that is by Volition." King also made the important point that "The Reason or End of every Action is always known to the Agent; for nothing can move a Man but what is perceiv'd" (p. xxviii). Colliber, in another work filled with detail on the physiology of thinking and acting (*Free Thoughts concerning Souls*, 1734), simply affirms that by an act of the will "a Power is exerted on our bodies, and the Motion of our Bodies follows immediately as quick as Thought" (p. 53). Another book of psychology with attention to physiology (*An Enquiry into the Origin of the Human Appetites and Affections*, 1747)[19] says the soul can "by a mere act of the will . . . produce certain motions *de novo*" (p. 65). These are samples of one strong theme in the accounts of action in the century.

Another theme, growing in strength through the century and linked with the controversy over thinking matter, was that human action could be explained solely in terms of the mechanism of the body. In some cases, this claim was advanced by the new materialists in the century, but the analysis given by some immaterialists helped erode the more traditional notion by giving too much to the body mechanism. Malebranche's influence may be discernible here: by denying the efficacy of second causes, but recognizing the detailed physiology required to move arms and legs, it was not too difficult for some writers to dismiss the extraordinary intervention of God and to settle for body mechanism alone. The basic challenge to the immaterialist claim that mind moves body was laid down in an anonymous tract in 1760. In between, Andrew Baxter's Malebranchian analysis failed to save much of a role for the person as agent in action.

The anonymous tract published in 1732, *A Philosophical Enquiry into the Physical Spring of Human Actions, and the Immediate Cause of Thinking*[20] (credited to Strutt; see Jacob, *The Radical Enlightenment*), notes that Locke locates the springs of action in thought and volition. He cites Locke's *Essay*, 4.10.19, where Locke says: "For example, my right hand writes whilst my left hand is still. What causes rest in one and motion in the other? Nothing but my will, a thought of my mind." Strutt wonders how this view is consistent with 2.21.16 of the *Essay*, where Locke ascribes the power of action to agents, not to the will or thought.[21] He agrees that thought and volition are powers or abilities of the person, but they do not cause any motion or rest:

"*Thinking*, *Willing*, or *Resolving*, can no more *act* upon a Body, or give it a new Determination, than *Length*, *Breadth*, or *Thickness* or *Rotundity* can, for that solely depends upon Physicks" (p. 28). The movement of my hand is a physical effect and must have a physical cause. Both the motion of my hand and the resolution to move it have a physical and mechanical cause (p. 29). Thought does not even produce thought or ideas, so it does not produce motion either. Change of thought is due to change of frame and texture of the subject (he seems to mean physical frame and texture). Strutt's argument here echoes Malebranche's necessary connection argument: "there is no certain Medium, by which the absolute physical Connection, between seeing the Reason of an Action and doing it can be prov'd" (p. 31). The motion of any body, including our own, is due to impulse and contact and is thus subject to physical laws. Since only matter has the power of impulse and contact, "*matter only can act upon or affect Body, so as to put it into Motion*" (p. 37). He notes that Cudworth had said that God moved the world not mechanically "but *vitally*, and by *Cogitation* only," and he points out that Cudworth had also said that we move our bodies merely by will or thought. Strutt does not want to comment on Cudworth's remark about God, but he thinks he (Strutt) has shown that men cannot move matter by taking thought (pp. 44-45).

Strutt then turns to the question of whether the springs of human action are external or internal. He takes rather odd examples of human action, any movement of the body, even those caused by a blast or jolt. He refers to the movement of one's body due to a gunpowder blast as mechanical, although he does not think we do know how the movement of air from blast moves the body. But he insists that "nothing can be more evident, than that Bodies cannot *act* upon each other *unless they* touch" (p. 48). All actions by external bodies must be by contact of bodies or by the air between them. If, as Clarke argues, the spring of human action is not in the understanding, then "it must necessarily arise, either from the Action of Bodies external, or from physical Causes, resulting from the very Being and Constitution of Man; by which some constituent Parts of the Frame, *necessarily* and *physically* and according to the Laws of Mechanism, act upon and move the other Parts so as to Produce the Effect" (p. 50). In either case—internal or external causes—the action is "equally unavoidable and necessary." The cause of all actions and of all ideas is physical.

The direct antithesis to Strutt's analysis is found in Baxter's *Enquiry into the Nature of the Human Soul* (1733). Baxter's general position is, as we saw in a previous chapter, that matter is passive and inert. Any powers it may have are imposed by God. Baxter tried to retain some powers for man, but man's powers are dependent upon those of God. He distinguished mechanical from spontaneous motion. The latter, he admitted, is not so easy to define or characterize. He is clear, however, that spontaneous motion does not exclude but rather supposes mechanical motion (pp. 144-45). The spontaneity of our moving our body "consists in setting the mechanism at work: we are free to excite motion in the hand, or foot, or not to excite it; but we are not free to excite it with, or without the help of mechanism; if it is begun spontaneously, it is executed or performed mechanically" (pp. 145-47). No movement of our body can take place without the bodily mechanism operating. To move some part of our body, "more is required . . . than simply to will it" (p. 154). For one thing, the muscles and bodily mechanism must be in order. He cites the examples of breathing: we can speed it up, slow it down, even for a moment stop it, but breathing is the same in its mechanism whether controlled by the will or not (p. 156). That we are not the cause of our own involuntary motions (e.g., the circulation of the blood) is shown by the principle that "*a Being can never be the cause of such an effect as it doth not concur to produce*": I cannot do what I do not know (p. 161). But when we will an action, we do not work alone. We can design and will the action and even set it in motion (in that, Baxter differs from Malebranche, although he does not tell us how we set it in motion); but God's causation is present in all the rest of the action, in the working of the muscles, the flight of the arrow. There are two immaterial beings at work when we act: ourselves when we will to move, and God who moves after that. What qualifies an action to be *my* action is (1) that I will and design it, and (2) that I do something that sets the mechanism in motion. What I do to set the mechanism in motion is to move my animal spirits. When I move the animal spirits as a way of moving some part of the body, I only will the motion: that is what it means to set the mechanism in motion (p. 139).[22] "No *agent* indeed can act without *willing* the action, but the difference to be taken notice of here is, that the human soul in particular only *wills* the action, and is forced to depend upon a *borrowed power* for the execution of what it *wills*" (p. 139). That power is borrowed from God, but it is the working of the mechanism of the body on which my willing also depends.[23]

The difficulty of fitting actions onto bodily motions is one confronting most action theorists. Baxter's solution is to give the mind or will of man a role in action analogous to God's role in the world. Without God's constant intervention in the universe, motion would cease. Without man's intervention in the motion of his body, voluntary motions would cease. The mechanism of the body clearly plays a role in voluntary action which cannot be denied. Yet once this has been admitted, there seems no easy way to graft spontaneous action, new forces, onto mechanical movements. Strutt's alternative comes easy to hand. Baxter's alternative tends to make all human actions supernatural, as Clarke remarked to Leibniz. Clarke's turn of phrase may, however, embody an important truth about human action, but a truth difficult to articulate. A direct reply to Strutt was attempted by an anonymous writer in 1760, in *An Essay Towards Demonstrating the Immateriality and Free Agency of the Soul*. This work contains an informed discussion of Strutt and Collins. The author sees a threat to religion in the materialism of these two men. He begins by distinguishing *necessary motion* (impulse of body on body) from *voluntary motion* (movement of my body or its parts by me) (pp. 31, 68). He suggests that voluntary motion has two forms: self-motion, when I move my whole body, as in walking, and voluntary movement of my head, hands, feet (p. 32). Necessary motion also has two forms: external (where the term 'necessary' properly applies) and internal (where the term 'mechanical' is proper) (pp. 72-73). The idea of voluntary motion is given me by reflecting upon what I feel within when I move my body or any part of it, e.g., when I try to walk from one end of the room to the other, or when I move my head or arms (p. 34). I find, he says, "upon Reflection, that I may either rise up or sit still; that I may move my Hand or Finger, or let it alone; that I may move my Hand upwards or downwards" (p. 102). He contrasts this with someone else pulling me or forcing my hand or finger to move. The former examples give me the idea of freedom or volition, the latter the idea of necessity. Both of these ideas arise from reflecting upon the conditions I was in when, e.g., my hand moved (p. 113). I can only judge by comparison that others are free or determined, but in my own case, I have a direct or intuitive knowledge of when I am free or determined (p. 105). Some mechanical motions can appear to be voluntary, and some voluntary can appear necessitated. For example, a man may pretend to have fits and hence deceive me into thinking his bodily movements are necessary. For all of these reasons, the idea of self-motion must come from our own case.

This author agrees that his body is a machine or modified piece of matter. Its movements depend upon nerves and muscles (p. 34). Matter is absolutely inactive. Strutt's error was to view the animal part of our nature as matter, whereas it is in fact "an organized Piece or Part of Matter, capable of self, or Voluntary motion." The nerves and muscles of the body can only pass on motion. If they are moved by animal spirits, something else must activate the animal spirits. Eventually we must conclude that some being not material starts all this bodily motion (pp. 37-39). The organization of matter which our animate body is, is ultimately activated by mind or spirit. Strutt's concept of frame and texture fits matter, but it is inappropriate for spirit. Strutt wrote of the *physical* springs of action. The author of this tract draws a distinction between the physical springs of action and the springs of action, the latter being appropriate only to human action. By assimilating the causes of action to the causes of physical motion, Strutt has misconceived human action. Another misconception, which also leads to the claim that all actions are determined, is to confuse motives with causes (p. 106). Probably echoing Clarke, this writer says that 'motive' and 'reason' are two words for the same idea (p. 109). As an example of cause, he cites the melting of lead by fire. Until the fire actually melts the lead, it is not a cause, only an active power of fire (pp. 110-11). When we say that I stood up because I was tired of sitting, we should recognize that it is my spirit or soul which "is properly the Cause of that motion," of my body standing. We also say that my seeing the connections in the steps of an argument is the cause for my assenting to the conclusion. When we use the word 'cause' of the motive of our actions, we either do so in the sense that 'cause' is equivalent to 'motive', in which case we say no more than that 'the motive was the motive'; or we misidentify the cause, for the cause of my acting is my spirit or soul, not my motive (pp. 112-13). It is the judgment we form when deliberating about what to do that might be said to be the cause or reason for our acting, not the motive. But strictly, it is I who judge and act; the person is the agent of his action (p. 116). Moreover, as the cause of his actions, the agent is a non-necessary cause: "every Cause is so far from being a necessary Cause, that no original Cause can be a necessary cause" (p. 127).

Other writers tried to find ways of recognizing the agent as the cause of his actions, but the distinction between necessary and non-necessary causes so clearly drawn by this last writer was, for the most part, missed in Britain. Kant's free-causality was an important elaboration of this concept in Germany. The emphasis in the works we have examined upon the spontaneity of action, the beginning of something new in nature, also reminds us of Kant's struggles with the concept of action and with ways of finding room in nature for agency.[24] The growing materialism in Britain, especially Priestley's popularizing of Hartley's physiology, made it difficult to graft moral causes onto physical causes. Hartley did try to reserve a category for the voluntary, for actions that "arise from Ideas and Affections," such as walking and speaking. Automatic motions were "those which arise from the Mechanism of the Body" (*Observations on Man*, p. 57). But since ideas for Hartley are traces in the brain, and since operations such as willing are for him brain activities, we are hard pressed to see how the voluntary really does differ from the automatic. Hartley says that if some motion of our body "follows that Idea, or State of Mind (i.e., set of compound Vibratiuncles), which we term the Will, directly, and without our perceiving the Intervention of any other Idea, or of any Sensation or Motion, it may be called voluntary in the highest Sense of this Word" (p. 103). Voluntary actions become automatic ones through skill and habit. A voluntary action, then, seems to be one controlled by certain brain traces and vibrations, while automatic actions are controlled by other kinds of vibrations, perhaps located elsewhere than in the cerebellum. In some of the early sections of his *Observations on Man* Hartley tries to be cautious, talking only of the best explanation, claiming not to be reducing thought to brain states. But by the end of the volume, he is speaking of "the mechanism of human action." By that phrase, he explains he means "that each Action results from the previous Circumstances of the Body and Mind, in the same manner, and with the same Certainty, as other Effects do from their mechanical Causes" (p. 500). He even now says that man does not have the power to begin motion (I think the brain for him is always in motion), and what power we do have to act, to choose, to will arises from the mechanism of our nature. Motives are said to be causes, even mechanical causes (pp. 501-02). "All human Actions proceed from Vibrations in the Nerves of the Muscles, and these from others, which are either evidently of a mechanical Nature . . . or else have been shewn to be so in the Account given of the voluntary Motions" (p. 503).

In *The Monthly Review* for July 1763, a review of *Freewill, Foreknowledge, and Fate*, by Edward Search (i.e., A. Tucker) contrasted Search's claim that mind is the efficient cause of what we do with Hartley's making "all human action necessary, being performed by the mechanical running of vibratiuncles from the sensory to the motory, without any intervention of the mind" (p. 53). The only way anyone could think that the mind or will could intervene in the body mechanism was by some direct control of some part of the physiology.[25] Search was a typical exponent of this view: we "work upon certain unknown nerves, they inflate the muscles, the muscles pull the tendons, the tendons move the limbs" (p. 29). If there is some obstruction, I will not be able to act; but Search's point is that the action of the mind upon the first nerve fibre is immediate (p. 30). Philip Dodd-ridge (in *A Course of Lectures*, 1763) marvels at but does not doubt our ability to affect our physiology:

The power which the mind evidently has of moving the various parts of the body by nerves inserted in the muscles is truly wonderful, seeing the mind neither knows the muscles to be moved, nor the machinery, by which the motion in it is to be produced: so that it is as if a musician should always strike the right note on a very complex instrument, which he had never seen before. That no laws of mechanism can produce this, is proved by its being voluntary, as well as by other considerations. (p. 7)

Doddridge also insists that action requires spontaneity, and he makes the point that only a thinking being can act, "for spontaneity implies an idea of the action to be performed" (p. 4). Bonnet makes this last point also, in his *Essai de psychologie* of 1754. He distinguishes sensing from acting. To have perceptions occasioned by the movement which objects excite in the brain, is to sense. To impress on the brain parallel movements, is to act. Ideas involve the faculty of knowing; movement involves the faculty of moving. The latter faculty presupposes the former: "One does not will what one does not know" (p. 132). Bonnet appreciates Malebranche's point that we lack sufficient physiological knowledge to affect the nerves, and hence he has some doubts over how much control we in fact have in acting. His resolution of this conflict between what he takes to be the case—that we do move our arm—and what he accepts as necessary for moving our arm—a knowl-edge of the relevant physiology—is as follows: "The soul feels that it moves its arm, by the reaction of the arm on the brain. That reaction affecting some of the senses, produces in the soul a feeling, an idea. From that sensible idea the soul is able to deduce with the help of language the reflective notions of existence, feeling, and volition" (pp. 133-34).

Whether this kind of control or intervention (if that is what it is) is sufficient for us to say that we act, may be doubtful. Other writers gave other reasons to deny our ability to intervene in the motions of the body. Priestley, for example, insisted to Price (in *A Free Discus-sion of the Doctrines of Materialism, and Philosophical Necessity*, 1778) that "every human volition is invariably directed by the cir-cumstances in which a man is, and what we call *motives*" (p. 145-46). For Priestley, to act freely would be to act without motives, without causes. Price charged Priestley with saying self-determination implies no cause, asking Priestley: "Does it follow that because I am *myself* the cause, there is no cause?" (p. 136) For Price, to be an agent means that man cannot act from forces acting upon him or from mechanical causes. To determine ourselves requires an *end* and a *rule* to guide us. Such a rule in no way takes away the self-determination, so long as we do not make "our reasons and ends in acting the physical *causes* or *efficients* of action" (p. 137). Reasons are not causes. Price cites Clarke's distinction between the operation of physical causes and the influence of moral reasons. The views or ideas we have may influence our actions but that influence is "not any kind of *mechanical* or *physical* efficiency" (p. 143).

The author of *Letters on Materialism* (1776), Joseph Berington, devotes one of his letters to Hartley's account of the mechanism of human action. He notes that for Hartley all actions and bodily motions arise from "previous circumstances, or bodily motions already existing in the brain, or from vibrations" (p.165). He recognizes that Hartley admits *motives* as one of the antecedent causes of actions and bodily motions, but Berington calls attention to the difference between motives and physical causes. Motives do not work in the way that weights in a balance do. In fact, motives do not cause actions at all: it is the agent who brings about his actions. Man, "from the view of the motives presented to his mind, *determines himself* to act" (p. 166). Berington also recognizes that actions cannot be separated from bodily motions. "When I term motives *moral causes*, I would not be understood to mean, that motives have no physical effect upon us; for all action is physical: my meaning is, that motives do not *themselves* produce our voluntary actions" (p. 167). That self-determining power belongs to the agent, self-activity for the metaphysics accepted by Berington being one of the essential properties of spirits.

The Significance of Action

Earlier in the century William Wollaston gave an analysis of agent-caused action, which caught the similarities between doing and saying, between actions as assertions or denials and linguistic utterances (*The Religion of Nature Delineated*, 1725). He was mainly concerned with those acts that are morally good or evil, but much of what he says applies to other actions. In order for an act to be morally good or evil it *"must be the act of a being capable of distinguishing, choosing, and acting for himself"* (p. 7). As he notes, "no act at all can be ascribed to that, which is not indued with these capacities." For a being who cannot choose, who lacks the opportunity to choose, and who does not act "from an internal principle," really acts not at all, or acts only "under a necessity incumbent *ab extra*" (p. 8). Such a being is not an agent, is only an instrument, and would be like inert and passive matter, only a machine.

Wollaston next remarks that "It is certain there is a meaning in many acts and gestures."[26] Weeping, laughing, shrugs, frowns are examples of meaningful gestures. Other acts even *"imply propositions,"* so evident is their signification. This latter sort of acts makes an assertion. A group of soldiers coming upon another group and firing are, by their actions, declaring that the second group is an enemy. If in fact they are friends, the first group have made a false assertion, just as much as if the captain had uttered the words, "They are enemies" (pp. 8-9). Any spectator watching that action "would have understood this action as I do; for a declaration, that the others were enemies." Since "what is to be understood, has a meaning: and what has a meaning, may be either *true* or *false*," these actions made truth claims. Wollaston reminds us that "in common speech we say some actions are *insignificant*, which would not be sense, if there were not some that are *significant*, that have a tendency and meaning. And this is as much as can be said of articulate sounds, that they are either *significant* or *insignificant*" (p. 11). He admits of course that "the *significancy* here attributed to mens acts, proceeds not always from nature, but sometimes from custom and agreement among people" (p. 12). Conventional meaning, whether in language or in action, usually depends upon customs and practices; but Wollaston insists that the actions that most interest him have an *"unalterable* significance, and can by no agreement ever be made to express the contrary to it" (p. 12). He offers as an example of such fixed meaning in action, a person who takes and disposes of another's property. Such action can "by no torture be brought to signify, *that it was not his*." Even some acts of omission carry signification in this strong sense. Wollaston offered the following as a negative definition or criterion of a right action: *"No act* (whether word or deed) *of any being, to whom moral good and evil are imputable, that interferes with any true proposition, or denies any thing to be as it is, can be right"* (p. 13). Thus actions that deny truths are wrong.

Although Wollaston placed the agent, with intentions and abilities, at the center of actions, his discussion of the signification of actions tends to locate the meaning in the act, not in the acting. John Clarke (in *An Examination of the Notion of Moral Good and Evil, Advanced in a late Book, entitled, The Religion of Nature Delineated*, 1725) took Wollaston to task for failing to see the *agent* as the affirmer or denier, as much in acting as in speaking:

I desire the Reader to take notice, that Affirming and Denying are Actions, which in strict Propriety of Language are only applicable to Agents; so that Actions, whether words or Deeds, can not be properly said to affirm or deny any thing; the Agent only can be properly said to affirm or deny Truth by his Actions, whether Words or Deeds. (p. 6)

Moreover, "in order to a Person's affirming or denying the Truth, an intention to affirm or deny is required" (p. 9).[27] In addition, the meaning I intend must be conveyed to others, otherwise I have not made an insertion. "A Man is then, and then only, said to affirm or deny a Thing, when he conveys a Proposition in his own Mind to the Minds of others; as expressing his own Sense, Apprehension or Persuasion of the Agreement or Disagreement of Things." Even if a man's actions excite in the minds of others meanings which he did not intend (as often happens), Clarke insists that "if he himself had no such Propositions in his own Mind, had no Intention of communicating any such Propositions to others, he cannot in any Propriety of Language be said to affirm or deny them." If I, knowing no Greek, pronounce, "in the hearing of others, Words in the Greek Tongue" which I do not understand but which are equivalent to 'there is no God', I have not asserted that there is no God. Similarly for deeds:

Let us suppose some Action should as necessarily convey the aforementioned Proposition into the Minds of such as should see or hear of it, as Words themselves could; yet suppose the Agent altogether insensible of it, and to have no such Intention at all, he could not be said to deny the Being of a God. (pp. 9-10)

A spectator's meaning may differ from an utterer's meaning. "Affirming or denying is neither more nor less than conveying our Sense (real or pretended) of things, their Agreement or Disagreement to others by Words" (p. 14). Clarke has no objection to extending the notion of affirming or denying to those actions which have "by Consent a Signification or Meaning apply'd to them." To extend, as Wollaston does, the notion of affirming or denying to actions where the consent is lacking is very misleading. Without any agreed-upon meaning for actions, different people will impute different meanings to the action. The action can be interpreted in a variety of ways. Clarke offers a number of instances to illustrate this feature of actions and their interpretation (pp. 16-22). He summarizes his point, indicating the different features and conditions relevant to the determination of the significance of actions:

The free and voluntary Actions of Men may have various significations, according to the various Sense and Discernment, the different Knowledge of Mankind, particularly of the Condition and Circumstances of the Person acting, and those his Actions has any Relation to, in different Observers. This is evident beyond all

Dispute, that different Persons may have different Senses, Notions, Apprehensions or Propositions conveyed to them by the same Action. And accordingly we find that Persons well acquainted with the World, such as have studied Mankind, will penetrate strangely into other Men, and discover by their way and manner of Action, their Notions, Humours, Inclinations, passions, real Designs and Intentions, where others of less Discernment will be altogether at a loss, or have very different Conceptions. (p. 26)

Implicit in many of Clarke's examples is the notion of what we know as "performatives." One example in particular catches this, along with the importance of there being not only agreed-upon meanings for actions but properly designated persons to perform them:

Let us suppose, again, Orders given in a Nation under the Apprehension of an Invasion from an Enemy, that Beacons should be fir'd, or Lights set up in such and such Places, to give Notice of his Approach; that Persons were appointed accordingly for the Purpose, and agreed to execute the said Orders: If they fire the Beacons, or set up the Lights, that Action would be equivalent to this Proposition, The Enemy is come; and they might be said thereby to affirm a Truth, if the Enemy was come, and a Lie if he was not, because this was really meant and intended. (p. 10)

What happens if unauthorized persons set up lights?

But supposing other Persons ignorant of the Orders and Use of Beacons, should fire the Beacons, or set up Lights, they could not be said thereby to affirm that the Enemy was come, notwithstanding their Action would necessarily convey that Proposition to the Minds of such as, being acquainted with the Orders given, should see the Lights; and that for this Reason only, because they had not the least Intention to affirm any such Thing. (p. 10)

Clarke's reference to those who have studied mankind and who have made discoveries about passions, inclinations, and intentions presages Hume's systematic examination of human nature later in the century. Hume did not write about action in the way in which Clarke or Wollaston did, although he indicates that he would disagree with Wollaston's notion about actions making truth claims. Passions, volitions, and actions for Hume are "original facts and realities, compleat in themselves. . . . 'Tis impossible, therefore, they can be pronounced either true or false, and be either contrary or conformable to reason" (*Treatise*, p. 458). Hume did note, as Wollaston had, the relativity of many actions, relative to the different customs and practices and beliefs of different countries (*Enquiry concerning the Principles of Morals*, pp. 198-99). In a fascinating footnote to this same work, Hume fills out, much as John Clarke did, the different components of an action.

Hume was concerned to point out that *consent* alone is insufficient to transfer property or to form the obligation of a promise: "Besides consent, the will or intention must be expressed by words or signs" (p. 199). Once expressed in words or signs, the person cannot take back the promise by secretly giving "a different direction to his intention" and by withholding "the assent of his mind." The expression used to make the promise must be one of which I know the meaning, and I must have some understanding of the consequences of the promise (p. 200). Another condition Hume cites for making the promise is that I use the expression seriously, not in jest: "it is necessary that the words be a perfect expression of the will, without any contrary signs."[28]

Conclusion

Lord Monboddo's letter to Price of 5 February 1781 may give a fair indication of where the philosophy of action was by the end of the century. He says that "the prejudice is so great in favour of the Mechanical Philosophy at Present, that I did not expect you were to be convinced by anything I have said against it."[29] Price had been arguing in a previous letter that the soul exists in a place, but not in such a way as to involve divisibility. Monboddo thought that anyone who said the mind was extended or in a place was bordering on materialism. But Price was not much different from Monboddo in his views on mind and its role in action. Monboddo thinks that some will admit that motion was at first begun by mind, though not many present philosophers do: that motion is still produced by mind, Monboddo says, is rejected by most. His own view is clear: "It is mind . . . that makes Body both move, and cease to move" (p. 148). Impulse from other bodies can move bodies, of course, but "That Bodies, moved by Mind, do not continue their motion in that way [via impulse] we know with as great a certainty as we know anything. I mean from consciousness of the motions of our own Body" (p. 148). He thinks we are conscious that we do not move our body by impulse; rather, we "learn from consciousness . . . that it [mind] moves it [body] by constant and incessant energies, in the same way that Dr. Clarke says that God Almighty, or some inferior Mind, moves the Celestial Bodies" (p. 149). Monboddo reflects a composite though not always consistent montage of most of the immaterialists' doctrines.[30] He praised Cudworth for his recognition that "body cannot move itself, and, therefore, what moves body must be incorporeal" (p. iv). He also praises Cudworth's plastic nature, a principle in all of nature which operates for a certain end but without consciousness or knowledge of that end. He cites Baxter's *Enquiry* for its insistence that body is not self-active. He criticizes those who, even admitting a god who created the universe, think that the universe now runs along on its own by the powers of matter and mechanism. For him, mind is required at every point. Descartes is a theist but his *"physiologie* is absolute materialism." Body continues to move, once started by mind, but any bodily movement which cannot be shown to be due to the impulse of another body has to be moved by mind. Monboddo even accepts some kind of animism, finding some sort of mind or motive principle in every body (p. 2). He recognized that in moving body, the human mind "operates by the mechanical powers of muscles, sinews, and bones" (p. 254), but his comment on the various accounts of bodily mechanism is that those writers *"physiologise* without Mind" (p. i).

Notes

1. *De la recherche de la vérité* (1674). The French text can be found in volumes I and II of the *Oeuvres Complètes*, edited by Geneviève Rodis-Lewis, Paris, 1972. The following quotations occur on pages 309 to 316 of volume II. The English used is that of the recent translation by Thomas M. Lennon and Paul J. Olscamp, Ohio State University Press, 1980.

2. The *Eclaircissements* are clarifications and discussions of various doctrines in the *Recherche*. They are printed as volume III of the *Recherche* in the Rodis-Lewis edition. The topic of XV is 'the efficacy attributed to second causes'. The passage cited here is on pp. 224-25 of volume III.

3. Ibid., p. 225.

4. Ibid., pp. 225-26. In *Eclaircissement* I, which takes up the topic of God as the cause of our movements, Malebranche speaks of motives as necessary for action, but he seems to locate man's power in the ability to suspend our consent. God has created us speaking, walking, thinking, willing, but he has not and does not make us consent (p. 31). We have the power to consent or to withhold our consent. We are physically predetermined towards the good, but our liberty resides in our power of consenting or suspending consent. To will some action, he says in *Eclaircissement* XII, is to consent to a motive which carries us to good (p. 177).

5. Ibid., p. 226.

6. Ibid.

7. Ibid., p. 227.

8. Ibid., p. 228.

9. Ibid.

10. Lennon-Olscamp, p. 498.

11. Ibid., p. 503.

12. Ibid., p. 504.

13. *Natural Obligation to Believe the Principles of Religion and Divine Revelation*, in *Boyle Lectures*, volume III, 1739.

14. Writing to More, Descartes remarked that "there are two different principles causing our motion." One is "purely mechanical and corporeal and depends solely on the force of the spirits and the construction of our organs, and can be called the corporeal soul; the other

is the incorporeal mind." (*Philosophical Letters*, ed. by A. J. P. Kenny, p. 243.) The first way in which bodies move is like the motion of animals or of automata. The physiological and motor apparatus works alone to move limbs. Descartes even suggests that the impressions depicted on our retina by objects can, without such 'seeing' being conscious, "cause our limbs to make various movements" (p. 36). Such physiological activities belong to the body alone and are "said to take place in a man rather than to be performed by him" (p. 51). Joseph Keble (*An Essay of Human Actions*, 1710) draws a distinction between acts and actions. The motion of a tree or the movement of a storm are acts, only men have or do actions (p. 32). It is the "Reason or Sensuality of the Agent that makes it an Action, and not the bare being an Act, for every Motion is an Act . . . but every Motion is not an Action."

15. Clarke may be echoing Locke here. In 4.10.19, Locke remarked that it is a matter of fact that my willing or thinking to move my hand is the cause of my hand moving. He then adds: "Explain this and make it intelligible, and then the next step will be to understand creation."

16. These letters are brief and succinct, as are Clarke's replies; none is more than two pages long. They were printed as part of and continuously paged with Clarke's exchange with Leibniz. The reply to Collins was also printed with this exchange but it was separately paged, with the title, *Remarks upon a Book Entituled, A Philosophical Enquiry, etc.* (1717).

17. In his reply to Collins, Clarke argues that "*Moral Necessity*, in true and Philosophical Strictness, is not indeed any *Necessity* at all, but 'tis merely a *figurative Manner of Speaking*" (p. 15).

18. Cf. John Jackson, *A Defense of Human Liberty*, 1730: "A Mind endued with perfect *Freedom*, which consists in having a perfect Knowledge of the eternal and immutable *Relations* and *Difference* of Things, and an unbiassed or unrestrained Power of Action upon such a Knowledge, will always as invariably *act one Way*, e.g., always do what is right and good, and best in the whole, as if it were impell'd by *Necessity*" (p. 21). He goes on to say: "*Moral* Freedom therefore does not consist in a Power of doing contrary Actions with the same *Indifference*, but in the Nature of Things it consists in being endued with *Reason* and the Perception of the Difference of *Good* and *Evil*, and in Consequence of that *Reason* having a Power of *choosing* and *doing* either the one or the other" (p. 23).

19. This work was published anonymously. It has been credited to a James Long, but it has been recently argued (fairly convincingly) that this is an early work of Hartley. See "Two Early Works by David Hartley," Stephen Ferg, in *Journal of the History of Philosophy*, XIX, April 1981, pp. 173-89.

20. This tract is very probably by Samuel Strutt (see Jacob, *The Radical Enlightenment*, p. 174); but while there are some similarities between this and the earlier tract which does carry his name, there are sufficient incompatibilities between the two tracts to cast some doubt on Strutt's authorship of both.

21. W. Windle (*An Enquiry into the Immateriality of Thinking Substance*, 1738) notes Strutt's suggestion of a possible contradiction in Locke. He says he hardly thinks Locke "could mean that the Attributes of *Thought* and *Volition* were Agents when he said that his *Will*, or *Thought*, determined his Right hand to write" (p. 63). Windle does not understand how "one by a Thought of his Mind can give Motion to the Parts of his Body," but he does not think anyone has a clearer conception of the manner of operation by impulse. "There is as little conceivable Connection between the *Impulse* of a Body in Motion, and the *Motion* of a Body that was at rest, as there is between *Thought* and *voluntary Motion*; that the one infers the other can be argued only from Experience" (p. 70).

22. Baxter also shows an awareness of some of the Newtonian physiologies, where the aether was used instead of animal spirits. In a later passage, he cites Newton's *Opticks* on animal motion being performed by the vibration of the elastic medium "*excited in the brain*

by the power of the will" (p. 328). He takes this as evidence that the fluid has to be put in motion by a non-material cause. His main concern is to say that, however the muscles work, we need a non-mechanical cause to initiate action.

23. Watts's Malebranchian way is more pronounced. He admits that experience does show us that we move our limbs, but this, he thinks, deceptive, since Spirit does not have a power to move bodies. When I will to move my limbs, God has so arranged it that spirit, nerves, muscles move (*Philosophical Essays*, 1733, p. 132).

24. For an analysis of some recent discussions of action, with attention to Kant, see my "Act and Circumstance," *The Journal of Philosophy* 59, 1962; "Agent Causality," *American Philosophical Quarterly* 3, 1966; and "My Hand Goes Out to You," *Philosophy* 41, 1966.

25. The strongest claim for mind's control of bodily mechanism was made by William Porterfield, in *A Treatise on the Eye* (1759) and in some earlier essays. He claimed that many of our vital functions were originally under conscious control.

26. Cf. Georg Henrik von Wright, *Explanation and Understanding* (1971): "Intentional behavior, one could say, resembles the use of language. It is a gesture whereby I mean something" (p. 114).

27. This page is consecutive to 6, page numbers 7-8 being omitted.

28. Hume was writing with an eye upon what he took to be "a doctrine of the Church of Rome, that the priest, by a secret direction of his intention, can invalidate any sacrament."

29. *Lord Monboddo and Some of His Contemporaries*, ed. by William A. Knight (London: J. Murray, 1900), p. 147.

30. See his *Antient Metaphysics*, volumes I and II (1779-82).

Chapter VIII

The Physiology
of
Thinking and Acting

One of the more interesting aspects of eighteenth-century British philosophy is the physiology underlying the accounts of cognition and action. There were four different physiological theories in the century: (1) the scholastic theory of species, (2) the physiology of animal spirits and brain traces, (3) the physiological application of Newton's subtle elastic fluid (the aether), and (4) the Hartleian theory of vibrations. The transition from the second to the third was especially smooth and easy, despite some structural differences. All four theories were used as explanations of awareness: perception, thinking, association, memory. What happens at the level of awareness has specific correlates with what happens in nerves and brain. The theory of animal spirits and that of the aether were also invoked as the physical or mechanical side to human action. Doctors writing on the nature of muscular movement applied the third theory to explain how we move our limbs. The first theory had just about disappeared by the time the century begins. The second theory is extensively cited and described up to mid-century. After that appears the theory of muscular contractions by the operation of the aether in nerves and brain; Hartley's theory begins to attract attention, receiving strong endorsement late in the century from Joseph Priestley's materialism.

From Scholastic Theory of Species to Animal Spirits

In the last few years of the seventeenth century and in the early years of the eighteenth, Henry Layton was citing the scholastic theory of species with approval. In a long catalogue and summary of early works of psychology (*A Search After Souls* [1693?]), he refers to Franciscus de Oviedo who had talked of "a Material Phantasy offered to the Intellect," which produces "a Species impressed upon it, or expressed in it, the Action which is here productive of this Spiritual Species received in the Soul, depends upon the Phancy, which is a Corporeal Thing" (p. 141). Layton further quotes Oviedo as saying "Anatomists do find, that from the outward Organs of the Sense there go Nerves which lead to the Brain, by which the Vital Spirits represent the Images received, unto the common Sense, or inward Faculty, that can discern" (p. 145). Oviedo talked interchangeably of a knowing principle or of an inward sense, even of the perceptive faculty. When this sense conserves the species, retains the impression, this is imagination; the assertive power of the soul is that of knowing and distinguishing the species; when it records and remembers then it is the memory. If Layton is right, Oviedo even spoke of the intellect "taking a View of the Ideas in the Phantasy."

Layton could have referred to Edward Reynolds's *A Treatise of the Passions* (1650), where the same theory is used. The principal parts or powers of the soul for Reynolds are the understanding and the will. The first apprehensions and perceptions of the soul are passive. Here "it receiveth the *simple* species of some object from immediate Impressions thereof of the Ministry of the Soule; as when I understand one Object to be a Man, another a Tree" (p. 445). Other passive operations grounded on the impressions received from objects "are *mixed Operations* of Compounding, Dividing, Collecting, Concluding, which we call *Discourse*." For Reynolds, knowledge is "the Assimilation of the Understanding unto the things which it understandeth, by those Intelligible Species which doe Irradiate it, and put the power of it into Act." He goes on to speak of the "Species and resemblances of things being conveyed on the Understanding" when they "work their own Images. In which respect the Philosopher saith, That the Intellect becometh All Things by being capable of proper impressions from them" (p. 446).

Layton might also have known a medical work, *A Mechanical Account of Poisons*, by Richard Mead (1702). Animal spirits are used along with species in Mead's account of the work of poisons. Normally,

Such is the Constitution of the *Humane Oeconomy*, that *as* upon the Impression of outward *Objects* conveyed to the *Common Sensory*, different *Species* are excited there, and represented to the Mind; so likewise upon this Representation, at the Command and Pleasure of the Soul, part of the same Fluid is determin'd into the Muscles, and mixing with the Arterial Blood there, performs all the Variety of Voluntary Motion and Actions. (p. 63)

The command of the soul is not always needed to move the body: "Representations made to the Mind do immediately and necessarily produce suitable Motions in the Bodily Organs." What happens in delirium, caused for example by poisons, is that various species and combination of species are aroused in the mind without any order, certainly without their normal order. When with this lack of order there goes "a wandering and irregular Motion of the Nervous Fluid, whereby several Objects are represented to the Mind, and upon this Representation divers Operations performed by the Body, tho' those objects are not Impressed upon the organs, nor those Operations or Motions deliberately Commanded by the Soul" (p. 64), the disorders of consciousness are easily understood. The spirits are disturbed in delirium.

In his tract against Broughton, *Observations upon a Treatise intituled Psychologia* (1703), Layton says that thought resides in the head and arises from the spirituous particles of the blood.[1] The different faculties are assigned places in the head or brain (p. 39). The perceptive faculty is located in the sensorium. The account which he earlier quoted from Oviedo is in this work accepted by Layton.

I pretend that the Object being represented by *Medium* of the Organ, to the Common Sense, passes thence to the Understanding where it is *receiv'd*, and distinguish'd in a particular manner, and thence so distinguished it passes, for further Examination, unto the proper Organ of the Phantasy, where such distinguished perceptions are framed and formed into several distinct shapes and fashions. (pp. 56-57)

It is this shaping and fashioning of the objects in the phantasy which produces ideas. This physiology invoked by Layton is of course very similar to that outlined by Descartes in his *Regulae* and developed in more detail in his treatises, except that motion, not species, is transmitted from object to sense organ and thence to the brain.

Descartes gave the theory of animal spirits an extended formulation and use in his description of the workings of the body. In his *Treatise on Man*, he writes about the part of the blood which goes to the brain. That blood is not only for nourishing the substance of the brain, "but also and principally to produce there a certain very subtle wind, or rather a very lively and very pure flame, which is called the 'animal spirits'."[2] These spirits also go to the pineal gland through nerves whose openings are just large enough to allow for the spirits to move through them. The spirits cease to have the form of blood. From the brain, they move out into nerves and are able to change "the shapes of the muscles into which these nerves are inserted and in this way to move all the members."[3] He goes on to give details of how this works.[4] He also speaks of four different features of animal spirits: they can be more or less numerous, their parts can vary in size, they can be more or less agitated, and they can be more or less equal at different times. These differences produce different operations of the natural humours or inclinations which result in liberality, love, confidence, etc. He also tells us how the physiology of animal spirits produces or occasions ideas. The spirits have specific nerves and specific places on the pineal gland to which they go.

In his *La Dioptrique*, Discourse IV, where he is discussing the way external objects affect the brain, Descartes tells us that we must understand the nature and workings of the nerves, especially of the animal spirits "which are like air or a very subtle wind which, coming from the chambers of cavities in the brain move through the nerve tubes to the muscles."[5] He goes on to talk of how the spirits move through nerves and move muscles in a number of specific ways. His *Les Passions de l'ame* repeats most of these details and adds some others. Article 7 of that work says that the movement of muscles depends on the nerves which contain animal spirits. The action of those spirits is due to the warmth of the heart, a kind of fire which is caused by the blood of the veins. Thus fire "is the corporeal principle of all the movements of our members."[6] Article 10 says that the spirits are bodies, very small with quick movement. When spirits come from the brain to the muscles, the spirits in the muscles are excited. He gives details of how this works. Article 13 insists that it is the movement in the brain, not in the eye, which "represent these [external] objects to the soul." Sounds, smells, tastes, heat, thirst, as well as our internal appetites "excite some movement in our nerves which by their means pass to the brain." These movements give to the mind various feelings, as well as send the animal spirits into specific nerves and muscles. Article 26 tells us that the spirits themselves can cause impressions similar to those aroused by external objects, but in the absence of those objects. It is in this way that imagination is explained: the fortuitous movement of spirits. The pineal gland can be moved by the spirits but also by the mind (Art. 34). When the mind moves the gland, that motion excites the animal spirits on the gland which are then sent into the nerves and muscles. The movement of the gland by the spirits is, he says, instituted by nature (Art. 36). Memory too is accounted for by the same physiology (Art. 42). My wish to recall something causes the gland to move in a certain, specific way, and the movement of the gland moves "the spirits towards different parts of the brain until they come across that part where the traces left there by the object which we wish to recollect are found" (Art. 42). Previous movements of the spirits have made it easier for specific areas to be opened by the spirits or by the gland-movements.

Animal Spirits in Locke's Essay

By the time of Locke's *Essay*, the theory of animal spirits appears to have become standard. The Cambridge Platonist John Smith (in *Discourse Demonstrating the Immortality of the Soul*, 1660) has considerable detail on the theory. Referring to Descartes's doctrine of the pineal gland as being the seat of sensation and the place where soul and body meet, Smith remarks that the animal spirits move the body. He also says that "all the motions of our soul in the highest way of reason and understanding are apt to stir those quick and nimble spirits."[7] The spirits attend the beck and call of our mind, if we are strong and rational enough. He also talks of the bodily mechanism being controlled by the spirits, blood, bile, etc. Similarly, Richard Bentley (in *Matter and Motion Cannot Think*, 1692) finds it necessary, in arguing against materialism, to say that no particular "Species of Matter, as the Brain and animal Spirit, hath any Power of Sense and Perception" (p. 16). Since for him no motion added to matter can produce sense or perception, no specific motion of animal spirits through the muscles and nerves can do so either.

Locke's references to the physiology of animal spirits are cautious and tentative (like most of his references to hypotheses), but he does invoke this physiology as a possible explanation of perception. In *Essay* 2.1.15, he speaks of impressions made on the brain and on animal spirits. He suggests that some people may say that the memory of thoughts is retained by the impressions on the brain and the traces left there after such thinking. *Essay* 2.8.4 offers as an account of the "natural causes and manner of perception," in relation to privative causes, "that all sensations being produced in us only by different degrees and modes of motion in our animal spirits, variously agitated by external objects, the abatement of any former motion must as necessarily produce a new sensation as the variation or increase of it, and so introduce a new *idea*, which depends only on a different motion of the animal spirits in that organ." Such an explanation belongs to those physical accounts which Locke tried to avoid, but he does advance it here as "a reason *why a privative cause might . . . produce a positive idea.*" In 2.8.12, in talking of how ideas of primary qualities are produced in us, he says "it is evident that some motion must be thence continued by our nerves and animal spirits, by some parts of our bodies, to the brain or the seat of sensation, there to *produce in our minds the particular* ideas *we have of them.*" In section 21 of this same chapter, the explanation of "how the same water, at the same time, may produce the *idea* of cold by one hand and of heat by the other" is given in terms of animal spirits. Locke says that "*warmth* as it is *in our hands*" is "*nothing but a certain sort and degree of motion in the minute particles of our nerves, or animal spirits.*" Different sensations of heat and cold are a function of "the increase or diminution of the motion of the minute parts of our bodies, caused by the corpuscles of any other body." If the motion of the minute particles or animal spirits in one hand is greater than that in the other, and if "a body be applied to the two hands, which has in its minute parts a greater motion than in those of one of the hands, and a less than in those of the other, it will increase the motion of the one hand and lessen it in the other, and so cause the different sensations of heat and cold."

Resort to the motion of animal spirits and to the particles of bodies in order to explain the hot and cold hand phenomenon is perhaps the most positive use of the animal spirit physiology in the *Essay*. There is, however, another similar appeal (thought a bit more cautious) in the section on retention, 2.10.5. After talking of the fading of ideas when memory fails, he then says:

How much the constitution of our bodies and the make of our animal spirits are concerned in this, and whether the temper of the brain make this difference that in some it retain the characters drawn on it like marble, in others like freestone, and in others little better than sand, I shall not here inquire, though it may seem probable that the constitution of the body does sometimes influence the memory.

In seeking for an explanation of the behaviour of birds in following and reproducing a tune (2.10.9), Locke again speaks of traces left on the brain by sounds. Similarly, in his efforts to understand sameness of consciousness, and why the same consciousness could not belong to more than one agent, Locke confesses to not having sufficient knowledge of the nature of thinking substance. But to the suggestions he makes in 2.27.13, he remarks in passing: "How far this may be an argument against those who would place thinking in a system of fleeting animal spirits, I leave to be considered." And in 2.27.27, he makes the same reference: "Did we know what it was or how it was tied to a certain system of fleeting animal spirits, or whether it could or could not perform its operations of thinking and memory out of a body organized as ours is." Both of these references in this chapter clearly are to views held by other writers, views which relied upon the physiology of animal spirits. In his chapter on the association of ideas (2.33.6), Locke cites this physiology in a more positive manner.

Custom settles habits of thinking in the understanding, as well as of determining in the will, and of motions in the body: all which seem to be but trains of motion in the animal spirits, which, once set a-going, continue in the same steps they have been used to; which, by often treading, are worn into a smooth path and the motion in it becomes easy and, as it were, natural. As far as we can comprehend thinking, thus *ideas* seem to be produced in our minds; or, if they are not, this may serve to explain their following one another in an habitual train, when once they are put into that track, as well as it does to explain such motions of the body.

He cites skilled, habitual action, such as the movement of a musician's fingers over the keys while the musician may be thinking of other things. He then remarks: "Whether the natural cause of these *ideas*, as well as of that regular dancing of his fingers, be the motion of his animal spirits, I will not determine, how probable soever, by this instance, it appears to be so; but this may help us a little to conceive of intellectual habits and of the tying together of *ideas*."

Later in the *Essay* (4.10.19), while talking of action and the fact that by willing or thinking I can move my hand, he says that how this is done is not clear, but some make use of animal spirits in explaining voluntary action: "the giving a new determination to the motion of animal spirits." Locke thinks this does not help us, for we still have to explain how we can give a new motion to those spirits. Either we immediately determine the spirits by our thoughts, or some other body moved by our thought moves the animal spirits; but in either case, we do not understand how our thought can move body.

In these references by Locke, we can hear most of the features of the theory of animal spirits.
1. Impressions are made on the brain.
2. Those impressions leave traces in the brain.
3. Those impressions are caused by (a) different degrees of motion in our animal spirits and by (b) the change of motion of those spirits.
4. Each change in the motion of animal spirits causes a new impression on the brain and these impressions cause or are followed by new ideas.
5. Memory is a function of the brain's ability to retain traces.

6. Thinking is the motion of animal spirits, or closely correlated with such motion.
7. Habits of body and of mind are due to trains of motion in the animal spirits which tend to move in established pathways in the brain.
8. Action is the result of movement of animal spirits.

Locke was strongly attracted to points 7 and 5, he finds 1, 2, 3, and 4 probable. The sixth claim was a bit extreme in its noncorrelative form, but it is allied to Locke's own suggestion that matter might have a power superadded to it of thinking. Point 8 is, as we have seen, accepted by some writers on action, rejected by others. Aside from 6 and 8, these points contain the essentials of the standard theory of animal spirits and brain traces in the first half of the eighteenth century in Britain. It was Malebranche's systematic and detailed account of this theory which Locke probably had in mind. Certainly, it was Malebranche whom Isaac Watts was following in his later account of the theory. Once again, Malebranche's influence on eighteenth-century British philosophy must be noticed.[8]

Malebranche on Animal Spirits and Brain Traces

In his chapter on the imagination in his *Recherche de la vérité* (II.I), Malebranche stresses the close connection between sense and imagination: they differ only in degree. He reminds us that in Book I of that work he said our sense organs are composed of small fibres which go from the surfaces of our body to the brain. These fibres can be moved either by motions originating in the brain or by motions from without. When the impressions from the object affect our nerves and transmit that effect to the brain, the mind feels and judges that that which it feels is external, that is to say, "it perceives an object as present."[9] This difference in the flow of animal spirits is just the difference between feeling and imagining. The disturbance of the fibres of the brain is much more lively by the impressions of objects than it is by the flow of animal spirits from within, but there are occasions when a person's animal spirits are strongly agitated by "fasting, vigils, by a high fever, or some violent passion" (p. 192). Then the spirits move the internal fibres of the brain with as much force as do external objects. On such occasions, we believe that we see objects before our eyes, when in fact we are only imagining they are there.

Malebranche says that every time there is a change in the part of the brain to which the nerves go, there occurs a change in the mind. We cannot have a new perception or image without a new change in the brain. The faculty of imagination consists only in "the soul's power of forming images of objects producing changes in the fibres of that part of the brain which can be called the *principal* part," because it is the place where the mind resides. This power of the imagination includes two features: the one is the action of the will, the other is the obedience which this power gives to the animal spirits which trace the images on the fibres of the brain. He distinguishes these two powers as the active and passive imagination. Thus the imagination consists only in the force or power which the mind has of forming images of objects, in imprinting them in the fibres of its brain. The larger and more distinct the vestiges of the animal spirits are, which are the traces of these images, the more the mind will imagine strongly and distinctly. In other words, the clarity of imagination depends upon the force of the animal spirits and the constitution of the fibres of the brain.

Malebranche says everyone agrees that animal spirits are only "the most refined and agitated parts of the blood, which is refined and agitated principally by fermentation and by the vigorous movement of the muscles constituting the heart" (p. 91). The air we breathe also causes changes in the animal spirits. This air gets into the arteries and disturbs the blood. The changes in the animal spirits brought about this way also produce changes in the faculty of the imagination. The nerves which go to the heart cause changes in the mind, without our control. When the passions are stirred up, the animal spirits are agitated and we imagine things that we would not think of when calm. He gives a detailed account of how this happens, the close connection between blood, animal spirits and imagination. These are instances of involuntary action taking place contrary to, or even against, the orders of the mind (chapters III-IV).

Chapter V deals with the connection between the ideas of the mind and the traces in the brain. It is not enough, Malebranche says, to know that there is a general relation between ideas and traces, that traces in the brain are connected with one another, that they are followed by movement of animal spirits, that the traces stir up changes of ideas, or that movement of animal spirits excites passions. He wants to pinpoint details of these connections and actions. He rejects the notion that the mind becomes the body, or that the body becomes the mind, when they are united together. The mind is not spread out in all parts of the body. Each substance, mind and body, remains what it is: the mind is not capable of extension and the body is not capable of sensations. But there is a natural correspondence between them, e.g., when the mind receives any new ideas, traces are imprinted on the brain, and when objects produce new traces on the brain, the

mind receives new ideas. Malebranche cites three causes for this natural correspondence. The first, which the others presuppose, is *nature*,
or the constant and immutable will of God. This produces natural
connections which are independent of our will, e.g., between the
traces produced by a tree or mountain which we see and the ideas of
the tree or mountain; between the traces produced in our brain by
the cries of a man or an animal suffering, or by the face of a man who
threatens us, and the ideas of pain, force, weakness and the sentiments
of compassion, fear, and courage. These natural connections are general for all men. They are also necessary for the conservation of life.
Identity of time is another cause of natural connections between
traces and ideas. If the time at which we have certain thoughts is the
same as the time at which we have certain brain traces, then if in the
future the traces occur again, these thoughts will also. Correlations
between words and thoughts work this way, the word sets up traces
in the brain which are correlated with thoughts. The third cause of
such natural connections is the will of man. That is, we are able to
control some relations so that we can plan and order our lives.

Traces also have mutual relations or connections with each other.
When one is agitated, the others are also, those that have been imprinted
at the same time. Association is also explained in this way. The identity
of time of impressions is especially important because "the animal spirits, finding the path of all the traces made at the same time half-open,
continue on them since it is easier for them to travel those paths than
through other parts of the brain" (p. 106). There are some natural connections, dispositions of the fibres, with which we are born. Memory
is explained by reference to the same phenomenon. All our different
perceptions are attached to changes which come to the fibres of the
principle part of the brain in which the mind most particularly resides.
Thus the fibres of the brain, having received certain impressions by the
flow of animal spirits and by the action of objects, hold for a while
the ability to have the same dispositions, to receive there the same
impressions. Memory consists only in this disposition of the fibres to
retain or to receive again the same impressions. We think of the same
things when the brain receives the same impressions. Habits also receive a similar explanation. Differences in infancy, middle age, and
old age also have their explanations in differences in the condition of
the fibres and the flow of animal spirits.

Animal Spirits in Eighteenth-Century Britain

The physiology detailed by Descartes and Malebranche, cited by Locke,
Bentley, and Smith, is found in eighteenth-century Britain in a wide

variety of writings. It appears in some of the Newtonians (e.g., James Keill, Pemberton, Derham, Cheyne); it is summarized by Chambers in his dictionary; it receives extended treatment by some writers whose interests were more on the issues raised by Locke's suggestion about thinking matter; it finds passing mention in popular publications like *The Spectator*; and Hume appeals to it in a variety of contexts.

In a work on anatomy, *The Anatomy of the Human Body* (first published in 1698 and reprinted many times, the seventh edition being in 1723), James Keill cites the accepted account of the structure of the nerves and muscles: "Threads or Tubes, of which there be different Kinds; for there are some soft, flexible, and a little elastick; and these are either hollow, like small Pipes, or spongeous, and full of little Cells, as the nervous and fleshy Fibres" (pp. 1-2). A nerve is described by Keill as "A long and small Bundle of very fine Pipes, or hollow Fibres, wrapt up in the *Dura* and *Pia Mater*" (p. 329). He also says that "The Medullary Substance of the Brain is the Beginning of all the Nerves; and 'tis probable that each Fibre of the Nerves answers to a particular Part of the Brain at one End, and to a particular Part of the Body at its other End, that whenever an Impression is made upon such a Part of the Brain, the Soul may know, that such a Part of the Body is affected." The nerves go with the arteries throughout all the body, so "that the Animal Spirits may be kept warm, and moving, by the continual Heat and Pulse of the Arteries" (p. 330).

Passing references to animal-spirit physiology are found in Derham's Boyle lectures for 1711–12, *Physico-Theology: Or, A Demonstration of the Being and Attributes of God* (3rd ed., 1714). For example, while talking of muscular motion, Derham says that voluntary motions of our limbs "are absolutely under the Power of the Will; so as that the Animal hath it in its power to command the Muscles and Spirits of any part of its Body, to perform such Motions and Actions as it hath occasion for" (p. 160, n.2). He also cites Willis's treatise on the brain[10] where Willis claims that it is in the brain that the spirits which relate to voluntary motion are found (p. 163, n.6).

A much more extended account of nerves, veins, and their operations is given by George Cheyne in his *Philosophical Principles of Religion* (2nd ed., 1715). Cheyne tells us that this new edition has been corrected in the light of comments from Dr. Gregory, John Craig, and also from Cheyne's reflections on the second edition of Newton's *Opticks* and the *Principia*. As well, as he has benefited from Cotes's Preface to the new edition of the *Principia* and also from Derham's recent books. Thus Cheyne's work is very much in line with the Newtonian group. In chapter III of this work, he talks of the voluntary motions of rational creatures. He says these motions cannot be accounted for by mechanism alone. Muscles are bundles of fibres, the nerves that are ducts of the brain are "for deriving an appropriated Juice or Spirit from the blood" (p. 133). He goes on to say: "Wherefore, since the nervous Juice or Spirit is form'd out of the Blood, and since the Nerves are very small arterial Tubes, this Spirit very probably must move in these Nerves after the same manner the blood does in the Arteries, only with this difference, that it moves abundantly more slow" (pp. 134-35). Cheyne's account of voluntary action is as follows:

And the only Conception we can form of voluntary Motions is, that the Mind, like a skillful *Musician*, strikes upon the Nerve which conveys Animal Spirits to the Muscle to be contracted, and adds a greater Force than the natural to the nervous Juice; whereof it opens its Passage into the Vesicles of which the Muscular Fibres consist, which it could not have done by its natural Power. (pp. 137-38)

Later, in chapter VI, he says that the veins leading to and from the brain distribute "throughout the whole *System*, the more pure, refin'd, and subtile part of the Blood, (as is suppos'd) which is then call'd the *Animal Spirits*" (p. 303). Wanting to be properly cautious before accepting this standard physiology, Cheyne says that "it is not impossible but these *Emissary* Vessels [the veins that go from the brain] of the small *Glands*, whereof the *Cortical* part of the Brain consists, may contain a Liquor, and that this Liquor may be the more refin'd and subtile part of the Blood" (p. 304). This liquor may be "something akin, or *Analogous* to those Spirits we gather from animal Substances, by Heat in an Alembick." He points out that the "nervous Fluid has never been discovered in live animals by the Senses however assisted" (p. 306). He also thinks the size of the nerve fibres so small that no fluid "cou'd move with Velocity to answer the Appearances." In short, it seems "pretty difficult to come to any certain Conclusion on either side," about the nature of the veins and any fluid they may contain. He suggests that either of two suppositions will "account for the appearances, in a gross and general manner": (1) either "the Fibres, contain a pretty consistent Fluid whereof they are constantly full, and then the least drop forced into the one Extremity will drive out as much at the other, and that instantaneously," or (2) "these *Fibres* are solid, and not pervious and some infinitely subtle Spirit pervades them, with as much Facility as it would the most *pervious* Tubes" (p. 306).

It is clear from later pages that Cheyne's caution concerns the nature of animal spirits, not whether there are any such: "And since it is not as yet positively Demonstrated, whether the *Animal Spirits*, be a fluid contain'd in the *Nervous* and *Membranous* Fibrils, as hollow

Tubes, or if they are only a *subtile Spirit*, or *Aura* pervading these, as solid Filaments" (p. 314). Animal spirits or something analogous to them fills the tubes and pipes of the nerves and veins (p. 316). He suggests that the spirits or fluid are driven through nerves by the dilation of small arteries. Sensation is caused by the action of "the finer and more fluid parts of Bodies, upon the *Organs* of Sense; the Impulse communicated by these subtle parts of Bodies, upon the *Organ* fitly disposed, is through them transmitted to the *Nerves*, Appropriated and contriv'd for such a Sense, and through them to the Brain" (pp. 318-19). He thinks it not inappropriate to say all sensation is nothing but touching, since impulses are involved in all sensation, impulses which go from organ to brain. The animal spirits "are the most precious things in all the *Animal Body*, by which we move, and our Blood *circulates* . . . by which all the Pleasures of Life are relished, and all *Sensation* perform'd" (p. 331). He notes that "in *Muscular* Motion the Expenses of *Animal Spirits*, are in much less Proportion, than the elevated Weight" (pp. 330-31). Spirits are the "Life of the Blood."

Another Newtonian, Pemberton, contributed a long introductory essay on muscular movement to one of the standard anatomical treatises, that of William Cowper, *Myotomia Reformata: Or an Anatomical Treatise on the Muscles of the Human Body* (1724).[11] In that essay, Pemberton examines the evidence and arguments for the nerves being tubes with fluid moving through them. He supplies detailed computations on the pull of tendons on joints, the forces involved, the role of gravity, etc. The second part of his essay addresses the problem of the causes of muscular contraction. Pemberton tells us that most recent writers suppose that the fleshy parts of muscles "are formed into Vesicles or Cells, whose inflation and distension by some fluid within them" contracts the fibres of the muscle (p. xxxiv). This view is an hypothesis only, has not been confirmed by "any direct proofs." He refers to this view as the vesicular hypothesis. If the inflation of the vesicles is to be great, "we must suppose the Fibres to be composed of compleat Bladders connected together." If less contraction is supposed sufficient to move muscles and limbs, then we need only suppose the fibres to be "hollow Cylinders." Pemberton then goes on to ask what shape or figure the cells will make when extended. This part of his essay works with the geometry of curves. He also tries to compute how much the muscles must contract, hoping to check this against what in fact is the case. This could be an indirect check on the vesicular hypothesis, if what that hypothesis requires is falsified by observation on muscle contractions. Pemberton thinks that future experiments will probably show that this hypothesis has to be rejected (p. lxvii).

In his careful analysis, Pemberton cites most of the current beliefs about the structure of muscle fibres and their operation. For example, he says that Leeuwenhoek thinks his microscopes reveal the fibres to be hollow tubes, but Pemberton is cautious about accepting this claim (p. lxix). He does not think any experiments so far have given sufficient evidence to say just what the structure of the fibres is or how they inflate. The alternatives are open. Either we can see whether we can "discover something existing in the Body, that we might know to be capable of inflating these Vesicles, were there any such; or in default of this," we can try "to frame in our Minds a Notion of some Principle suited to produce the Effect required" (p. lxix). He does not think anyone has yet given careful enough attention to the proper construction of such an explanatory principle. He will in the end advance Newton's subtle, elastic fluid as providing the best explanation, but en route to that conclusion he reveals the state of the animal-spirit physiology in Britain. He agrees that the nerves are necessary for the action of the muscle.

This Office of the Nerves is generally allow'd to be perform'd by the means of some very fine and subtle Fluid, which is called by Authors the Animal Spirits, and that Contraction of the Muscles concerned in Voluntary Motion arises from this Spirit being some way Operated upon at the Original of the Nerves. (p. lxx)

Pemberton even seems to accept the supposition that "the Blood assists in muscular Motion only by preserving the Parts in a proper state for the Spirits to pass through the Extremities of the Nerves and perform their Office on the muscular Fibres" (p. lxxi). He thinks Cowper's experiments have given added support to this supposition. But other writers give a more specific function to the animal spirits, a function Pemberton is quite suspicious of: "they suppose the Fluid in the Nerves to inflate the Cells of the muscular Fibres by rarifying the Blood within them," the usual way it was supposed animal spirits were produced. Fermentation of juices, he thinks, is hardly sufficient to account for the working of muscles. Like Malebranche, Pemberton favours mechanical explanations, although he shows some sympathy with James Keill's suggestion that muscles are moved by attraction of blood particles to animal spirit particles (p. lxxii).[12]

There is also a discussion of the animal spirit physiology in Chambers's *Cyclopaedia; Or, An Universal Dictionary* (1728), a dictionary which in all matters relating to science relied heavily upon Newton. Under the entry for 'sensation', Chambers describes the action of external objects on the animal spirits, which in turn activate the nerves. The soul is said to reside in that part of the brain where the soul perceives the effects of external objects. The only way objects can act on us is by exciting changes in the surfaces of the fibres of the nerves.[13] Animal spirits are defined as "an exceedingly thin, subtle, moveable Fluid, Juice or Humour separated from the Blood in the Cortex of the Brain, hence received into the minute Fibres of the Medulla, and by them discharged into the Nerves, by which it is convey'd through every Part of the Body, to be the Instruments of Sensation, muscular Motion, etc." Chambers points out that the existence of animal spirits is controverted by some writers, but he thinks appeal to them is effective as an explanation. Moreover, he thinks Boerhaave's work in biology and anatomy has gone a long way towards demonstrating their existence.

Isaac Watts's *Philosophical Essays on Various Subjects* (1733) was a kind of compendium of learning on space, substance, body, spirit, the operations of the soul, the place and motion of the soul, etc. These were, he tells us, written many years before their publication. The third essay in this collection, on perception and ideas, starts off by referring to Malebranche's doctrine of seeing all things in God. He cites the doctrine of intelligible objects and agrees that bodies do not cause ideas in us. Rather, when certain motions occur in our body, God has ordained that we will have certain perceptions (pp. 73-77). Similarly, all that we know about action is that when the soul wills, the body moves (p. 78). He also talks of traces on the brain (p. 83). With primary qualities, we may suppose that the brain traces "may in the Shapes or Motions thereof have some Resemblance to the external Objects which are the Occasions of them" (p. 84). The very figure of a triangle or a square, of a house or tree is traced upon the retina and probably conveyed to the brain. But these figures cannot of themselves cause similar ideas, since body cannot influence mind: "we cannot conceive how any corporeal Motions or Figures impresst or traced in the Brain, should have an efficacious Power in and of themselves, to give any notices to the Soul, or to raise Perceptions or Ideas in a Mind or Spirit" (p. 84). God has ordained that when such traces are on the brain, we will have such perceptions and ideas.

Watts also repeats Malebranche on memory. It is the arousal of brain traces which give occasion to our having the same ideas as before, in the imagination or in the memory. Even ideas of thought, willing, reason have their brain traces aroused by the words which are attached to the ideas (p. 92). When the words are repeated, the ideas arise because of the brain traces: "and thus we are assisted in the Memory or Recollection even of intellectual Things by Animal Nature." The relation is not always from brain trace to thought.

When the Soul sets itself by an Act of its Will to recollect any former Ideas, corporeal or Intellectual, it is very probable that it employs some finer and Spirituous Parts of Animal Nature to open all the kindred Traces that lye in that part of the Brain, till at last it lights upon that particular Trace which is connected with the desired Ideas, and immediately the Soul perceives and acknowledges it. (pp. 92-93)

Animal spirits are characterized as "those subtle Corpuscles, whatsoever they are, whereby such Traces or Impressions are formed or revived in the Brain which correspond to our Sensations or Ideas, and which are usually the occasion of them" (p. 119).

Some physiologists offered explanations of emotional states and nervous disorders. While Robert Whytt in 1765 finds the existence of animal spirits only probable, and hence does not use them in his *Observations on the Nature, Causes, and Cure of those Disorders which have been Commonly called Nervous Hypochondriac, or Hysteric*,[14] Bernard Mandeville uses them extensively in his *A Treatise of the Hypochondriack and Hysterick Passions* (1711; 3rd ed., 1730). In the dialogue form in which Mandeville's work is written, the two speakers represent the two views: the nerves are strings that vibrate, or they are tubes through which flow animal spirits. The persons in the dialogue debate whether there are animal spirits.

How do you know that there are Animal Spirits at all? The Nerves, through which they are supposed to flow, are not hollow, made like Pipes, as Arteries, Veins, Lympheducts, Lacteals, and other Vessels, that are contriv'd to convey Liquids: They are solid Bodies like Strings, or Cords made up of many lesser Strings: No Liquid is found in them, nor have they any Cavity to contain it. Therefore this Business of the Animal Spirits is only a Dream. (p. 135)

The other person replies that the existence of animal spirits "is a point that never was controverted. That the Blood is a Compound of various Parts very much differing from one another, and that many of these are volatile, is certain" (p. 136). He offers other reasons for saying that "many things are transacted in the Brain, that could not possibly be perform'd but by means of volatile Particles originally derived from the Blood." The contrary hypothesis is that the nerves are strings "in which the Motion impressed on one End is immediately communicated to the other" (p. 137).

Rejecting the notion that matter can think, Mandeville asserts that "as the Soul acts not immediately upon Bone, Flesh, Blood, etc., nor they upon that, so there must be some exquisitely small Particles, that are the *Internuncii* between them, by the help of which they manifest themselves to each other" (p. 156). These intermediaries are of course the animal spirits. These spirits are employed in the act of thinking (p. 158). Those involved in thinking are no more subtle than those "that continually extend the several Muscles of our Legs and Thighs in walking." The person opposing animal spirits in this dialogue counters by saying that "Thought is wholly incorporeal, and is perform'd by the Soul it self," not by means of animal spirits. The point is that the spirits do not think, but they are "employed in the Act of Thinking." Thinking is the "various Disposition of Images received." This disposition of the images is "the Work of the Spirits, that act under the Soul, as so many Labourers under some great Architect" (p. 160). An example is given of trying to recollect something:

how nimbly those volatil Messangers of ours will beat through all the Paths, and hunt every Enclosure of the Brain, in quest of the Images we want; and when we have forgot a Word or Sentence, which yet we are sure our Memory, the great Treasury of Images, has once been charged with, we may almost feel, how some of the Spirits flying through all the *Mazes* and *Meanders* rommage the whole Substance of that medullary Labyrinth, whilst others ferret through the inmost Recesses of it with so much Eagerness and Labour, that the Difficulty they meet with sometimes makes us uneasie, and they often bewilder themselves in their Search, 'till at last they light by chance on the Image that contains what they look'd for, or else picking it up, as it were, by Piece-meal, from the dark Caverns of Oblivion, represent what they can find of it to our Imagination. (pp. 160-61)[15]

Another important, extended statement of this theory of animal spirits and brain traces is found in Samuel Colliber's *Free Thoughts concerning Souls* (1734). Colliber says that it is universally agreed that the brain is the seat of sensation (p. 8). Anatomists have shown that though it seems to us that sensation is diffused throughout the body, it is in reality nowhere but in the brain, "to which the Sensible Impressions made either on the External or Internal Parts of the Body, are as it were convey'd by means of the Nerves." He cites Dr. Willis in support. He also speaks of "the finest and most volatile Spirits" filling the hollow spaces around that part of the brain where the nerves terminate. These are, he says, commonly called animal spirits. Colliber was concerned to argue against the new materialists, those who were suggesting that matter might think, that thought was a property of the brain. As does Samuel Clarke, Colliber argues that no single particle of the brain could be the sensitive or thinking faculty. He says that "our Modern Corporealists seem to be aware of" this difficulty and hence they now speak of the soul being a result of a composition of such particles (p. 15). Colliber does not see how thinking could be identical with a composition of animal spirit particles, because they are volatile and in perpetual motion, unlike our thought. He agrees that the animal spirits of the brain are the "immediate Instruments of the Soul's Sensation of external Objects," but he insists that "the Human Soul is no constituent Part of the Body, nor any thing resulting from or essentially depending on it" (p. 21). The soul is a substance simple and uncompounded, capable of receiving impressions from sensible objects and also capable of acting on the animal spirits (p. 22).[16]

Colliber says that the soul, while embodied, sees "by the means of Images of Visible Objects form'd by the Rays of Light on the Bottom of the Eyes" (p. 25). These images affect the nerves and animal spirits of the brain, in the same way "as the Objects affect or work upon the Particles of the Light or Air" (p. 26). His specific account of sense perception is as follows:

External Objects making Impressions on the *Sensories*, either immediately, or else by means of the Light of the Air, or of certain *Effluvia* or . . . subtile Particles proceeding from themselves, form by these Impressions certain Figures or Images of themselves in the *Sensories* (as is plainly to be seen in the Bottom of the Eyes) and at the same time, move by means of these Impressions and Images, the Animal Spirits in the Nerves. These Spirits communicate a like Motion to some of the Animal Spirits in the Cavities or hollow Spaces of the Brain [and] may form by their means some very minute Images or Signatures (as so many Copies from Originals) on the soft interiour Surface of those Cavities; which Images or Signatures (Tho' undiscernible to the Eye) by reflecting the Spirits towards the Seat of the Soul, may excite the Sensitive Faculty to attend to and perceive them. (p. 40)

The same motions of the reflected spirits, which "are the immediate Occasions of exciting the first Sensations and Ideas in the Soul," are also the occasion of retaining those sensations and ideas, so long as these motions are continued between "the Seat of the Soul and those Images" (p. 41). The sensations of the "suppos'd Images in the Brain" can be "no other than various Sorts of Feeling." Colliber also accepts that part of this theory which sees the difference between memory and imagination as proceeding from the different "Sorts and Degrees of Motion in the Spirits of the Brain." And the same appeal to the soul remembering by moving the spirits is made:

If therefore the Soul is willing to revive its Ideas (or renew its Sensations of Objects) it may be conceived to do it by moving the Spirits in Streight Lines towards those Images; by which means it may perceive or distinguish their several Properties, so as we distinguish the Inequalities in the Surfaces of Bodies, and the various Figures they compose by the means of a Staff or some other Instrument; but in a manner far more refined and perfect. (p. 41)

John Jackson (*A Dissertation on Matter and Spirit*, 1735) agrees that spirit or soul cannot think without the help of body and animal spirits. As we have earlier seen, he was writing in that controversy over thinking matter. His point here is that without ideas and perceptions the soul is as "dead, inert, or unactive as the Body is without *vital* motion." The soul is changed from inactive to active by the action of matter and animal spirits. In order to be active in thinking, the soul must be united to a body, for "'tis certain the Soul no more *reflects* than it *perceives* without the help of the animal Spirits and Organs; it may as well speak without a *Tongue*, or move the Body without *Muscles* and Limbs" (pp. 31-32).

Another compendium of knowledge, *The Philosophical Grammar: Being a View of the Present State of Experimental Physiology, or Natural Philosophy* (1735), by Benjamin Martin, describes a nerve as "a long and small Bundle of very fine Pipes, or hollow Fibres, wraped up in the Membranes of the Brain, from whence they have their Beginning" (p. 273).[17] The parts of the body are rendered sensible by "the Motion of an exceeding fine and invisible Fluid" contained in the nerves, called Animal Spirits, by "which Impressions are communicated to the Mind (whose seat is in the Brain) from all Parts of the *Animal Body*" (p. 274). The use or function of the brain "is to separate from the Blood brought thither, the finest and subtlest Parts thereof, called *Animal Spirits*" (p. 277). The nerves then convey the animal spirits to the parts of the body.

In his "An Essay concerning the Motions of the Eyes,"[18] William Porterfield uses animal spirits to explain two anomalies of vision. In discussing double vision due to nonuniform movement of the two eyes, he speaks of "The uniform Motion of our Eyes requiring an easy and regular Motion of the Spirits" (p. 194). At death, he says the spirits are worn out and exhausted. He cites a woman who, two days before her death, saw all things double: "The true Cause thereof seems to have arisen from the languid irregular Motion of the animal Spirits disqualifying them for executing the Commands of the Will, and directing both Eyes to the same Object" (pp. 194-95). Later, while discussing the question of why we have one image even though both eyes look at an object, Porterfield cites Brigg's hypothesis which talks in terms of tension and vibrations of the fibres of the retina. Porterfield rejects this explanation, saying it is "more probable, that the Impressions made upon our Organ produce an Undulation and Refluctuation of the Spirits, or of Newton's *materia subtilis* in the Nervous Fibrils, which reaching the *Sensorium*, gives us the Ideas of objects, than that these Ideas should be excited by these Vibrations themselves" (p. 205-6). Porterfield clearly accepted the usual theory that the rays of light excite motions in the "Organs of Vision, and . . . in the Animal Spirits, which are propagated through the nervous Fibres to the *Sensorium*" (p. 219).

Voluntary Muscular Motion

The Royal Society's interest in the physiology of muscular motion, especially of voluntary motion, continued beyond Cheyne's and Pemberton's earlier accounts. Instrumental in this continued interest in experimentation and explanation of voluntary muscular motion was the establishment of the Croonian Lectures. Two sets of lectures were established, one to be given to the Royal College of Physicians, the other to the Royal Society. These latter were to concern themselves with muscular motion. The first of these Croonian Lectures were given before the Royal Society in 1738 by Alexander Stuart.[19] In his account (presented with demonstrations of experiments), Stuart invoked attraction (repulsion is only a result of attraction, not a separate force) and elasticity of fluids and of arteries and veins. The nerves are vesicles but non-elastic. They serve "to convey an aqueous fluid, called the animal spirits, from the brain, *cerebellum*, or spinal marrow, to the muscles" (p. xlii).[20] Fluids are necessary as a medium for attraction over distance: "The power of attraction does not reach much, if at all, beyond contact, either mediate or intermediate; and . . . it takes effect in solids only by the mediation of fluids" (p. xxv). These fluids, when in contact with solids, "acquire a degree of motion by attraction into their pores, capillary tubes, and interstices . . . so as to swell, extend, or expand them" (p. xxxii).

One of the experiments Stuart demonstrated to the Royal Society was performed on a live frog, suspended by string attached to its forelegs, but with its head newly cut off. The aim of this experiment was to "shew the existence of a fluid in the nerves, and that Muscular Motion is begun by an impulse on it through the nerves into the muscles" (p. ii). He showed this by inserting a probe into the area around the first vertebra and gently pushing. When this is done, the hind legs contract. His explanation of this phenomenon is that the probe compresses the fluid in the nerves and forces it to move through the nerves and out the other end. Thus at least the beginning of the motion of muscles "may be justly ascribed to a propulsion of a small quantity of the contained fluid, through the slender canals into the muscles, in which they terminate" (p. xxxix). Since these muscles work in the same way when moved by the animal, Stuart concludes that "voluntary muscular motion in a living animal is begun in the

same manner, by an impulse through the nerves, into the muscles."
In other words,

The effect of the impulse by the probe is the same, which is or may be produced
in these muscles by the mind as well; or is the very same in its manner as voluntary or spontaneous motion, and performed by mediation of the same instrument,
to wit, the animal spirits, or fluid of the nerves, and the muscles of voluntary
motion. (p. xxxix)

He thinks that since "the quantity of animal spirits propelled into the
muscles in this Experiment must be supposed very small; it follows,
that the waste of this fluid by moderate voluntary motion in life is
very inconsiderable" (p. xl). This fluid or animal spirit, then, is "the
immediate subject of impulse, or the immediate instrument of the
mind for beginning muscular motion" (p. xliii). We are not told how
the mind controls the animal spirits, how its action is a substitute for
the mechanical starting of the impulse, but Stuart insists that "the
mind has a distinct power of distinct nerves for determining the animal spirits, and there the blood" to go to whichever side of a given
muscle it wishes to move (for contracting or extending). If the mind
"impels but a very little more of the nervous fluid than usual, through
the slender tubes of the nerves, into those extended vesicles [of the
muscle fibres], they will be uniformly dilated" (p. xlvi). And "the
mind may keep up this inflation, as long as it pleases, only by impelling
constantly such a small quantity of the nervous fluid into the distended
vesicles." When the mind desists from sending that fluid through the
nerves, the vesicles contract.[21]

A somewhat similar analysis using animal spirits had been dedicated
to the President of the Royal Society, Hans Sloane, in 1733. This
analysis was by Browne Langrish, who was to give his Croonian lectures in 1747. In this earlier work, *A New Essay on Muscular Motion*,
Langrish starts from the principle that every corpuscle of matter has
two poles, attraction and repulsion. He also claimed to have demonstrated "from the Structure of the Nerves, that neither Muscular Motion nor Sensation could be performed distinctly if they arose from
any Vibrations in the Nerves themselves" (Advertisement). He does
say that "the use of the Ganglia on the Nerves, is to interrupt any vibratory Motion which may happen in them." In that way, they help
to convey "the Ideas of Pleasure or Pain, or the various Impressions
made on the Nerves, distinctly, from the several Parts of the Body, to
the *Sensorium* in the *Brain*." He does not think anyone has yet explained muscular motion. Many hypotheses have been advanced. He
is convinced that "*Muscular Motion* is mechanically performed," and

is governed by laws of matter and motion (p. 10). He thinks it probable, given the form and figure of muscle fibres, "that there is some Subtile, volatile, spirituous Matter, as animal Spirits secreted from the Blood by the Glands of the Brain, and continually flying into the Nerves" (p. 13). But he thinks he has shown that blood is not the sole cause involved in muscular motion. He did this by tying up certain arteries leading to the legs of frogs and finding no impairment of motion. If all blood is prevented, of course motion ceases, but he thinks the pulsation or vibrations of the arteries assist the motion of the animal spirits moving through the nerves. The flow of blood also keeps the fibres "warm, supple, distended, and every Way ready for the Influx of the Animal Spirits into them; and by its expansive and progressive Motion to assist the Motion of the Animal Spirits through the Nerves" (p. 19).

Langrish cites Pemberton's Introduction to Cowper's *Myotomia Reformata*, but he thinks Pemberton is wrong to give such a prominent role to muscular motion. What the spirits do is greatly to increase "the Force of the corpuscular Attraction in the Fibres themselves" (p. 22). He is convinced that were we able to divide muscle fibres, we would find them to be "little Hollow Cylinders" (p. 23). He cites various phenomena of magnetism, electricity, chemical reaction to support the conclusion (with Newton's help) that "all the *Phaenomena* of Nature do arise from the constituent Particles of Bodies being either impelled towards each other. . . or else by being repelled" (p. 39). An impressed force on muscle fibre causes the corpuscles to fly past each other; when the force is relaxed, the attractive power of each corpuscle brings them back to its normal position. The spirits flowing in the fibres increase the attractive power of the corpuscles (p. 55).

Langrish admits that "many learned Men have denied the Existence of Animal Spirits, because they are not within the reach of our Senses." We are not yet able to see the spirits, but he thinks it reasonable, given what we do know, to say there are such spirits. If we deny animal spirits we cannot explain muscular motion (p. 62). He rejects vibrations of nerves as a sufficient cause of muscular motion (p. 63). Nor does Langrish think Bryan Robinson's very elastic aether an acceptable explanation.

It does not seem agreeable to those sublime Speculations which Mr. Locke and Others have made, concerning the Soul, to think that it is capable of giving so great an Impulse to the Origin of a nervous Cord, as to vibrate so solid a Substance with such prodigous Velocity as *Muscular Motion* is well known to be performed, after it is once determined by the Will. (p. 69)

He admits that we do not know how soul or thought influences matter, "but it is most natural to believe that it acts only the most subtile, rare, and elastic *Aura* in the Body." These are the animal spirits. The nerves are always full of such spirits. Thus, "the least imaginable *Impetus* will be sufficient to give an undulating Motion to them" (p. 66). Animal spirits are the most refined and most agile matter. Their velocity may equal that of lightning. Hence, voluntary motion can be almost instantaneous (p. 77). He distinguishes voluntary from involuntary muscles, the former being those which never contract except by the direction of the will or mind (p. 78). The will "directs or propells a greater Quantity of Spirits, or the same quantity with a greater Force, into the Nerves which go to those Muscles" that it wishes to use (p. 79). The nerves "which supply the voluntary Muscles, have a Power of denying a Passage to the Animal Spirits into the muscular Fibres at all other times but when they receive an additional Impulse from the will" (p. 80). How the will gives the impetus to the animal spirits, Langrish does not know.

Hume's Spirits and Traces

With the theory of animal spirits and brain traces so much in evidence in a wide variety of writers, it should come as no surprise to find Hume citing and appealing to this theory. Hume knew Malebranche's *Recherche*, his references to the theory closely resemble Malebranche's and Watts's account of it. He very likely was aware of the various accounts of this physiology by doctors and scientists in England and Scotland. Hume had also directly experienced the close connection between bodily states and emotions during his depression, which began at the end of 1729. He sought advice from a doctor (perhaps Cheyne) in 1734. Hume compared his mental and emotional condition then to the "Coldness and Desertion of the Spirit" described by mystics and fanatics.

As this kind of Devotion depends entirely on the Force of Passion, and consequently of the Animal Spirits, I have often thought that their Case and mine were pretty parallel, and that their rapturous Admirations might discompose the Fabric of the Nerves and Brain, as much as profound reflections, and that warmth or Enthusiasm which is inseparable from them.[22]

Many of Hume's references to this theory involve the link between animal spirits and the passions, but he also cites the theory to explain belief and imagination as well as mistakes in association.[23]

In the *Treatise*, there is early on an explicit appeal made to the relation between spirits, traces and ideas. He speaks of making "an imaginary dissection of the Brain" as a way of showing "why upon our conception of any idea, the animal spirits run into all the contiguous traces, and rouze up the other ideas, that are related to it" (p. 60). Mistakes in association are explained in this way:

as the mind is endow'd with a power of exciting any idea it pleases; whenever it dispatches the spirits into that region of the brain, in which the idea is plac'd; these spirits always excite the idea, when they run precisely into the proper traces, and rummage that cell, which belongs to the idea. But as their motion is seldom direct, and naturally turns a little to the one side or the other; for this reason the animal spirits, falling into the contiguous traces, present other related ideas in lieu of that, which the mind desir'd at first to survey. (pp. 60-61)

Employing the chemical language used by Malebranche, Hume later says the imagination can be disordered by "any extraordinary ferment of the blood and spirits" (p. 123).[24] In writing on the passions, Hume invokes the spirits to account for the relation of one passion to another: "The predominant passion swallows up the inferior, and converts it into itself. The spirits, when once excited, easily receive a change in their direction; and it is natural to imagine, that this change will come from the prevailing affection."[25]

In dealing with belief in the *Treatise*, Hume remarks that "All the operations of the mind depend in a great measure on its disposition, when it performs them; and according as the spirits are more or less elevated, and the attention more or less fix'd, the action will always have more or less vigour and vivacity" (p. 98). In the section on scepticism with regard to reason, Hume explains why reason, seeking firm foundations for belief, does not in fact undermine all belief, by speaking of the mind's attention being "on the stretch" and "the spirits being diverted from their natural course"; they are then "not govern'd in their movement by the same laws, at least not to the same degree, as when they flow in their usual channel" (p. 185). Throughout, Hume stresses that psychological and physiological states work together, a truth any man can discover in his own case: "the different dispositions of his body change his thoughts and sentiments," as Hume knew from his own illness (p. 248). The physiological states are characterized by the theory of animal spirits and traces. That theory is invoked when he writes about perception, as well as about belief and the passions. For example, in discussing the double image caused by pressing one's eyeball, he says that this phenomenon shows "that all our perceptions are dependent on our organs, and the dispositions of our nerves and animal spirits" (p. 211). Similarly, "Original impressions or impressions of sensation are such as without any antecedent perception arise in the soul, from the constitution of the body, from the animal spirits, or from the application of objects to the external organs" (p. 275). As Malebranche and Locke both said, Hume also remarks that "any new object naturally gives a new direction to the spirits, and changes the disposition of the mind" (p. 99). Objects work by motion. When they press upon any sense organ, they "meet with resistance; and that resistance, by the motion it gives to the nerves and animal spirits, conveys a certain sensation to the mind" (p. 230). There is also in Hume a reference to the physiology of action: "We learn from anatomy, that the immediate object of power in voluntary motion, is not the member itself which is moved, but certain muscles, and nerves, and animal spirits."[26]

The Aether and Vibrations

The General Scholium at the end of Book III of Newton's *Principia* had thrown off the suggestion of "a certain most subtle Spirit which pervades and lies hid in all gross bodies," the force and action of which might account for the attraction of particles, the cohesion of particles, the operation of electric bodies, the emission, reflection, refraction of light. In addition, Newton suggested that this subtle spirit is that by which "All sensation is excited," and by means of which "the members of animal bodies move at the command of the will." The specific action of this spirit is vibrations "mutually propagated along the solid filaments of the nerves from the outward organs of sense to the brain, and from the brain into the muscles." The Queries in the second edition of the *Opticks* extended this suggestion. Query 12 applied to perception: "Do not the rays of light in falling upon the bottom of the eye excite vibrations in the tunica retina: Which vibrations, being propagated along the solid fibres of the optic nerves into the brain, cause the sense of seeing." Query 24 applied the suggestion to muscular motion: "Is not animal motion performed by the vibrations of this medium, excited in the brain by the power of the will, and propagated from thence through the solid, pellucid and uniform capillaments of the nerves into the muscles for contracting and dilating them?"

Some of the Newtonians in the century stayed with animal spirits in their physiology. Others who started with them, later spoke in terms of vibrations and the aether. Pemberton was one of the earliest Newtonians to prefer vibrations of the aether to animal spirits and inflation of nerves and fibres. After carefully analyzing the fibres of muscles, and after a careful consideration of the various alternatives then advanced, Pemberton (in his introductory essay to Cowper's work on anatomy) declared for Newton's hint of a fluid "contained in the Nerves" as probably being "no other than part of that subtle, rare, and elastic Spirit, he [Newton] concludes to be diffused through the Universe" (p. lxxiii). Thus we can suppose, he suggests, that "the Mind, when it wills a Part to be moved, acts upon this Spirit at the Extremity, to which it is present, of the Nerves, so as to communicate a proper Pulsation and vibratory Motion of this Spirit through the whole Nerve," and these "excited Pulses" make their way to the muscle fibres, where they stir up the elastic spirit there (p. lxxiv). When the mind ceases to act on the elastic spirit nearest it, the muscle relaxes.

Bryan Robinson (*A Treatise of the Animal Oeconomy*, 1732) declared his indebtedness to Newton also. He says that "Muscular motion is *performed by the Vibrations of a very Elastic Aether, lodged in the Nerves and Membranes investing the minute Fibres of the Muscles, excited by the Power of the Will, Heat, Wounds, the subtile and active Particles of Bodies, and other Causes*" (p. 82). Robinson thinks that experiments have failed to confirm either that nerves are pipes or that "such a Fluid as they conceive *Animal Spirits* to be, is separated from the Blood in the Brain" (p. 84). Moreover, animal spirits are unfit for moving the muscles (p. 85). Other writers have taken the nerves to be "solid Threads extended from the Brain to the Muscles and other Parts of the Body." He claims that

We find by Experience, that by the Power of the Will we can move the Muscles of our Limbs with various Degrees of Force; that there is not the least sensible Difference in point of Time between willing the Motion of the Muscles, and the Motions themselves; that Muscles contracted by the Power of the Will, dilate again the very Instant in which the Soul ceaseth to exercise that Power. (pp. 88-89)

The nerves are thus "the Instruments whereby the Will gives Motion to the Muscles" (p. 89). The will works the muscles by "producing some kind of Motion in those Ends of the Nerves which terminate in the Brain, which Motion is propagated" from there to the muscles (pp. 89-90). The will operates at the origin of the nerves in the brain. He thinks that the speed at which the motion passes from the brain to the nerves of distant muscles shows that the speed is due to the "vibrating Motion of a very elastic Fluid," the same elastic fluid that is in all bodies (p. 92). When my will excites a vibratory motion in the ends of nerves that terminate in the brain, that motion is in an instant propagated to the muscles "and excites a like Motion in the Aether lodged within those membranes" (p. 96). The vibratory motion in the aether makes the aether expand (its expansive force), which swells the membrane and causes a contraction of the fibres. The attractive powers of the membrane take over as soon as the will ceases (p. 98).

Cheyne, who earlier in the century had been cautiously drawn toward animal spirits, in 1740 opted for vibrations alone, seemingly even without the medium of fluid or aether (*An Essay on Regimen*). Cheyne cites the subtle matter, animal spirits, and Newton's *Spiritus Subtilissimus*. None, he now says, have been satisfactory as explanations.

How much more natural, *philosophical* and *simple* is it, to suppose the *Nerves* to be infinitely delicate and *mechanically* adjusted membraneous *Tubes*, *Twists*, or *Ropes*, whose *Elasticity* and *Mechanism* is preserv'd by an internal milky soft *Pith*, which Membranes receive their first Impression and *Impulse* from the *self-moving Principle* within us. (pp. 150-51)

The self-moving principle in us must communicate the first impulse either on the intermediate fluid or directly on the membrane. Cheyne opts for the latter, as being simpler. He speaks of the first impulse being continued by oscillation of the mechanism. Undulations, vibrations and tremors on the membraneous pipes: this is how muscles work.

In his *The Natural Method of Cureing the Diseases of the Body, and the Disorders of the Mind* (1742), Cheyne rejects Bryan Robinson's appeal to the aether.

As to *muscular Motion*, it is very ingeniously, and with great Probability, accounted for by Dr. *Bryan Robinson*, from Sir *Isaac Newton*'s Principles of an infinitely rare and elastic Fluid; (*spiritus quidam*) which is the *Theory* of some other *Mathematicians*. Now nothing can be more elegant, *mechanical*, natural and *adequate* to all this Appearance, than this Account of *muscular* Motion, if this elastic Fluid could be proved. But surely the *Elasticity* of the Fibres, especially of their *membraneous* Coats of the infinitesimal *nervous Fibrils*, which they have from the *Meninges*, which every one allows to be extremely *elastic*, must have the far greater Share in all the animal Functions, and in *Muscular Motion*. (pp. 31-32)

Whether the nerves need to be inflated "by a *Materia Subtilis*, or *Liquidum Nervosum*," Cheyne insists that no one "doubts that the first *Impulse* proceeds from the *immaterial Substance*" (p. 33). That this immaterial substance is able to impress "proper *Vibrations* and *Tremors*" in certain nerve fibres and muscles, and that external objects set up vibrations also, he firmly asserts (p. 94).

In his lectures to the Royal Society, Browne Langrish (*The Croonian Lectures on Muscular Motion*, 1748) acknowledges the suggestion made by Newton in the Queries, along with "what Dr. Pemberton has said in his very learned Introduction to Cowper on the Muscles." His question is, "by what means a Muscle so instantly and forcibly contracts itself, or shortens its Length, at the Command of the Will" (p. 2). Each muscle fibre is tubular. Muscular motion "proceeds from the *attractive* Quality of the constituent Particles, every fibre being increased and strengthened by the addition of some *aethereal Matter* flying out from the Extremities of the Nerves; and that this is instantly occasion'd by the Will, and ceases again as soon." The contractive "or muscular action, does not depend upon any Fluid dilating or distending the Fibres; but, on the contrary, they shrink and grow less" (p. 29). Such action can only be caused by aethereal matter, not by blood or lymph juices. This aethereal matter may be mixed with the blood and "secreted from it by the Glands of the Brain," thereby bringing his version of the aether theory into close similarity with his earlier account of animal spirits. He thinks that the delicate texture of the brain indicates that "the Fluids they convey to the Muscles must be exquisitely fine" (p. 30). This nervous fluid, like animal spirits, is at the command of the will, it moves "as quick as Lightening" (p. 32). It is the most refined matter in nature. The fluid acts upon the particles of the muscular fibre by increasing their attractive virtue (p. 33). As Stuart did, so Langrish thinks that the influence "which the *Soul* has upon the *aethereal Medium* in the nerves must be by Impulse; for though our finite Capacities are not able to comprehend the Nature of immaterial Impulse, yet nothing is more certain than that the most Subtile Matter in the Universe cannot be moved without some impressed Force" (p. 37). He confesses that the human mind is limited, hence we cannot fully understand the workings of muscles and will. We can only refer to second causes such as the immaterial impulse, the subtle fluid, etc.

That the *Supreme Being* hath implanted an immaterial Spirit in every living Creature, for the Purposes of Sensation and voluntary Motion, I think cannot be denied by anyone in his senses: But perhaps it may not become us to be too sollicitous about the Reach of human Reason. (p. 41)

Langrish ends his lectures with a warning not to settle for vibration only, without some immaterial impulse. To suppose muscles to work solely by the elasticity of the nerves or by an impulse not started by the will is "so immaterial a Notion as not to deserve an Answer."

Langrish's warning against settling for vibration alone in the physiology of thinking and acting may have been anticipating what was on the horizon. David Hartley's account, published one year after Langrish's Croonian lectures, was viewed by some writers in the century in that way. An interesting transition to Hartley's account is found one year earlier than Langrish's lectures, in a book which summarizes some of the earlier views on physiology, suggesting difficulties with the animal spirit account, and opting for vibrations, or at least for motions of brain particles without spirits or aether. This is the work to which I referred earlier, the work sometimes attributed to a James Long but recently argued to be by Hartley himself: *An Enquiry into the Origin of the Human Appetites and Affections, Shewing How Each Arises from Association* (1747). The author points out that some of the writers on the structure of nerves (he mentions mainly the physicians and anatomists) took them to be round and tubular and "filled with a certain fine subtle fluid, generally called and known by the name of animal spirits" (p. 61).[27] This author also reports a difficulty raised against this physiology: if animal spirits carry the messages of our will, it seems unlikely they could move fast enough. There is no time gap between my will or thought to move my arm and my arm moving. For those, like Malebranche and Watts, who denied that we do move our limbs or animal spirits, this objection would be no problem. But for those who thought there was some connection between thought and action, a connection bridged by animal spirits, the problem of time and the speed of the animal spirits would be a difficulty. For this reason, this author says some writers made the nerves a combination of chords and tubes. Chords would account for the quickness of execution of action, because by touching one end of a chord, the motion is carried instantaneously to the other end. This author favours the chord vibration theory, but he suggests that God could easily fill the nerves with fluid capable of moving fast enough to meet the objection.[28] What this author takes to be important is the close correlation between motion and activity of the nerves *and* our perceptions. This correlation *is* typical of Hartley's *Observations on Man*.

If every distinct particular perception of the soul excites a distinct particular motion of the nerves, and reciprocally, every distinct particular motion of the nerves produces a distinct particular perception in the soul, it will ever be, that when the same motions of the nerves are repeated, the same perceptions shall be felt by the soul, and, *vice versa*, when the same perceptions are felt in the soul, the same motions shall be excited in the body. (pp. 62-63)

As Hartley did in his *Observations on Man*, so this author speaks of the medullar substance in the brain vibrating. When objects impress a specific motion on that substance, the regular vibrations change. If that specific motion is reinforced sufficiently, the normal vibrations of the brain will be permanently changed to that specific one produced by the object (pp. 66-67). In both works, the association of ideas is better accounted for with vibrations of nerve chords than by the activity of animal spirits moving about in tubular pathways in the brain.[29] What precisely the nature of ideas is is not clear from the account in this 1747 work, but the correlation is firm: when I have ideas, there are motions in the brain. To recall an idea, the same motions must occur again in the brain. "Every distinct sensation in the soul is ever accompanied with a distinct motion in the body" (p. 77). Different motions of the nerves differently affect the soul. But nothing "can affect her otherwise than by the alternations it causes in the state, site, and disposition of the medullar particles in the brain" (p. 78). Association is similarly explained: "when two or more objects present themselves at the same time, the impressions on the sensory caused by them lying so near each other that in turning to that part of the sensory, the mind cannot view one without the other, and so the idea answering to those objects ever after keep in company together" (pp. 71-72).

Hartley's account in his *Observations on Man* adds very little to the statement of the vibration theory in this 1747 work; there are more details in the later book. Hartley traces his theory of vibrations back to Newton's Queries, as so many writers in this century did. He identifies the white medullary substance of the brain as the immediate instrument of sensation and motion, as well as the means by which ideas are presented to the mind (*Observations*, pp. 7-8). External objects cause vibrations in the medullary particles (p. 11). He thinks the aether is the medium of transmission of motion, even inside the brain, thereby departing perhaps from the earlier work. Sensations leave traces after the object has ceased; ideas are more permanent traces caused by the repetition of sensations (p. 57). Ideas copy impressions. He disclaimed the thesis that matter can be endowed with the power of sensation: he insisted that ideas and sensations are of a 'mental nature' while vibrations are corporeal. But his distinction between ideas and vibrations is not too clear. The link between sensations and ideas is firm. When sensations are associated together a sufficient number of times, they gain a power over the corresponding ideas such that, if the sensation is subsequently impressed alone, the other associated ideas are excited in the mind (p. 65). In turn, this association is explained by reference to the corporeal causes of sensation and the vibrations in the brain. "When Objects and Ideas, with their most common Combinations, have been often presented to the Mind, a Train of them, of a considerable length, may, by once occurring, Leave such a Trace, as to recur in Imagination as in this single Occurrence" (p. 78).

Action, too, is accounted for in these terms. If some motion of our body "follows that Idea, or State of Mind . . . which we term the Will, directly, and without our perceiving the Intervention of any other Idea, or of any Sensation or Motion, it may be called voluntary, in the Highest Sense of this Word" (p. 103). In a more cautious mood, he treats his account as an explanatory hypothesis: we are

enabled to account for all the Motions of the Human Body, upon Principles which, tho' they may be fictitious, are, at least, clear and intelligible. The Doctrine of Vibrations explains all the original automatic Motions, that of Association the voluntary and secondarily automatic ones and, if the Doctrine of Association be founded in, and deducible from, that of Vibrations, in the manner delivered above, then all the Sensations, Ideas, and Motions of all Animals, will be conducted according to the Vibrations of the small medullary particles. (p. 109)

In his account of Hartley's theory, Priestley (*Hartley's Theory of the Human Mind*, 1775) points out that the different degrees of vibrations and the place of a vibration in the brain can account for different ideas. Priestley is convinced that some "mechanical affection of the nerves and brain must necessarily correspond to all our sensations and ideas" (p. xiv). Repeating vibrations establish dispositions for those specific vibrations in the future, differences in strength between vibrations originally impressed and those occurring in recollection account for the difference in sensory and memory ideas. Both in the physiology of animal spirits and in that of vibrations, these same principles of similarity, disposition, and association are found. The principles used by Malebranche are still at work at the end of the eighteenth century in Britain. There is perhaps another link, besides Malebranche, between the Cartesian physiology and the Hartleian account. We saw in a previous chapter that one of Priestley's critics, Joseph Berington (*Letters to a Materialist*), linked the name of Charles Bonnet with that of Priestley. Priestley had in fact recommended Bonnet's work. Bonnet was in the same tradition as the British authors we have been discussing: he knew Malebranche's work well and he articulated Descartes's suggestion of natural signs as that to which ideas respond.[30] Bonnet also gave a detailed account of the physiology of animal spirits, occasionally using vibrations as well.[31] He says that God wished that all our ideas should be dependent originally on movement or vibrations excited in certain parts of our brain. The recall of the same idea "probably depends on a similar cause. It is a modification of the motor force of the soul, which, in acting on the fibres or the spirits, occasions movements similar to those which the objects made" (*Essai de psychologie*, 1754, p. 11). Bonnet attempts to explain all the

operations of our mind in a mechanical way (p. 13). There is, as with
Malebranche, constant reference to nerve fibres and brain movements.
The production of ideas is always occasioned by some movement in
the brain, a movement either from "the actual impression of objects
on the senses" or by the movement-force of the mind acting directly
on the brain (p. 39). There are also different nerve fibres for different
sensations and ideas (pp. 44 ff.). He also speaks of degrees of force and
vivacity in the reproduction of ideas (p. 57).

Conclusion

In commenting on the Hartelian physiology, Thomas Reid (*Essays on
the Intellectual Powers of Man*, 1785) cites Newton's conjectures in
the Queries, about aether and its vibrations around the optic nerve.
What Newton advanced as conjecture only, Hartley, Reid says, has offered as demonstration. Reid makes no mention of the many treatises
on anatomy and muscular motion which also applied Newton's suggestions. He is not prepared to take these hypotheses as explanations
of thinking and acting. Reid is worried about the mechanism inherent
in Hartley's use of Newton's suggestions. He thinks the tendency "of
this system of vibrations is to make all the operations of the mind
mere mechanism, dependent on the laws of matter and motion" (Vol.
I, p. 93). Reid does not think there is any evidence for vibrations,
vibratiuncles, elastic aether, etc.[32] He recognizes that Hartley dis-
claims being a materialist, that he does not say thought is produced in,
only that it is connected with, the medullary substance of nerves and
brain. But, Reid argues, unless we have reason to think vibrations exist,
we cannot even advance this notion of connections (p. 101). Reid
thinks it unlikely, also, that the great variety in degrees of sensations
could find an equal number of different vibrations.

But Reid did not reject all physiology. Along with the defenders
of these specific physiologies, he took it as a law of our nature that
for perception of objects, "the impressions made upon the organs of
sense must be communicated to the nerves, and by them to the brain"
(p. 87). He rejects animal spirits and tubes for the notion of nerves
as "fine cords" which pass "from the brain, or from the spinal marrow . . . to all parts of the body." All voluntary and involuntary
motions of the body are performed by these cords. Without nerves to
muscles we cannot move; without nerves to sense organs we cannot
perceive. The movement is from object, to sense organ, to nerve, to
brain. There "the material part" of perception ends (p. 88). Reid uses
the term 'impression' for all changes brought about by objects through

this process. Without these impressions, we cannot perceive; but just having physical impressions in nerves and brain does not constitute perception. Reid confesses not to know why the physical process is necessary for 'mental' perceiving, but there is, he insists, an exact correspondence between impressions and "the nature and conditions of the objects by which they are made; and a correspondence between our perceptions and sensations and those impressions." He does not specify the nature of these correspondences, but on it depends the accuracy of the information about the world (p. 89).

Reid tried to follow a sign theory of ideas, but it is clear from his remarks on physiology that he saw the importance of the physiological correlate for perception. In that, he reflects one of the attitudes towards physiology in the century: for every mental activity—whether it be perceiving, remembering, associating, willing—and to each idea, there corresponds a specific activity or state in the brain. Reid does not seem to think we have control over brain processes, as many writers thought we could send the animal spirits into their proper channels; but even those writers who talked in such an intentional way only meant to say, I think, that when I try and succeed in recalling a name or an idea, my efforts at recalling cause (but not intentionally cause) the spirits or the vibrations to work in specific ways. Even in willing and acting, the account was that by taking thought I cause the spirits to move in specific ways or the aether to vibrate in specific nerves and muscles. What happens after that is due to the mechanism of the body. This distinction between cause and intentional cause marks the fragility of the connection between mind and matter. On the side of human action, that fragility can in fact break the connection: *I* do not move my arm or activate my body—its action is all due to mechanism. Man the machine may be eased into action by God, but thereafter physics, chemistry, anatomy, and optics will give us the account of human thought and action: this was, as we have seen, always a near and an easy alternative in the eighteenth century. The more difficult alternative was to specify a link between bodily mechanism and conscious control. The attempts to specify such a connection were exactly parallel with those efforts to avoid the possibility of thinking matter.

Notes

1. Broughton agreed with Layton in accepting this physiology: he speaks of "A Fluid in the Human Body, as we call *Animal Spirit*" (*Psychologia*, 1703, p. 205). He also says that no physician is so ignorant as to doubt that such a fluid exists. Animal spirit physiology is found earlier still in Britain. One of the standard medical works in the Elizabethan period, Thomas

Vicary's *The Anatomie of the Bodie of Man* (1548), distinguished several kinds of spirits: animal, vital, natural. The soul of man was located in the head, the brain made animal spirits out of blood sent to it. For a discussion of this early form of the animal spirit physiology, see "Physiology and Psychology in Shakespeare's Age," *Journal of the History of Ideas* 12, 1951, by Patrick Cruttwell. Also, Lisa Jardine's *Francis Bacon: Discovery and the Art of Discourse* (Cambridge: Cambridge University Press, 1974), pp. 89-96.

2. *Treatise on Man*, translation and commentary by Thomas Steele Hall (1972), p. 19. The French text is given in this edition after the English translation. I have used Alquié's handy three-volume edition of Descartes, *Oeuvres philosophiques*, Garnier. The citation here is to volume I, p. 388.

3. Hall, p. 21; Alquié, pp. 389-90.

4. Hall, pp. 22-27; Alquié, pp. 391-402. Cf. *La description du corps humain*, Alquié, volume III, p. 824: "And finally the parts of the blood most agitated and most lively being carried to the brain by the arteries which come from the heart in a straight line, constitute air or a very subtle wind which is called animal spirits; the spirits dilate the brain and ready it to receive the impressions of external objects and the impressions of the soul; that is, makes the brain become the organ or seat of the common sense, the imagination and the memory."

5. *La Dioptrique*, in Alquié, volume I, p. 683.

6. Art. 8, Alquié, volume III, p. 957; English translation by Haldane and Ross, p. 335.

7. In *Select Discourses* (1660), p. 119.

8. Joseph Priestley (*Disquisitions Relating to Matter and Spirit*, 1777) remarked that Malebranche is "said to have been the first who brought into vogue the doctrine of *animal spirits*" (p. 217). Priestley may have been quoting La Mettrie, who said of Malebranche, he was "the first of the philosophers who put in vogue the animal spirits" (*L'Homme Machine*, ed. A. Vartanian, 1960, p. 73. Vartanian also tells us that La Mettrie considered Malebranche's *Recherche* as "the best general treatise on physiological psychology." La Mettrie accepted the animal-spirit account but identified the mind with the configuration of parts of the brain).

9. Lennon-Olscamp, p. 88.

10. Thomas Willis, *Cerebri anatome*, 1664.

11. This work had the sanction of the Royal Society and the help of a number of Newtonians. In an advertisement to the reader, Richard Mead says that Cowper died thirteen years ago, leaving this revision of an early work in the hands of Mead. Mead, along with Joseph Tanner and with help from Dr. Jurin, the then secretary of the Royal Society, put the material in order. Mead also invited Pemberton to contribute his introductory essay.

12. This last suggestion is also found in Browne Langrish's *New Essay on Muscular Motion* (1733). J. A. Bennett has recently pointed out that the debate over a mechanical versus a chemical explanation of muscular motion goes back at least to Christopher Wren. (See Bennett's article, "A Note on Theories of Respiration and Muscular Action in England, c. 1660," in *Medical History* 20, January 1976, pp. 59-69.) In an address before the Royal Society, Wren said that "a mechanical account must be complemented by a chemical explanation" (in Bennett, pp. 63-64). Wren continued: "in the Body of a Man, if we consider it only mechanically, we may indeed learn the Fabrick and action of the organical Parts, but without Chymisty, we shall be at a Loss to know, what Blood, Spirits, and Humours are, from the due Temper of which (as of the Spring in the Barrel Wheel) the Motions of all the Parts depend."

13. Pemberton is cautious about the explanation of perception. "For notwithstanding we are able exactly to trace the Species of things manifested by Sight to their Impression on the Optick Nerve, and have discovered by what Principles, and by what Mediums, the Images of external Objects are formed in the Eyes; yet what effects those Images have on the Nerves,

whereby the Perception of the things themselves is caused, remains wholly a secret to us" (p. ii in his Introductory essay to Cowper's work on anatomy).

14. Whytt really mocks the appeals to animal spirits (pp. v, vi), but he does offer arguments and reasons as well for rejecting them. At least, he says that he finds no reason to use "the *irregular motion, increasing derivation, repercussion, confusion,* or *hurry* of the animal spirits, in accounting for the symptoms of nervous hypochondriac or hysteric disorders" (p. 8, n.). Whytt appeals to the notion of *sympathy* for his physiological explanations.

15. This example, and this metaphorical way of talking about animal spirits, keeps appearing in the literature. We have seen it in Locke and it occurs later in Hume. Some indication of the general and widespread knowledge of the animal-spirit physiology, as well of this same example, is given by its appearance in several issues of *The Spectator*. In issue 86, for 8 June 1711, we find the following: "Whether or no the different Motions of the animal Spirits in different Passions, may have any effect on the Mould of the Face when the Lineaments are pliable and tender . . . I shall leave to the Consideration of the Curious." A more detailed account, which is identified with the Cartesians, is found in issue 417 for 28 June 1712. The question is, how is it that the sight of a lovely scene brings with it other ideas, awakens ideas in the imagination. "The set of Ideas which we received from such a Prospect or Garden, having entred the Mind at the same time, have a Set of Traces belonging to them in the Brain, bordering very near upon one another; when, therefore, any one of these Ideas arises in the imagination, and consequently dispatches a flow of Animal Spirits to its proper Trace, these Spirits, in the Violence of their Motion, run not only into the Trace, to which they were more particularly directed, but into several of those that lie about it: By this means they awaken other Ideas of the same Set, which immediately determine a New Dispatch of Spirits, that in the same manner open other Neighbouring Traces, till at last the whole Set of them is blown up, and the whole Prospect of the Garden flourishes in the Imagination." This account also offered an explanation of why, "when the Fancy thus reflects on the Scenes that have past in it formerly, those which were at first pleasant to behold, appear more so upon Reflexion, and that the Memory heightens the Delightfulness of the Original." This is the case because "the Pleasure we received from these Places far surmounted, and overcame the little Disagreeableness we found in them; for this Reason there was at first a wider Passage worn in the Pleasure Traces."

16. In a later work, *The Known God: Or, The Author of Nature Unveil'd* (1737), Colliber characterizes the soul as being of a middle nature between God and matter. In being active, it resembles God; in receiving impressions from matter, it is like matter. He still rejects the notion that thought can proceed from matter or from blood and animal spirits.

17. *The Spectator* again indicates the general dissemination of this physiology: "I consider the Body as a System of Tubes and Glands, or to use a more Rustick Phrase, a Bundle of Pipes and Strainers, fitted to one another after so wonderful a manner as to make a proper Engine for the Soul to work with" (No. 115, 12 July 1711).

18. In volume III of *Medical Essays and Observations of the Royal Society of Edinburgh*, 1737.

19. *Three Lectures on Muscular Motion*, 1739, Supplement to *Philosophical Transactions* of the Royal Society of London, volume 40.

20. Stuart says that with two exceptions, himself and Boerhaave, everyone writing on muscular motion has supposed the nerves to be elastic. In his inaugural thesis at Leyden in 1711, he says he advanced the claim that the nerves were not elastic. Boerhaave subsequently, in 1713, acknowledged this.

21. William Porterfield was even suggesting at this time that the mind controls many muscles involved in perception as well as some governing the vital functions. "No Body denies but the Mind presides over those Muscles which tune the Ear, and yet we are not conscious

of their Acting; the Motions of the Eyelids are also all voluntary, though we are often insensible of them, and even in many Cases, cannot by any Act of Volition hinder them to move in a particular Manner." In these and more vital function cases, custom and habit have made such actions appear necessary and mechanical, but it is simply that the mind has imposed upon itself a law "whereby it regulates and governs them to the greatest advantage." Porterfield does not think vital motions can be accounted for by mechanism alone ("An Essay concerning the Motions of the Eyes," Part II, in *Medical Essays*, volume IV, 1737). In this last remark, Porterfield agrees with Stuart (and as we saw earlier, with Malebranche) that "Original impulse, and therefore every new motion, must arise from some immaterial being, as its immediate cause." Since "Impulse, as the begining of every new muscular motion, is in the power of the mind or will," the mind or will must be an immaterial being (Stuart, *Three Lectures*, p. xli). The origin of the "chain of natural causes" must, Stuart says, "be an omnipresent and immaterial agent as the prime cause." He even suggests that this chain may not be so long "as is generally imagined." Hence God himself may be "the immediate acting, ubiquitary cause of centrepetal power" (p. xlii).

22. Letter to Cheyne, dated March 1734, in *The Letters of David Hume*, ed. by J. Y. T. Greig, volume I, p. 17.

23. For a detailed discussion of Hume's use of this physiology, see R. F. Anderson's excellent study, *Hume's First Principles*, 1966.

24. In his essay, "The Epicurean," Hume says (probably on behalf of this particular philosophy which he is there characterizing) that "the brain separates and refines the spirits" (*Essays, Moral, Political and Literary*, 1741, reprint of 1974, p. 141). There is also an interesting entry in Hume's memoranda on his reading during the period 1729-40: "There is a remarkable study to confirm the Cartesian Philosophy of the Brain. A Man hurt by the fall of a Horse forgot about twenty Years of his Life, and remember'd what went before in a much more lively Manner than usual" (quoted by Mossner, "Hume's Early Memoranda, 1729-40," in *Journal of the History of Ideas* 1948, p. 502). Is Hume suggesting that the fall from the horse disturbed the flow of animal spirits, turned them out of their established ways and hence upset the memory?

25. See Hume's *Dissertation on the Passions*, in volume IV of the Green and Grose edition of Hume's works (1874, p. 123).

26. *Enquiry concerning Human Understanding*, p. 66.

27. A somewhat lesser-known anatomist, Malcolm Flemyng, is another example of one who argued for nerves as "hollow canals or tubes . . . which contain and transmit a peculiar juice or fluid, the animal spirits" (*The Nature of the Nervous Fluid, or, Animal Spirits Demonstrated*, 1751). Flemyng had argued the same claim earlier in the century. He also cites for support the work of Haller and Boerhaave.

28. In his presentation of Hartley's version of vibrations, Priestley (*Hartley's Theory of the Human Mind*, 1775) says that "This hypothesis does not require that the nerves be *tubes*, or consist of bundles of tubes, for the purpose of containing any *fluid*, though it is in no way inconsistent with the supposition of their being of that structure" (pp. x-xi).

29. He reports the defenders of animal spirits as saying that the pathways are "kept open by the resorting of animal spirits thither for that purpose" (p. 71). The loss of ideas in sleep is said to be because the animal spirits are kept out of the appropriate areas. The author was obviously well read in the animal spirit physiology.

30. For a discussion of the notion of natural signs, and the role they play in perception, see my *Perceptual Acquaintance from Descartes to Reid*, chapter I.

31. A similar combination of the two physiologies is found in an anonymous tract, *Theological Survey of the Human Understanding* (1776). In a work heavily influenced by Locke, this author adds a section at the end entitled, "A Psychological Stricture." Animal spirits are

said to be the *"Medium of Discernment"* for the percipient. He gives the usual characterization of such spirits, as a fine, subtle fluid separated from the blood by the brain. These spirits are communicated to the veins and they make us sensible of impressions from without, *"probably* by a Kind of *undulating* Motion" (pp. 250-53). Cf. also Mead's *A Mechanical Account of Poisons* (1702): he says the muscles are put into action by tremors of the nerves which cause their fluid to be "draft into the moving Fibres." This can be done "by the determination of the Will," or by the "outward *Impulsions* of an *Elastic* Fluid" such as air (p. 72).

32. Reid rejects most of these physiological notions because no one had observed what they claimed to refer to, especially the tubular structure of nerves. The talk of animal spirits was for him pure conjecture. James Harris had earlier rejected mindlike entities — aether, animal spirits, nervous ducts, vibrations — as modern substitutes for occult qualities (*Hermes*, 1751, p. 393).

Conclusion

In the eighteenth-century literature we have been examining, there were two ways in which the person as agent was by-passed. One way was when the mechanism of the body was so detailed that all our movements were said to be caused (or at least, accounted for) by the physiology of the body. The bodily mechanism functioned with the precision and regularity of a machine, of a clever and sophisticated automaton. The other way was the extreme immaterialist route, where God intervenes to move muscles which then move our limbs. Although no one made this point, this extreme Malebranchian ontology left man something like a puppet with spiritual strings, a mere neurospast, as John Edwards charged. On this view, the difficulties of understanding how our intentions and volitions could interfere with material physiology were replaced by the mysterious and miraculous intervention of the infinite mind in human affairs.[1]

For some writers, this extreme immaterialist view about the cause of human action was generalized to the whole of nature: all physical movement is caused by God. William Jones (*An Essay on the First Principles of Natural Philosophy*, 1762)[2] traced the source of this ontology to the belief in a vacuum. With the acceptance of a vacuum, "some have confidently affirmed, that natural effects are no way to be accounted for, but by the power of the Deity immediately interested" (p. 216). Those who reached this conclusion assume, falsely,

190

that if God did act by second causes, we would be unable to reject the belief that "such causes were able to contrive and frame a world without his [God's] interposition." Jones conjectures that those who for religious motives object to second causes, "must imagine surely, that matter, if there is but enough of it, can move, act and think, by its own nature."

Jones cites Baxter's *Enquiry* in a number of passages, whose author appealed to "the power of the Deity immediately interested"; but the object of Jones's attack turns out to be most of the scientists and theological writers of the century: Keill, Desaguliers, Friend, Rowning, Derham, Maclaurin, Cotes, and of course Newton and Samuel Clarke. Two features of the generally accepted view of matter bothered Jones: the use of immaterial principles and the acceptance of a vacuum. Jones argued (from observation and experiment, he insisted) for material causes, for explaining all events in nature by reference to mechanism. He was aware that not all writers went the extreme Malebranchian route of resolving all effects in the immediate intervention of God; but the reluctance of some of the Newtonians to say that attraction and repulsion were inherent in matter, reserved for God the self-activating causal role. Jones was sympathetic to the point of view of Leibniz, that God created a world which did not need his constant attention, nor did Jones believe God would mix together material and immaterial principles for the working of nature.

The appeal to a vacuum, to empty space, was, however, the main object of Jones's carefully constructed attack upon modern writers. His book is not unlike Cudworth's *True Intellectual System of the Universe* in its discussions of ancient writers, and in its assessing modern writers against the ancients. While Cudworth was much more directly concerned to combat atheists, Jones also has an interest in what does and does not support atheism. The possible grounds for atheism were especially important for Jones, since he was fully conscious that his own acceptance of mechanical explanations might be considered atheistical. However, the basic ground for atheism was, Jones insisted, the acceptance of empty space. In his summary of "The Judgment of Antiquity on the System of Nature" (pp. 185-216), Jones claimed that all the ancient authors, except the atomists, supported his conclusions. It was the "*Democritic* atheists" who, "by the help of an internal power or *gravitating force* in *atoms*, and a *vacuum* wherein these atoms might have room enough to move without being resisted, had dextrously contrived to account, as well for the *formation* as the *preservation* of the world, without a *divine providence*" (p. 214). In drawing on the Greeks for support against Leibniz, Samuel Clarke was appealing, Jones slyly remarks, to the 'Democritic atheists'. Clarke's reference to the Greeks in his exchange with Leibniz was to their use of matter and the vacuum. Since Clarke's Boyle lectures were written to attack atheism and to defend religion by reference to the phenomena of nature, Jones takes some delight in calling attention to this association between atheism, a vacuum, and Clarke. The "*Democritic* method of philosophising," Jones stresses, recommended itself to Clarke "by its doctrines of a *vacuum*, and an inherent quality of motion in the parts of matter; by which it differed from the best and most universal philosophy of antiquity, and was distinguished as a foundation for atheism" (p. 215).

This ancient foundation of atheism, the vacuum, is "now recommended as the only sure foundation of natural religion." On the suspicion that, were God not entirely involved in the activity of nature, matter might activate itself, it might even think, writers like Clarke have seized on the concept of a vacuum or empty space, the space in which God can work at a distance. But seizing on this concept is, Jones argues, to "make ourselves materialists, that is, atheists, in order to confute atheism more effectually" (p. 216). Jones is not far from Hume's sardonic twist, that an immaterialism is an atheism, except that his route to that conclusion differs from that of Hume.

In a more serious vein, Jones finds the immaterialist's argument for God devious and precarious.

If you will follow their new prescription, you must bring yourself, in the first place, to believe *a vacuum*; the steps to which are not understood by one in a thousand: then you are to remove the notion of *actio in distans*, which in the last age had some great authorities on its side: then you arrive at this conclusion, though not without a considerable stride, that God himself is the sole agent, to whose immediate power, exclusive of all secondary agents, the lowest effects in the world are to be imputed. And if these things are so, then it follows, that there is a God, and you triumph over atheism. (p. 217)

Much easier, Jones thinks, to refute atheism by calling attention to final causes, e.g., the structure and organization of the eye which "was *contrived for seeing*" (p. 216). Jones recognized that he and Baxter used similar premises to reach different conclusions: "The end I have proposed in mentioning these things, is to shew the necessity of a material agency in the heavens, subordinate to the divine power: whereas it is his design to shew from the same premises, that God himself is the agent immediately" (pp. 112-13). Planetary motion must either be regulated "*physically*, by the instrumentality of some material agent properly adapted; or *supernaturally*, by some immediate influence of divine power" (p. 113). He objected to the supernatural appeal because, among other reasons, "every pretender to philosophy" will then have "a liberty of proposing what powers he pleases, and all of them equally good, if they are to be mended at every turn by a miracle" (p. 113). The "established order of natural things" is always to be preferred to "a miraculous interposition." If, instead of God's direct interposition, writers appeal to immaterial secondary causes, such as attraction and repulsion, Jones charges that this is to "ascribe unintelligible and innate powers to inert matter" (pp. 180-81).

Earlier in his book, Jones tried to charge (as Leibniz did in writing to Clarke) that the Newtonian's gravity was a form of occult power (pp. 60-61). This charge was often made. What is more interesting about Jones's discussion of the concept of gravity is the way in which he discloses the ambiguities and even ambivalences in the use of that concept. Sometimes 'attraction' is said to be a term used to refer to the effects or phenomena only. At other times, attraction is spoken of as an active principle, as a cause, or as a tendency of bodies. At the end of a presentation of what different writers have said about gravity, Jones nicely summarized what he has shown about the ambiguities.

Sir *Isaac Newton*. "Gravity exists and *acts*."

Dr. *Friend*. "In *explaining* gravity, *Newton* has demonstrated it to arise from an *attractive force*."

M. *Maupertuis*. "It should be remembered in justice to Sir *Isaac Newton*, he has never considered *attraction* as an *explanation of gravity*. He considers it not as a *cause*, but as an *effect*."

Mr. *Cotes*. "Gravity is the most simple of *causes*."

Dr. *Clarke*. "It has often been distinctly declared, that by the term *attraction*, we do not mean to express the *cause* of bodies tending toward each other, but barely the *effect*, the *effect itself*, the *phaenomenon*, or *matter of fact*."

Dr. *Desaguliers*. "Attraction seems to be settled by the great creator as the *first of second causes*."

Mr. *Rowning*. "When we use the term *attraction*, we do not determine the physical cause of it, but use it to signify an *effect*: nevertheless, to attraction effects are manifestly owing."

Sir *Isaac Newton*. "There are *agents in nature* able to make the particles of bodies stick together by very strong *attractions*, and it is the business of experimental philosophy to *find them out*."

Dr. *Desaguliers*. "We are not sollicitous about the *cause of attraction*."

Dr. *Friend*. "I believe *attraction* will always be *occult*."

Jones's own account "attributes all motion to the action of matter upon matter" (p. 53). The agency in matter is mechanical, those mechanical causes being fire in its two forms as light and heat. He conceived of fire as a fluid that pervades all things, not unlike, it would seem, that subtle fluid mentioned by Newton in his General Scholium. Jones shared this view about fire with a group of anti-Newtonians.[3] He also cites a passage from Berkeley's *Siris* in support. Thus his matter is not the inert, passive matter of the corpuscularians; the activity of his matter through light and heat is not an intentional or conscious cause; but nature for Jones does have God as its creator and designer. God does not, and should not, play any role in the explanations of science. The mechanism of nature, when fully understood, will provide us with the explanations of all phenomena.

The mechanism of the body matches the mechanism of nature. Breath in the lungs and heat in the vessels are the moving forces of the body: "all the animal functions, are sustained and carried on by an internal heat, which keeps the blood fluid, and by the external *air* pressing into the lungs" (pp. 15-16). Jones does not devote much attention to animals and man, but his few brief accounts of bodily movement suggest the sort of mechanical picture which many writers feared as the result of Locke's suggestion. There is no mention of the mind or of consciousness in this account.

The body of man, which is the highest piece of machinery in nature, is made to *see*, and *hear*, and *speak*, upon mechanical principles; and it dies without the constant impression of a *material force* upon it from the element of *air*. (p. 179)

I have not found any reactions to this stark, impersonal picture of man's body seeing, hearing, and speaking, seemingly independent of or without any relation to man himself. Jones may only have meant to indicate the workings of the physiology in seeing, hearing, and speaking. But his language does not give us any reason to think his account of human action, had he constructed one, would have found any need for the person. Just as the universe, the machine of nature, works through second, material causes without any intervention from God, so the machine of our bodies works through the same second, material causes without any need for the intervention of our minds, of our intentions or volitions. Jones does not draw this last firm conclusion, but everything that he says strongly suggests that he would have had difficulty avoiding that conclusion.

Aside from the extreme Malebranchian view, where I do not cause my arm to move (God does the causing), the other writers who used the physiology of thinking and acting found some role for intentions and volitions. Even Malebranche found a role for them, only it was not a causal one. No one was very clear about how intentions and volitions do fit into or help cause actions, but, contrary to the fears of the orthodox immaterialists who were convinced that Locke's suggestion would quickly lead to automatism in man, we have not found anyone defending a British 'L'homme machine'.

David Hartley, whose *Observations on Man* was often thought to lead to such a notion, was careful to distinguish automatic from voluntary motions of the body (p. iii). "The *Automatic* Motions are those which arise from the Mechanism of the Body in an evident manner." Hartley admitted the reference to automata: the automatic motions "are called *Automatic*, from their Resemblance to the Motions of *Automata*, or Machines, whose Principle of Motion is within themselves." These automatic motions are not Jones's seeing, hearing, and speaking: they are such things as "the Motion of the Heart, and peristaltic Motion of the Bowels" (p. iv). Voluntary motions for Hartley arise from ideas and affections, they are referred to mind. Here he cites "the Actions of Walking, Handling, Speaking, etc.," adding the important qualification: "when attended to, and performed with an express Design."

Hartley was interested in the correspondence of changes in the white substance of the brain and changes in ideas. He remarked that since external objects are corporeal, they "can act upon the Nerves and Brain, which are also corporeal, by nothing but impressing Motion on them" (p. 12). His physiology, as we have seen, made use of the notion of the vibrations of nerve fibres, a notion borrowed from Newton. From Newton also he used the active powers of attraction and repulsion. These powers belong to the small "Particles of the medullary Substance." Jones does not mention Hartley, but he could have used him as another instance of those who followed Newton on attraction and repulsion, as those who were not clear about what those terms referred to. Hartley says that what Newton meant by those terms was "a mere mathematical Tendency to approach and recede, be the Cause what it will, Impulse, Pressure, an unknown one, or no physical Cause at all, but the immediate Agency of the Deity" (p. 20). Hartley even confesses that "we are intirely at a Loss to determine, in what mechanical Way each Atom contributes to the Gravity of the whole Mass," even if we say, as some do, that "this Effect" is "immechanical," arising from the "immediate Agency of God" (p. 33).

Hartley readily admits that the correspondence between motion in nerves and sensation or ideas is such that we can "either make vibrations the Exponent of" sensations and ideas, or take sensations and ideas to be the exponents of the vibrations (p. 33). That is, either the vibrations are the corporeal interpretations of ideas, or the ideas are the mental interpretation of vibrations (pp. 33-34). What his physiology claims is that there is a systematic correlation. Hartley continues to speak of the rational and sensitive souls (p. 81), and he takes some care to say he is not denying the immateriality of the soul. The difficulty of supposing "that the Soul, an immaterial Substance, exerts and receives a real physical Influence upon and from the Body, a material substance," is avoided by Leibniz's pre-established harmony and also by Malebranche's system of occasional causes (p. 111). Similarly, Hartley says his own theory avoids that same difficulty. All he requires is "that there is a Change made in the medullary Substance, proportional and correspondent to every Change in the Sensations." While he does use the phrase, 'the mechanism of the mind', and while the physiological correlates presented in his account are very specific and detailed, and while he recognizes that his system results in the necessity of human action,[4] he insists that his basic correspondence thesis "precludes all Possibility of proving the Materiality of the Soul" (p. 511). Moreover, he points out more than once that he does not suppose "Matter to be endued with Sensation" (pp. 33, 511). He does not want to rule out this possibility, either. In fact, "It does indeed follow from this Theory, that Matter, if it could be endued with the most simple Kinds of Sensation, might also arrive at all that Intelligence of which the human Mind is possessed" (p. 511). Hartley even echoes Locke by saying that "the Immateriality of the Soul has little or no Connection with its Immortality" (p. 512). It was remarks like this one which, in the eyes of many, placed Hartley among the materialists, but his last word on the thinking-matter debate tries to clear his theory of that charge: "I see clearly, and acknowledge readily, that Matter and Motion, however subtly divided, or reasoned upon, yield nothing more than Matter and Motion still" (p. 512).

In his edition of *Hartley's Theory of the Human Mind* (1775), Priestley recognized that correspondence is what Hartley's theory claims, a correspondence between "the affections of the brain" and sensations, a correspondence between "all the varieties of sensations and ideas" and vibrations (p. xii). Priestley assures us there are sufficient differences in vibrations for such correspondences to occur, e.g., difference in degree of vibrations corresponding to strong or weak sounds, differences marked by the place of the vibrations in the brain and by *"its line of direction*, as entering by a particular nerve" (pp. xiii-xiv). Priestley speaks of ideas and sensations existing in the brain and also existing in the mind. He apparently means by the former the corresponding vibrations, the exponent of the ideas and sensations (p. vii). Vibrations accompany ideas, they may even cause ideas, but Priestley is not much concerned in these introductory essays to his edition of Hartley with the causal connection. If a physiological explanation for memory, or for association of ideas can be given in terms of type, place, degree and direction of vibration, the theory will be justified.

Priestley does not always stay with the language of correspondence and explanation. Sometimes he speaks of dependence. "It will stagger some persons, that so much of the business of thinking should be made to depend upon mere *matter*, as the doctrine of vibrations supposes" (p. xix). The "simple power of perception" apparently escapes this dependence, for Priestley goes on to remark that "if it were possible that matter could be endued with this property, *immateriality*, as far as it has been supposed to belong to man, would be excluded altogether." The simple power of perception seems to be awareness, although Priestley does not define that term. As both Locke and Hartley did, so Priestley dissociates immortality from immateriality, but he fails to see why Hartley was reluctant to ascribe perception to matter. As we know, Priestley did make this ascription. He does not think we can say how or why thought "can have any more relation to immateriality than to materiality" (p. xx). His notion of man as "of some *uniform composition*" is found here also. Perception, "as well as the other powers that are termed *mental*, is the result . . . of such an organical structure as that of the brain."

In this presentation of Hartley's theory, there are only a few references to Priestley's new concept of matter. In one passage, he hints at "the more subtle and important laws of matter exhibited in chymical operations," suggesting that, since "the laws and affections of mere matter are infinitely more complex than we had imagined, we may, by this time, I should think, be prepared to admit the *possibility* of a mass of matter like the brain, having been formed by the almighty creator, with such exquisite powers, with respect to vibrations, as should be sufficient for all the purposes above mentioned" (p. xviii). There is also a reference to the notion, found in Boscovich and Rowning, that the particles of bodies, and hence of nerves and brain, are never "in actual contact with each other, but kept at a certain distance from one another, by a repulsive power" (p. xi). Similarly, another passage gives a quick reference to the rejection by Father Boscovich and Mr. Michell of the idea of impenetrability.

Thus, of the two writers in eighteenth-century Britain who were associated with the immaterialist's prophecy of automatism, Hartley and Priestley, neither eliminated the mental. A few writers, Anthony Collins most prominently, anticipated Priestley's predication of thought to the brain; but no one, aside from these few, was able to understand why such an ascription to one substance was not materialism. The issue as it came to be characterized by Collins and Priestley was not over *substances*, but one over *predicates*. Many people still think that if those predicates we designate as 'mental' (e.g., the conscious sensory experiences or the affective ones) do not belong to mind, that these are predicates of the brain, we wrongly characterize the nature of those predicates. Does the *nature* of a predicate depend upon, is it dictated by, the subject to which it belongs? To answer this question, we need to contrast it with another question: 'what is it to *be* a predicate, especially to be a predicate *of* something?', for example, of a body, or of a person. Must all of the predicates of a thing be of the same sort? In suggesting that matter might be made to think, Locke did not suppose that, if that were to happen, the predicates of thought (believing, willing, feeling, sensing, perceiving) would then turn into motion or states of the brain. For Locke it was a question only of the *subject* of the predicates. His point was that, whatever the nature of the subject of the predicates, its nature did not affect or alter the nature of the predicates, although the appearance of the predicates will be in part dependent upon the subject.

The extent to which the predicates *are* dependent upon the subject, or, indeed, whether some predicates are independent of the substance or subject (from its nature) because they are superadded by God, is a question raised by Locke's suggestion. One recent writer, Margaret Wilson, has argued that Locke's talk of superaddition conflicts with his strong claim for a necessary connection between properties and their substance (and for a deductive knowledge of the properties, were our knowledge of the substance adequate or complete). Not only does Locke use this language about thought as a possible property of matter, gravity is presented in the same language. Wilson cites a passage from Locke's second reply to the Bishop of Worcester:

The gravitation of matter towards matter, by ways, inconceivable to me, is not only a demonstration that God can, if he pleases, put into bodies powers and ways of operation, above what can be derived from our idea of body, or can be explained by what we know of matter, but also an unquestionable and every where visible instance, that he has done so.[5]

Wilson's conclusion from this remark is: "I take this pronouncement about gravity to be an indication that the powers of a body are not fully derivable, even in principle, from the primary qualities of its insensible particles." Wilson even extends the role of God in adding properties and powers to bodies to the secondary qualities, basing this extension on Locke's talk of those qualities as "effects produced by the appointment of an infinitely Wise Agent, which perfectly surpasses our Comprehension" (*Essay*, 4.3.28).

The main question raised by Professor Wilson's discussion, the question which preoccupied the immaterialists who attacked Locke's suggestion, is whether superaddition is the imposing of a property which is antithetical to the nature of the substance to which it is added. Michael Ayers is right to stress what he refers to as Locke's agnosticism about our knowledge of the nature of substance.[6] Locke's suggestion was made as an illustration of the limitation of our knowledge. Ayers reminds us of Samuel Bold's remark about Locke's suggestion: "there is no demonstrative proof either that [God] can, or that he cannot superadd a power of thinking to some systems of matter fitly disposed. . . . [For] we cannot possibly . . . comprehend how far his power can extend, nor be certain of the capacity of substance, which is an unknown nature."[7] Ayers points out that just because Locke finds no contradiction in the possibility of thinking matter indicates that there would be, as far as we can determine, no unnatural (or nonnatural) imposition on corporeal substance, should God add thought to matter ("Mechanism," p. 220). The strongest case for saying that Locke's suggestion does not go against nature comes from Ayers's discussion of the traditional account of properties and accidents (pp. 225-28). This account is reflected in Locke's exchange with Stillingfleet, where God is said to create matter without motion, only later deciding to add that attribute. "It is, so Locke thought, contingent that matter should move: its motion is an 'accident'. But what could be less miraculous or contrary to the essence of matter than motion" (p. 229). In the same way, for all we know, God could have decided to add yet another accident to matter, thought.

It is also important to recognize that Locke's suggestion is linked with a *system* of matter *fitly* disposed. An organized system of matter of a certain complexity may acquire properties (or accidents) which a less complex system, or which any of the parts of the complex system, cannot have. Even if the deductive, necessary relation between the nature of a substance and its qualities is not denied by Locke's suggestion, the *nature* of those qualities is not fixed by the substance. We might know (were our knowledge more complete than it is) that thought was a property of the brain, just as we might also know in advance that any body would move, is extended, or of a certain size, but knowing that one of its properties is thought is not to know the nature of thought. Establishing that, for example, anger is a property of the body or of the brain does not establish that anger *is* a bodily occurrence, is motion or states of the brain. Mentality can be a property of physical structures without being identical with those structures, or without having the same nature as other properties of that structure.[8]

Even without an appreciation that a two-substance man is not required in order to preserve a two-predicate distinction, it is a bit surprising that no one picked up on Priestley's force concept of matter, even if his theory was considered materialistic, as a way in which the harsh materialism of inert, passive matter was replaced by a quite different matter. An active, dynamic matter, a world in which the vast amount of 'matter' is centers of force and power (attracting and repelling, but never touching) might have been viewed as less objectionable, might have been seen as a proper subject for a plurality of kinds of predicates. A materialism along these lines need not be opposed to a humanistic conception of man; nor did Priestley, who wrote extensively on religion, believe his system was so opposed. The compatibility of a certain kind of materialism with a nonmechanistic view of man is found in Diderot, a recent commentator (Jean Mayer) has argued. Attacking, as Priestley did also, "partisans of liberty, of final causes, of the two substances," Diderot's account of matter and of man ends in a "wider conception of human destiny."[9] What this commentator finds in Diderot is an account of man far richer in biological and psychological understanding than Priestley's (or than anyone else's in Britain save possibly Hume's). While this richness remains undeveloped in Priestley's writings, its presence in Diderot's writings can serve as a reminder of other possibilities for materialism than those we have found in our study.

When partisans of liberty, limited by religious tradition, conceive of a stable world, where unchangeable species perpetuate themselves, the determinist philosopher displays before our eyes the picture of an evolution always in motion, there he gives life to plastic, adaptable, perishable species. Human personality, even when under the yoke of a causality quite near to ancient *fatum*, appears modifiable, dynamic, capable of unleashing prodigious quantities of energy.[10]

Like Priestley's, Diderot's monism was opposed to the inert, passive matter of many immaterialists. Even when Diderot compared man to "a sensitive and living watch, that might have been made by a iatro-mechanist," it is, Mayer remarks, "Diderot who opposes to the sterility of spiritualism in psychology a new vision of personality, precisely because he considers man as a fully organized being, and no longer as a free soul locked in a slave body."[11]

Diderot relied more heavily on physiology and biology: he was up to date with the most recent developments in these areas. The reliance upon biological conceptions of living matter probably accounts for much of the difference between Diderot and any of his British contemporaries. Robert Whytt in Scotland, whose work Diderot knew, provided a more biologically oriented physiology, but he was a staunch supporter of two substances.[12] He talked in terms of the feeling, the consent, and the sympathy of nerves, terms not meant entirely as metaphors. Whytt's physiology does not seem to have been enlisted by either side in the thinking-matter debate in Britain. The fruitful and promising science of man did not emerge from that debate, nor from the useful work of Whytt. The science of man in Britain is found in Hume's *Treatise* and his two *Enquiries*, and before him in Pope's *Essay on Man*. While Diderot's account of human nature had strong roots in physiology and biology, Hume's is firmly planted in psychology, the psychology of his own experiences and introspection on his passions, emotions, and beliefs.

To the question, 'could Priestley's power concept of matter have helped dissipate the immaterialist's fear about thinking matter?', the answer probably lies in saying 'only if that concept had been given an explicit biological application'. Even then it may depend upon the type of biology employed. The issues surrounding the thinking-matter controversy in Britain, especially those issues of mechanism or active principles, are found in Europe during the eighteenth century, and are typified by the debate between Haller, the defender of preformationism, and Caspar Wolff, the proponent of epigenesis. Shirley Roe points out that in Haller, "matter possesses no abilities whatsoever on its own, without these having been designated by God."[13] Haller developed the very important force concept of irritability, a force "inherent in a particular type of matter (animal muscle tissue) that operates automatically under proper conditions of stimulation."[14] Unlike Whytt, "who believed that muscular contraction is based on the soul," Haller believed "that irritability is a force of matter not based on the soul or any other immaterial force, yet he was also concerned to show that matter could not on its own possess the power of irritability."[15]

Irritability operates mechanically: "Living organisms thus may possess forces that are not found in non-living matter; yet these forces operate mechanically in exactly the same way as physical forces do."[16] Roe even cites a passage from Haller that shows how close he was to Malebranche on action: "We create no movement: our soul wills that the arm lift itself. But it gives to it neither the force nor the movement; God has put the force in the muscle."[17] Reductive materialism was avoided by Haller's insistence on God's being the source of all the activity of matter, even when He gives to muscle fibres the power of irritability.

In contrast, Caspar Wolff contended that the essence of life "need not be attributed to a soul but can, rather, depend upon an attractive and repulsive force."[18] Wolff was not a materialist, in the sense of one who denied that the soul is an immaterial substance, or believed that all human actions are to be explained (as William Jones insisted) by reference only to the mechanism of the body. His view of living organisms cannot, then, be compared with those of Priestley in these respects. Where some comparison is possible is on Wolff's use of

mechanical principles, with their emphasis on secretion, solidification, attraction, repulsion, and the like. But Wolff's mechanism was not based on passive particles in motion, to which life processes were to be reduced. Rather, Wolff's rationalist view of substance allowed for a more complex sort of mechanism, as such a view had for Leibniz and for Christian Wolff, and thereby opened up avenues of explanation that were closed to so many of Wolff's contemporaries.[19]

It is the attention given to man's body as a living organism, with the appeal to mechanical principles of explanation, that could possibly have led Priestley to employ his new concept of active matter in the articulation of a philosophy of mind that might have shocked his contemporaries less, might have led him towards an account of man closer to that of Diderot. Nevertheless, Priestley's contribution to the thinking-matter controversy is significant, combining as it did the metaphysics of one substance but two predicates, with the new concept of physical matter as centers of force.

The interest in and use of active principles in matter in eighteenth-century Britain undergoes a kind of dialectical change. If Cudworth is correct, the hylozoick's life was nonconscious and nonintentional, without direction. Cudworth's plastic nature (and perhaps Grew's vital force) gets intention into the account by being expressions of God's intentions in the world. Newton's world picture retains God's activity in the world, since attraction is added to matter by God. Subsequent Newtonians were inclined to view attraction and repulsion as natural to matter, part of God's creation, rather than imposed from without. The plan and direction which Cudworth found in the world, and which the appeals to the argument from design invoked, is retained by eighteenth-century writers in the notion that God has planned and is directing the world. God's presence in the world is his acting in the world. Except for those who were tempted by the metaphysic of space and the *sensorium Dei* (where God's presence was explicated in quasi-literalist terms), the further explication took a cognitive form. God's presence is his knowledge of the world. But knowledge could be contemplative only, could be removed from action. The application of these notions to man, especially to the presence of his body to his mind (and of external objects to that mind) drew comparisons between the brain, where the images of objects are present to us, and God's cognitive presence.

The next step was then to link knowing with doing. We are conscious of moving our limbs, of moving about in the world. While most writers confessed ignorance as to how one is able to move his limbs, the immaterialist notion that God is the only genuine cause of motion was easily transferred to man: man as a spiritual being, as an immaterial substance, is also able to initiate motion, is also a genuine causal agent. But in the attempt to understand more about the workings of the body when one moves his arm, many writers were forced to recognize the near-autonomy of physiology. For those writers who accepted the view that we do move our bodies and our limbs when we want to do so, their accounts of how we move our bodies could go no further than to say we are able to interfere with our physiology. The interference occurs in areas of the brain which then activate the physiological processes of the body. In willing and acting, by taking thought I cause the spirits to move in specific ways or the aether to vibrate in specific nerves and muscles. The interference with our physiology ceases at that point: from then on, the mechanism of the body works the nerves and muscles. The contact between mind and body is thus very tenuous and brief.

One way in which the physiological mechanism of the body was made less objectionable was by thinking of the animal spirits as less material than the nerves and muscles. These spirits interact with the grosser matter of the body. They were corporeal but fine and rarefied. Moreover, while the anatomical features of nerves and muscles made the connectors with the body seem like strings of a puppet, the language used in talking about the animal spirits, in describing their action, was frequently intentional and purposeful: they seek ideas or impressions, they rummage in cells, they try to find old pathways, in much the way you or I sort through the papers on our desks to find some old notes. Newton's 'subtle aether' was also less material than hard corpuscles. Nevertheless, these physiological components were still material and the model for interaction between the mental and the material was causal.

One other way of avoiding the problems raised by the difference between mental and physical is to take Priestley's alternative. In holding that matter itself has sensibility or irritability, or that particles of nerve fibres are little centers of force, the difference is reduced. The immaterializing of matter, as Priestley thought of his account, not only involved the change from hard particles to centers of force; it carried as well the ascription to that force-matter of the property of thought. The source of genuine causality became a property of matter itself. Immaterialism had, one might be tempted to say, become a materialism, albeit an altered form of materialism. The plastic nature of Cudworth which was conscious but not expressly so, was replaced by thought itself. If matter is mind-like, and if thought and volitions are properties of that kind of matter, then physical and mental properties already belong to the same substance. *Interaction* is no longer needed, it is replaced by *action* of various sorts.

The nature of the causal link between mental and physical (whether on Priestley's account or on the more traditional account) was never specified. Perhaps the causal interaction model is misleading. There were a few writers who moved away from the causal model, both in accounts of perception and in the accounts of human action. Just as some writers replaced spatial presence by cognitive presence (and stressed the *significatory* reactions of the perceiver rather than the *causal* reactions),[20] so some writers about human action talked of meaning and significance. Recognition of meaning as the proper category for the mental directs our attention toward more fruitful concerns. Not that the body and its mechanism are not needed for action, but bodily movement and speech, for both spectator and user, are imbued with meaning. It is the knower as cognizer who is the signifier and the perceiver of meaning. If we could understand how physical movements, as well as physical objects, become meaningful, we might be able to give up the talk of causal interactions between mind and matter.

These various strands which kept the debate over the nature of matter and of thought going throughout the eighteenth century were never assimilated into a coherent system, as La Mettrie had managed to do with his *L'Homme Machine*. Nevertheless the debate reveals for us some of the assumptions behind traditional doctrines, some of the tensions created by the challenge to those assumptions, and the tenacity which engrained beliefs have. The debate also provides us a useful supplement to the cognitive theories of writers in the way of ideas, for the concepts of space, place, and extension were invoked by perceptual theories as well as by those metaphysical concerns over mind and body. The debate as well shows us some of the background behind the concerns over human nature, moral responsibility, and the nature of action and agency. The extensive eighteenth-century interests in moral philosophy, especially in liberty and necessity, should be placed within the context of the debate we have examined in this study. The nature of thought and of matter, as well as their connection, turns out to have been basic to most of the topics in science, philosophy, and religion.

Notes

1. Cf. Chambers's *Cyclopaedia*, entry under 'Natural Inclination'. Such an inclination "according to F. *Malebranch*, is the same thing with regard to Minds, that motion is with regard to Bodies; and as all the Varieties in the Material World arise from the several Motions of Bodies, so do all those of the Intellectual World arise from Inclinations and as all Motions are the Results of Impressions immediately communicated by the Finger of the Creator; so all Inclinations are certainly nothing else but continual Impressions of the Will of the Creator, on that of the Creature."

2. The second edition of Dublin, 1763, is the one used in the following discussion.

3. For a good discussion of this group, called the Hutchinsonians (after John Hutchinson's *Moses Principia*, 1724), see Arnold Thackray, *Atoms and Powers*, pp. 244-52.

4. Since voluntary motions are included in his correspondence theory, the necessity of actions may not be antithetical to moral responsibility.

5. "Superadded Properties: the Limits of Mechanism in Locke," in *American Philosophical Quarterly* 16, 1979, p. 148.

6. "Mechanism, Superaddition, and the Proof of God's Existence in Locke's *Essay*," in *The Philosophical Review* XC, 1981, p. 224.

7. The passage from Bold is from his *A Discourse concerning the Immateriality of the Soul* (1705), p. 165.

8. In our time, F. A. Hayek has developed this notion. See his "The Theory of Complex Phenomena," in *The Critical Approach to Science and Philosophy*, ed. by M. Bunge (1964), reprinted in *Studies in Philosophy, Politics and Economics*, F. A. Hayek (1967). Hayek points out that J. S. Mill drew attention to the difference between properties of complex wholes and simple properties. In his *System of Logic* (1843), Mill discusses the difference between the joint effect of causes being "the sum of their separate effects, and the case in which it is heterogeneous to them" (Bk. III, Ch. VI, Sect. 2). Mill cites some properties which stay the same when the subject of those qualities is combined with others. "The weight of a body, for instance, is a property which it retains in all the combinations in which it is placed. The weight of a chemical compound, or of an organized body, is equal to the weights of the elements which compose it." Similarly, "the component parts of a vegetable or animal substance do not lose their mechanical and chemical properties as separate agents, when, by a peculiar mode of juxtaposition, they, as an aggregate whole, acquire physiological or vital properties in addition." The acquisition of physical or vital properties is a function of the combination, they are not properties which the component parts have.

9. Jean Mayer, in his edition of Diderot's *Eléments de physiologie*, 1964, p. lxxvii.

10. Ibid.

11. Ibid., pp. lxxvii-lxxviii.

12. His main work is *An Essay on the Vital and Other Involuntary Motions of Animals* (1763). He also wrote *Physiological Essays* (1755), and *Observations on the Nature, Causes and Cure of Those Disorders Which Have Been Commonly Called Nervous Hypochondriac, or Hysteric* (1765).

13. *Matter, Life, and Generation: Eighteenth-Century Embryology and the Haller-Wolff Debate* (1981), p. 30.

14. Ibid., p. 33.

15. Ibid., p. 35.

16. Ibid., p. 97.

17. Ibid., p. 98. Roe identifies the source of this remark as Haller's *Briefe über einige Einwürfe nochlebender Freygeister wieder die Offenbarung*, vol. 3, p. 148.

18. Ibid., p. 116.

19. Ibid., p. 147.

20. As with so many of the concepts and doctrines in this study, this use of the category of meaning is developed in perception theories in my study, *Perceptual Acquaintance from Descartes to Reid*.

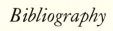

Bibliography

Bibliography

PRIMARY SOURCES

Biographical notes presented under the names of some authors have been supplied chiefly from the *Dictionary of National Biography* or from *Biographia Britannica*.

[Applegarth, Robert.] *A Theological Survey of the Human Understanding; Intended as an Antidote against Modern Deism*. Salisbury: Printed for J. Hodson, 1776. 276 pp.

Arnauld, Antoine. *Des vraies et des fausses idées, contre ce qu'enseigne l'auteur De la recherche de la Verité* [N. Malebranche]. A Cologne: Chez N. Schouten, 1683. 339 pp. Also published in *Oeuvres*. Paris: Chez S. d'Arnay, 1775–83. Vol. 38, pp. 177-362.

Baxter, Andrew (1686–1750). Philosophical writer, born and educated in Aberdeen, maintained himself chiefly by private tutoring.

[——.] *An Enquiry into the Nature of the Human Soul; Wherein the Immateriality of the Soul Is Evinced from the Principles of Reason and Philosophy*. London: Printed for J. Bettenham, [1733?]. 376 pp.

[——.] ——. The Third Edition. London: Printed for A. Millar, 1745. 2 vols.

[——.] *An Appendix to the First Part of the Enquiry into the Nature of the Human Soul, Wherein the Principles Laid down There, Are Cleared from Some Objections; and the Government of the Deity in the Material World is Vindicated, or Shewn not to Be Carried on by Mechanism and Second Causes* . . . London: Printed for the Author, and Sold by A. Millar, 1750. x, 280 pp.

[——.] *Matho: or The Cosmotheoria Puerilis, a Dialogue in which the first Principles of Philosophy and Astronomy are accommodated to the Capacity of young Persons, or such as have yet no Tincture of these Sciences. Hence the Principles of Natural Religion are deduced*. Translated, and enlarged by the Author. The Second Edition. London: Printed for A. Millar, 1745. 2 vols.

Bayle, Pierre. *Dictionnaire historique et critique*. 3d. ed. Rotterdam: Chez M. Bohm, 1720. 4 vols.

Bayle, Pierre. *Réponse aux questions d'un provincial*. A Rotterdam: Chez R. Leers, 1704. 2 vols.

——. *Oeuvres diverses*. A la Haye: Chez P. Husson [et al.], 1727. 4 vols.

Bentley, Richard. *Matter and Motion Cannot Think: or, A Confutation of Atheism from the Faculties of the Soul*. A Sermon preached at St. Mary-le-Bow, April 4, 1692. Being the Second of the Lectures Founded by the Honourable Robert Boyle, Esquire. London: Printed for T. Parkhurst and H. Mortlock, 1692. 39 pp.

[——.] *Remarks upon a Late Discourse of Free-Thinking* [by Anthony Collins]; in a Letter to F.H., D.D. by Phileleutherus Lipsiensis. London: Printed by J. Morphew, 1713. 85 pp.

Berington, Joseph (1746–1827). Catholic priest educated at the College of St. Omer, friendly when in Staffordshire with Joseph Priestley; later lived in London, and died in Berkshire.

[——.] *Letters on Materialism and Hartley's Theory of the Human Mind*; Addressed to Dr. Priestley. London: Printed for G. Robinson, 1776. 229 pp.

Berkeley, George. *Works*. Edited by A. A. Luce and T. E. Jessop. Bibliotheca Britannica philosophica. London: Nelson, 1948–57. 9 vols.

——. *An Essay towards a New Theory of Vision*. Dublin: Printed by A. Rhames for J. Pepyat, 1709. xiv, 187 pp.

——. *Philosophical Commentaries*. In Works (1948–57), vol. 1, pp. 7-139.

[——.] *Siris: a Chain of Philosophical Reflexions and Inquiries concerning the Virtues of Tar Water, and Divers Other Subjects connected together and Arising one from another*. By G.L. B. O. C. Dublin: Printed by M. Rhames for R. Gunne, 1744. 261 pp.

——. *A Treatise concerning the Principles of Human Knowledge. Part I. Wherein the Chief Causes of Error and Difficulty in the Sciences, with the Grounds of Scepticism, Atheism and Irreligion, are inquir'd into*. Dublin: Printed by A. Rhames for J. Pepyat, 1710. iii, 214 pp. No more published.

——. ——. *First Printed in the Year 1710. To Which are added Three Dialogues between Hylas and Philonous* . . . London: Printed for J. Tonson, 1734. 355 pp. Facsim. reprint by Scolar Press, 1971.

Bold, Samuel (1649–1737). Nonconformist divine, for many years rector of Steeple on the Isle of Purbeck; defender of Locke's *Reasonableness of Christianity*, later his friend, for whom he recorded "Mr. Locke's Extempore Advice, &c." [concerning reading and study for a gentleman] (Brit. Mus. Sloane MS. 4290, f. 11-14).

[——.] "A Discourse concerning the Immateriality of the Soul." In *A Discourse concerning the Resurrection of the Same Body; With Two Letters concerning the Necessary Immateriality of Created Thinking Substance* . . . London: Printed by S. Holt for A. and J. Churchill, 1705, pp. 95-176.

Bonnet, Charles (1720–93). From Geneva; considered one of the fathers of modern biology; his experimental research and his philosophy exerted great influence upon naturalists in the eighteenth and nineteenth centuries; he corresponded with almost all scientists of his time, despite being deaf when young, asthmatic, and almost completely blind at an early age; known as a remarkable experimentalist and theoretician.

——. *Essai analytique sur les facultés de l'ame*. A Copenhague: Chez C. & A. Philibert, 1760. xxxii, 552 pp.

——. *Essai de psychologie; ou, Considerations sur les operations de l'ame, sur l'Habitude et sur l'education*. A Leyde: Chez E. Luzac, 1754.

Boscovich [i.e. Bošković], Rudjer Josip. *Philosophiae naturalis theoria, redacta ad unicam legem virium in natura existentium*. Viennae Austriae: Apud A. Bernardi, 1754. 16, [22], 322, [2] pp.

——. *A Theory of Natural Philosophy, Put Forward and Explained* . . . Latin-English Edition from the Text of the First Venetian Edition. Published under the Personal Superintendence of the Author in 1763 . . . Chicago: Open Court Publishing Co., 1922. xix, 463 pp. Translation of previous item by James M. Child.

Broughton, John. *Psychologia; or, An Account of the Nature of the Rational Soul. In Two Parts. The First, Being an Essay towards Establishing the Received Doctrine of an Immaterial and . . . Immortal Substance, United to Human Body. The Second, a Vindication of that Doctrine, against a late Book, call'd Second Thoughts, &c.* [by William Coward]. London: Printed by W.B. for T. Bennet, 1703. 19 prelim. leaves, 418, 14 pp.

Browne, Peter (d. 1735). Dublin native, educated at Trinity College, Dublin, later fellow and provost, Bishop of Cork and Ross; attacked Toland and Berkeley; an austere and charitable man, and an impressive preacher.

[——.] *The Procedure, Extent, and Limits of Human Understanding.* London: Printed for W. Innys, 1728. 477 pp.

[Bulkeley, Richard.] *Letters to Dr. Clarke, concerning Liberty and Necessity; from a Gentleman of the University of Cambridge; with the Doctor's Answers to them.* London: Printed in the Year, 1717. In *A Collection of Papers . . . by Samuel Clarke,* q.v., pp. 401-16.

[Butler, Joseph.] *Several Letters to the Reverend Dr. Clarke, from a Gentleman in Glocestershire, Relating to the First Volume of the Foregoing Sermons; with the Dr.'s Answers thereunto.* London: Printed for J. Knapton, 1716. 42 pp. First published at the end of the 4th ed. of Samuel Clarke's *A Demonstration of the Being and Attributes of God* (1716).

Chambers, Ephraim (1680?-1740). F.R.S.; inspired by John Harris's *Lexicon Technicum* to compile a more inclusive work, he was also co-translator of the *Philosophical History and Memoirs* of the Royal Academy of Science at Paris (1742); thought to be a freemason; Diderot's and d'Alembert's *Encyclopédie* was originally conceived as a revision of his Cyclopaedia.

——. *Cyclopaedia; or, An Universal Dictionary of Arts and Sciences . . .* London: Printed for J. and J. Knapton [et al.], 1728. 2 vols.

Cheyne, George. *An Essay on Regimen. Together with Five Discourses, Medical, Moral, and Philosophical: Serving to Illustrate the Principles and Theories of Philosophical Medicin, and Point out Some of Its Moral Consequences . . .* London: Printed for Rivington [et al.], 1740. [448] pp.

——. *The Natural Method of Cureing the Diseases of the Body, and the Disorders of the Mind Depending on the Body. In Three Parts. Part I. General Reflections on the Oeconomy of Nature in Animal Life. Part II. The Means and Methods for Preserving Life and Faculties; and also concerning the Nature and Cure of Acute, Contagious, and Cephalic Disorders. Part III. Reflections on the Nature and Cure of Particular Distempers . . .* London: Printed for G. Strahan and J. and P. Knapton, 1742. 10 prelim. leaves, 316 pp.

——. *Philosophical Principles of Religion; Containing the Elements of Natural Philosophy, and the Proof for Natural Religion Arising from Them . . .* London: Printed for G. Strahan, 1705. 282, 68 pp.

——. ——. *In Two Parts. Part I. Containing the Elements of Natural Philosophy, and the Proofs of Natural Religion Arising from Them. The Second Edition, Corrected and Enlarged. Part II. Containing the Nature and Kinds of Infinities, Their Arithmetick and Uses; together with the Philosophick Principles of Reveal'd Religion.* London: Printed for G. Strahan [et al.], 1715. 2 vols. in 1.

Clarke, John (1682-1757). The younger brother of Samuel Clarke and Dean of Salisbury; was educated at Cambridge (Gonville and Caius College) and spent most of his life there. He translated into English Grotius's *De Veritate* and Rohault's *Traité de physique* from his brother's Latin translation.

[——.] *A Defence of Dr. Clarke's Demonstration of the Being and Attributes of God. Wherein is Particularly Consider'd the Nature of Space, Duration, and Necessary Existence. Being an Answer to a late Book entitul'd, A Translation of Dr. King's* Origin of Evil, *and Some Other Objections. Together with a Compendium of a Demonstration of the Being and Attributes of God.* London: Printed for J. and J. Knapton, 1732. iv, 163 pp.

Clarke, John (1687–1734). Classical scholar, educated at St. John's College, Cambridge, later Master of the grammar school at Hull; he also wrote about Samuel Clarke on moral obligation.

——. *An Examination of the Notion of Moral Good and Evil, Advanced in a late Book, Entitled, The Religion of Nature Delineated* [by William Wollaston]. London: Printed for A. Bettesworth, 1725. 63 pp.

Clarke, Samuel. *A Collection of Papers, Which Passed between the Late Learned Mr. Leibnitz and Dr. Clarke, in the Years 1715 and 1716; Relating to the Principles of Natural Philosophy and Religion. With an Appendix. To which are added, Letters to Dr. Clarke concerning Liberty and Necessity, from a Gentleman of the University of Cambridge* [Richard Bulkeley]: *with the Doctor's Answers to Them. Also, Remarks upon a Book, Entituled, A Philosophical Enquiry concerning Human Liberty* [by Anthony Collins] . . . London: Printed for J. Knapton, 1717. xiii, 416, 46 pp. French and English texts are on facing pages of the correspondence (pp. 2-399); Bulkeley's work occupies pp. 401-16; and the "Remarks" on Collins's work are given on the 46 pp. at the end.

——. *A Demonstration of the Being and Attributes of God; More Particularly in Answer to Mr. Hobbs, Spinoza, and Their Followers. Wherein the Notion of Liberty is Stated, and the Possibility and Certainty of It Proved, in Opposition to Necessity and Fate. Being the Substance of Eight Sermons Preach'd at the Cathedral-Church of St. Paul, in the Year 1704, at the Lecture Founded by Robert Boyle.* London: Printed for J. Knapton, 1705. 8 prelim. leaves, 264 pp.

——. *A Letter to Mr. Dodwell; Wherein All the Arguments in His Epistolary Discourse against the Immortality of the Soul are Particularly Answered, and the Judgment of the Fathers concerning That Matter Truly Represented* . . . London: Printed for J. Knapton, 1706. 103 pp.

——. ——. *The Sixth Edition. In this Edition are inserted The Remarks on Dr. Clarke's Letter to Mr. Dodwell, and the several Replies to the Doctor's Defences thereof.* London: Printed for J. and J. Knapton, 1731. 475 pp. Includes, as issued, with separate title pages: (1) A Letter to the Learned Mr. Henry Dodwell; Containing Some Remarks on a (pretended) Demonstration of the Immateriality and Natural Immortality of the Soul, in Mr. Clarke's Answer to his late Epistolary Discourse, &c. [by Anthony Collins] (pp. 71-81). First published 1707.
(2) A Defence of an Argument Made use of in a Letter to Mr. Dodwell, To prove the Immateriality and Natural Immortality of the Soul. By Samuel Clarke (pp. 83-103). First published 1707.
(3) A Reply to Mr. Clarke's Defence of his Letter to Mr. Dodwell: With a Postscript relating to Mr. Milles's Answer to Mr. Dodwell's Epistolary Discourse . . . [by Anthony Collins] (pp. 105-44). First published 1707.
(4) A Second Defence of an Argument Made use of in a Letter to Mr. Dodwell, to prove the Immateriality and Natural Immortality of the Soul. In a Letter to the Author of *A Reply to Mr. Clarke's Defence*, &c. By Samuel Clarke (pp. 145-86). First published 1707.
(5) Reflections on Mr. Clarke's Second Defence of his Letter to Mr. Dodwell . . . [by Anthony Collins] (pp. 187-239). First published 1707.
(6) A Third Defence of an Argument made use of in a Letter to Mr. Dodwel, to prove . . . By Samuel Clarke (pp. 241-311). First published 1708.
(7) An Answer to Mr. Clarke's Third Defence of His Letter to Mr. Dodwell . . . [by Anthony Collins] (pp. 313-90). First published 1708.

(8) A Fourth Defence of an Arguement made use of in a Letter to Mr. Dodwell, to prove . . . With a Postscript, relating to a Book, entitled, A Vindication of Mr. Dodwell's Epistolary Discourse, &c. . . . By Samuel Clarke . . . (pp. 391-450). First published 1708.

(9) Some Reflections on that Part of a Book called Amyntor, or The Defence of Milton's Life [by John Toland] which relates to the Writings of the Primitive Fathers and the Canon of the New Testament, In a Letter to a Friend. [By Samuel Clarke] (pp. 451-75). First published 1699.

——. *Remarks upon a Book Entituled, A Philosophical Enquiry concerning Human Liberty* [by Anthony Collins]. London: Printed for J. Knapton, 1717. 46 pp. With, as issued: Clarke, Samuel: A Collection of Papers (*q.v.*)

Clayton, Robert (1695-1758). Irish bishop, educated at Trinity College, Dublin; became a friend of Samuel Clarke; though many of his writings deal with religious topics, he also had antiquarian interests.

[——.] *An Essay on Spirit.* Dublin: Printed by S. Powell, 1750. lxv, 171 pp.

[Cockburn, Catharine (nee Trotter).] "Some Cursory Thoughts on the Controversies concerning necessary Existence, the Reality and Infinity of Space, the Extension and Place of Spirits, and on Dr. Watts's Notion of Substance." In *The History of the Works of the Learned*, for August 1743; Article V, pp. 79-101. The article, to which this is prefixed, is headed "Remarks on some Writers in the Controversy concerning the Foundation of Moral Virtue and Moral Obligation; particularly the Translator of Archbishop King's Origin of Evil, and the Author of the Divine Legation of Moses." (pp. 102-62)

Colliber, Samuel (fl. 1718-37). Known chiefly for *Columna Rostrata*, a history of the seventeenth-century Dutch naval wars, and the three tracts listed below.

[——.] *Free Thoughts concerning Souls: In Four Essays. I. Of the Humane Soul consider'd in its own Nature. II. Of the Human Soul compared with the Souls of Brutes. III. Of the supposed Prae-existent State of Souls. To which is added, An Essay on Creation . . . By the Author of the Impartial Inquiry, &c.* London: Printed for R. Robinson, 1734. xiii, 168 pp.

——. *An Impartial Enquiry into the Existence and Nature of God: Being a Modest Essay towards a More Intelligible Account of the Divine Perfections. With Remarks on Several Authors, Both Ancient and Modern; and Particularly on Some Passages in Dr. Clarke's Demonstration of the Being and Attributes of God . . . With an Appendix concerning the Nature of Space and Duration.* By S.C. London: Printed, and Sold by the Booksellers, 1718. 230 pp. Pages 212-30 contain "Two Discourses concerning the Nature of Space and Duration."

——. *The Known God; or, The Author of Nature Revealed. Being an Explanation and Vindication of What Seems Most Exceptionable in The Impartial Enquiry into the Existence and Nature of God, The Christian Religion Founded on Reason, and Free Thoughts concerning Souls. With Remarks on . . . Mr. Jackson's Defence of his Vindication of Dr. Clarke's Demonstration of the Being and Attributes of God; As Far as it regards the Absolute Infinity of the Divine Nature.* London: Printed for R. Robinson, 1737. v, 74 pp.

[Collins, Anthony.] *A Discourse of Free-Thinking, Occasion'd by the Rise and Growth of a Sect call'd Free-Thinkers.* London, 1713. vi, 178 pp.

[——.] *A Philosophical Enquiry concerning Human Liberty.* London: Printed for R. Robinson, 1717. vi, 115 pp.

[——.] *A Letter to the Learned Mr. Henry Dodwell* . . .
Included in Samuel Clarke's A Letter to Mr. Dodwell . . . 6th ed. (1731) as first item (pp. 71-81), *q.v.*

[——.] *A Reply to Mr. Clarke's Defence of His Letter to Mr. Dodwell* . . .
Ibid. as third item (pp. 105-44).

[——.] *Reflections on Mr. Clarke's Second Defence* . . .
Ibid. as fifth item (pp. 187-239).

[——.] *An Answer to Mr. Clarke's Third Defence* . . . Ibid. as seventh item (pp. 313-90).

[Coward, William.] *The Grand Essay: Or, A Vindication of Reason, and Religion, Against Impostures of Philosophy. Proving according to those Ideas and Conceptions of Things Human Understanding is capable of forming to it self. I. That the Existence of any* Immaterial Substance *is a Philosophic Imposture, and impossible to be conceived. 2. That all Matter has Originally created in it, a principle of Internal, or Self-Motion. 3. That Matter & Motion* must *be the Foundation of* Thought *in Men and Brutes. To which is Added, A Brief Answer to Mr. Broughton's Psycholo. &c.* By W. C., M.D., C.M., L.C. London: Printed for P.G. and Sold by J. Chantry, 1704. vi, 197, 177-248 pp.

Cowper, William. *Myotomia reformata: Or, A New Administration of All the Muscles of Human Bodies; Wherein the True Uses of the Muscles Are Explained, the Errors of Former anatomists concerning Them Confuted, and Several Muscles Not Hitherto Taken Notice of Described; to which are subjoin'd, A Graphical Description of the Bones; and Other Anatomical Observations. Illustrated with Figures after the Life*. London: Printed for S. Smith and B. Walford, 1694. 12 prelim. leaves, 280 pp.

——. ——. *To which is Prefix'd, An Introduction concerning Muscular Motion*. London: Printed for R. Knaplock [et al.], 1724. lxxvii, 194 pp. Pemberton is alleged to have written the introduction and assisted Mead in editing this edition.

Cudworth, Ralph. *The True Intellectual System of the Universe: The First Part; Wherein, All the Reason and Philosophy of Atheism Is Confuted; and Its Impossibility Demonstrated* . . . London: Printed for R. Royston, 1678. [19], 899, [83] pp. No more published.

——. ——. *The Second Edition, in which are now first added References to the Several Quotations in the Intellectual System; and an Account of the Life and Writings of the Author: by Thomas Birch*. London: Printed for J. Walthoe [et al.], 1743. 2 vols.

——. *Systema intellectuale huius universa* . . . *Ioannes Laurentius Moshemius reliqua omnia ex anglico latine vertit, recensuit, variisque observationibus et dissertationibus illustravit et auxit*. Ienae: Sumtu viduae Mayer, 1733. 2 vols.

——. ——. *Editio secunda ex autographo Moshemiano emendatior & auctior*. Lugduni Batavorum: Apud S. et J. Luchtmans, 1733. 2 vols.

Cumberland, Richard. *De Legibus Naturae Disquisitio Philosophica, in qua Earum Forma, Summa Capita, Ordo, Promulgatio & Obligatio è Rerum Naturae Investigantur; Quinetiam Elementa Philosophiae Hobbianae cùm Moralis tum Civilis Considerantur & Refutantur*. Londini: Typis E. Flesher, prostat verò apud N. Hooke, 1672. 32 prelim. leaves, 421 pp.

——. *A Treatise on the Laws of Nature. Made English from the Latin by John Maxwell* . . . *To which is prefix'd, An introduction concerning the Mistaken Notions Which the Heathens had of the Deity, and the Defects in their Morality, Whence the Usefulness of Revelation may appear. At the end is subjoin'd, An Appendix, containing two Discourses, I. Concerning the Immateriality of Thinking Substance. 2. Concerning the Obligation, Promulgation, and Observance, of the Law of Nature, by the Translator*. London: Printed by R. Phillips, and Sold by J. Knapton [et al. Pref. 1727]. 13 prelim. leaves, clxviii, 377, 167, [24], xxviii pp.

Derham, William (1657–1735). Graduate of Trinity College, Oxford, vicar of Wargrave, fellow of the Royal Society, chaplain under George I to the Prince of Wales (later, George II) and later canon of Windsor.

——. *Physico-theology; Or, A Demonstration of the Being and Attributes of God, from His Works of Creation. Being the Substance of XVI Sermons* . . . *at the Honble. Mr. Boyle's Lectures, in the Year 1711 and 1712*. London: Printed for W. Innys, 1713. 483 pp.

Descartes, René. *Oeuvres de Descartes, publiées par Charles Adam & Paul Tannery, sous les auspices du Ministère de l'instruction publique*. Paris: L. Cerf, 1897–1910. 12 vols.

——. *Oeuvres philosophiques*. Textes établis, présentés et annotés par Ferdinand Alquié. Paris: Garnier Frères, 1963-73. 3 vols.

——. *The Philosophical Works*. Rendered into English by Elizabeth S. Haldane and G. R. T. Ross. Cambridge: University Press, 1911-12. 2 vols.

——. *Philosophical Letters*. Translated and edited by Anthony Kenny. Oxford: Clarendon Press, 1970. xiii, 270 pp.

——. *Les Traitez de l'homme et de la formation du foetus, composez par Mr Descartes & mis au jour depuis sa mort par Mr Clerselier* . . . Paris: Chez C. Angot, 1664. [72], 456 pp.

——. *De homine. Figuris et latinitate donatus a Florentio Schuyl*. Lugduni Batavorum: Apud F. Moyardum & P. Leffen, 1662. 17 prelim. leaves, 122 pp.

——. *Treatise on Man*. French text, with translation and commentary by Thomas Steele Hall. Cambridge: Harvard University Press, 1972. xlviii, 115; facsim.: 107; 227-32 pp. Facsimile is of first French edition.

——. *Les passions de l'ame*. A Paris: Chez H. LeGras, 1649. 24 prelim. leaves, 286 pp.

——. "Regulae ad directionem ingenii." In *Opuscula posthuma physica et mathematica* (Amstelodami: Apud Janssonio-Waesbergios, 1701. 6 parts in one vol.), part IV.

Diderot, Denis. *Eléments de physiologie*. Edition critique, avec une introduction et des notes, par Jean Mayer. Paris: M. Didier, 1964. lxxxi, 387 pp.

[Dilly, A.] *Traitté de l'ame et de la connoissance des bêtes, ou après avoir demontré la spiritualité de l'ame de l'homme, l'on explique par la seule machine, les actions les plus surprenantes des animaux, suivant les principes de Descartes*. Par. A. D****. A Amsterdam: Chez G. Gallet, 1691, 276 pp.

Ditton, Humphrey (1675-1715). Mathematician and dissenting preacher, offered a method for determining longitude to Newton, Clarke, and Cotes.

——. *A Discourse concerning the Resurrection of Jesus Christ. In Three Parts. Wherein, I. The Consequences of the Doctrine are Fully Stated. II. The Nature and Obligation of Moral Evidence, are explain'd at large. III. The Proofs of the Facts of our Saviour's Resurrection are Propos'd, Examin'd, and Fairly Demonstrated, to be Conclusive. Together with an Appendix containing the Impossible Production of Thought, from Matter and Motion: the Nature of Humane Souls, and of Brutes: the Anima Mundi, and the Hypothesis of the Tò πᾶν; as also, concerning Divine Providence, the Origin of Evil, and the Universe in General*. London: Printed by J. Darby, and Sold by A. Bell, 1712. xvi, 568 pp.

——. *The New Law of Fluids: Or, A Discourse concerning the Ascent of Liquors, in Exact Geometrical Figures between Two Nearly Contiguous Surfaces. To which is added, The True State of the Case about Matter's Thinking*. London: Printed by J. Roberts for B. Cowse, 1714. 2 parts in one vol. Part 2 has a separate title: Matter Not a Cogitative Substance: Or, The True State of the Case about Matter's Thinking . . . [ibid.] 1713.

Doddridge, Philip (1702-51). Nonconformist divine; aided, as a student, by Samuel Clarke and Edmund Calamy; voluminous religious writer.

——. *A Course of Lectures on the Principal Subjects in Pneumatology, Ethics, and Divinity; with References to the Most Considerable Authors on Each Subject*. London: Printed by Assignment from the Author's Widow, for J. Buckland [et al.], 1763. 10 prelim. leaves, 595 pp.

Edwards, John. *Some Thoughts concerning the Several Causes and Occasions of Atheism, Especially in the Present Age. With Some Brief Reflections on Socinianism; and on a Late Book, entituled The Reasonableness of Christianity, As Deliver'd in the Scriptures [by John Locke]* London: Printed for J. Robinson and J. Wyat, 1695. 4 prelim. leaves, 134, 119-26 pp.

An Enquiry into the Nature of the Human Soul, Its Origin, Properties, and Faculties; Considered Both in Regard to Itself, and Its Union with the Body. In Which Several Received Opinions Are Confuted concerning Both. London: Printed for E. Owen, 1750. 65 pp.

An Enquiry into the Origin of the Human Appetites and Affections, Shewing How Each Arises from Association. With an Account of the Entrance of Moral Evil into the World. To which are added, Some Remarks on the Independent Scheme Which Deduces All Obligation on God's Part and Mans from Certain Abstract Relations, Truth, &c. Written for the Use of the Young Gentlemen at the Universities. London: Printed for R. Dodsley, 1747. 194 pp. Attributed variously to James Long, also to – – – – Barr (Halkett & Laing); more recently to David Hartley (see Stephen Ferg, infra.).

An Essay towards Demonstrating the Immateriality and Free-Agency of the Soul, in Answer to Two Pamphlets: one intitled, A Philosophical Enquiry into the Physical Spring of Human Actions, &c., Supposed to Have Been Wrote by Mr. Samuel Strutt; and the Other, Intitled, A Philosophical Enquiry concerning Human Liberty, Supposed to Have Been Wrote by Anthony Collins, Esq. London: Printed for J. Shuckburgh, 1760. xvi, 136 pp. Incorrectly attributed in library catalogues to Samuel Clarke.

Flemyng, Malcolm (d. 1764). M.D., Scottish physiologist, correspondent of Haller; eventually practised medicine in Lincoln.

——. *The Nature of the Nervous Fluid; Or, Animal Spirits Demonstrated; with an Introductory Preface.* London: Printed for A. Millar, 1751. xxiii, 40 pp.

[——.] *A New Critical Examination of an Important Passage in Mr. Locke's Essay on Human Understanding. In a Familiar Letter to a Friend. To which is added, An Extract from the Fifth Book of Anti-Lucretius, concerning the Same Subject; with a Translation in Prose.* London: Printed for J. Robinson, 1751. 57 pp.

Gassendi, Pierre. "The Fifth Set of Objections; Letter from P. Gassendi to M. Descartes." In Descartes's *Philosophical Works* . . . (1911-12), vol. II, pp. 135-203.

Gerdil, Giacinto Sigismond. The most famous Malebranchian in the eighteenth century, became a cardinal in 1777, and at the death of Pius VI, would have succeeded him as pope if not for Austrian opposition to someone from Savoy.

——. *Defense du Sentiment du P. Malebranche sur la nature & l'origine des idées, contre l'examen de M. Locke* . . . A Turin: De l'Imprimerie royale, 1748. 8 prelim. leaves, xxxix, 246 pp., 10 leaves.

——. *L'Immaterialité de l'ame demontrée contre M. Locke, par les mêmes Principes, par lesquels ce Philosophe démontre l'Existence & l'Immaterialité de Dieu, avec des nouvelles preuves de l'Immaterialité de Dieu, et de l'ame, Tirées de l'Ecriture des Peres & de la raison, par le P. Gerdil Barnabite* . . . A Turin: De l'Imprimerie royale, 1747. 11 prelim. leaves, 283 pp.

Gifford, Richard (1725-1807). Balliol student and miscellaneous writer.

——. *Outlines of an Answer to Dr. Priestley's Disquisitions relating to Matter and Spirit.* London: Printed for T. Cadell, 1781. viii, 128 pp.

Greene, Robert (1678?-1730). Physicist, educated at Clare Hall, Cambridge, of which he became a fellow; his "self-esteem was by all accounts entirely out of proportion to his due."

——. *The Principles of Natural Philosophy. In Which is Shewn the Insufficiency of the Present Systems, To Give Us Any Just Account of That Science; and the Necessity There Is of Some New Principles, in Order to Furnish us with a True and Real Knowledge of Nature.* Cambridge: Printed at the University Press, for E. Jeffery [etc.], 1712. [67], 391 pp.

——. *The Principles of the Philosophy of the Expansive and Contractive Forces; Or, An Inquiry into the Principles of the Modern Philosophy, that is, into the Several Chief Rational Sciences, which are Extant.* In Seven Books. Cambridge: Printed at the University Press, by C. Crownfield, and are to be sold by him [et al.], 1727. 981 pp.

Grew, Nehemiah. *Cosmologia Sacra: Or, A Discourse of the Universe, As It is the Creature and Kingdom of God. Chiefly Written, To Demonstrate the Truth and Excellency of the Bible; Which contains the Laws of His Kingdom in this Lower World.* In Five Books . . . London: Printed for W. Rogers [et al.], 1701. 7 prelim. leaves, xviii, 372 pp.

Haller, Albrecht von. *Briefe über einige Einwürfe nochlebender Freygeister wieder die Offenbarung* . . . Bern: Bey der Typographischen Gesellschaft, 1778. 3 vols. in one.

Hampton, Benjamin, of the Middle Temple. *The Existence of the Human Soul after Death Proved from Scripture, Reason, and Philosophy. Wherein Mr Lock's Notion that Understanding May Be Given to Matter, Mr Hobbs's Assertion That There Is no Such Thing as an Immaterial Substance . . . Dr Coward's Books of Second and Further Thoughts . . . are . . . confuted . . . With an Appendix, Shewing That the Above Mentioned Principles Are the Occasion of Civil Wars* . . . London: Printed for S. Popping, 1711. ii, 44 pp.

[Harris, James.] *Hermes; Or, A Philosophical Inquiry concerning Language and Universal Grammar* . . . By J.H. London: Printed by H. Woodfall for J. Nourse [et al.], 1751. xix, 426 pp.

[——.] *Philosophical Arrangements*. London: Printed for J. Nourse, 1775. xiv, 485 pp.

Hartley, David. *Observations on Man, His Frame, His Duty, and His Expectations*. In Two Parts. London: Printed by S. Richardson; for J. Leake [et al.], 1749. 2 vols.

——. *Hartley's Theory of the Human Mind, on the Principle of the Association of Ideas; with Essays relating to the Subject of It*. By Joseph Priestley. London: Printed for J. Johnson, 1775. lxii, 372 pp. Contains selections from his *Observations on Man*.

Hume, David. *The Philosophical Works*. Edited by T. H. Green and T. H. Grose. London: Longmans, Green, 1874–75. 4 vols.

——. *Dialogues concerning Natural Religion*. London, 1779. 264 pp.

——. *Enquiries concerning Human Understanding, and concerning the Principles of Morals. Reprinted from the Posthumous Edition of 1777, and Edited with Introduction, Comparative Table of Contents and Analytical Index by L. A. Selby-Bigge*. Third Edition, with Text Revised and Notes by P. H. Nidditch. Oxford: Clarendon Press, 1975. xl, 417 pp.

——. *Essays Moral and Political*. Edinburgh: Printed by R. Fleming and A. Alison, for A. Kincaid, 1741. v, 187 pp.

——. *A Letter from a Gentleman to His Friend in Edinburgh; Containing Some Observations on a Specimen of the Principles concerning Religion and Morality, Said to Be Maintain'd in a Book lately publish'd, Intituled, A Treatise of Human Nature, &c*. Edinburgh, 1745. 34 pp. Facsim. reprint edited by Ernest C. Mossner & John V. Price. Edinburgh: University Press, 1967.

——. *The Letters of David Hume*. Edited by J. Y. T. Greig. Oxford: Clarendon Press, 1932. 2 vols.

——. *Philosophical Essays concerning Human Understanding. By the Author of the Essays Moral and Political*. London: Printed for A. Millar, 1748. lv, 256 pp.

——. *A Treatise of Human Nature; Being an Attempt to Introduce the Experimental Method of Reasoning into Moral Subjects* . . . London: Printed for J. Noon, 1739. 2 vols.

——. ——. *Vol. III, Of Morals. With an Appendix, Wherein Some Passages of the Foregoing Volumes Are Illustrated and Explain'd*. London: Printed for T. Longman, 1740.

Hutchinson, John (1674–1737). Self-taught physicist, later worked under Dr. John Woodward, of Scriblerian fame; deeply influenced Duncan Forbes, Bishop George Horne, and William Jones.

——. *Moses Principia; Of the Invisible Parts of Matter; of Motion; of Visible Forms, and of Their Dissolution, and Reformation. With Notes*. London: Printed by J. Bettenham, 1724. 100 pp.

Jackson, John (1686–1763). Divine and pamphleteer, educated at Jesus College, Cambridge; known as a defender of Samuel Clarke.

——. *A Defense of Human Liberty; In Answer to the Principal Arguments Which Have Been Alleged against It; and Particularly to Cato's Letters on That Subject. In Which Defense the Opinion of the Antients, concerning Fate, Is Also Distinctly and Largely considered*. London: Printed for J. Noon, 1725. 207 pp.

——. ——. The Second Edition. To which is added, *A Vindication of Human Liberty; in Answer to a Dissertation on Liberty and Necessity Written by A. C., Esq.* [Anthony Collins]. London: Printed for J. Noon, 1730. 207, viii, 63 pp.

——. *A Dissertation on Matter and Spirit. With Some Remarks on a Book, Entitled, An Enquiry into the Nature of the Humane Soul* [by Andrew Baxter]. London: Printed for J. Noon, 1735. viii, 56 pp.

Jenkin, Robert (1656–1727). D.D., Master of St. John's College, Cambridge, which post he lost when he refused to take the oath of allegiance to William III.

——. *The Reasonableness and Certainty of the Christian Religion.* London, 1696–97. 2 vols.

Jones, William (1726–1800). Divine, physicist, educated at University College, Oxford; Fellow of the Royal Society from 1775; known as an influential high churchman late in the century.

——. *An Essay on the First Principles of Natural Philosophy: Wherein the Use of Natural Means, or Second Causes in the Œconomy of the Material World, Is Demonstrated from Reason, Experiments of Various Kinds, and the Testimony of Antiquity. In Four Books* . . . London, 1762. 277 pp. Reprint edition, Oxford: Printed, and Dublin Re-printed for W. Watson, 1763. 277 pp.

Keble, Joseph (1632–1710). Barrister and essayist, fellow of All Souls College, Oxford; known for his law reports.

——. *An Essay of Human Actions.* London: Printed for S. Keble, 1710. 55 pp.

Keill, James. *The Anatomy of the Humane Body Abridg'd: Or, A Short and Full View of All the Parts of the Body. Together with their Several Uses, Drawn from Their Compositions and Structures.* London: Printed for W. Keblewhite, 1698. 12 prelim. leaves, 328 pp., 3 leaves.

King, William. *De origine mali.* Authore Guilielmo King. Dublinii: A. Crook, 1702. 2 prelim. leaves, 214 pp., 13 leaves.

——. *An Essay concerning the Origin of Evil. Translated from the Latin, with large Notes; Tending to Explain and Vindicate Some of the Author's Principles against the Objections of Bayle, Leibnitz, the Author of a Philosophical Enquiry concerning Human Liberty* [i.e. Anthony Collins]; *and Others. To which is prefix'd, A Dissertation concerning the Fundamental Principle and Immediate Criterion of Virtue. As also, The Obligation to and Approbation of it. With Some Account of the Origin of the Passions and Affections.* London: Printed for W. Thurlbourn, Bookseller in Cambridge; and Sold by R. Knaplock [et al.], London, 1731. lvi, 330 pp. The "Dissertation" is by John Gay; the translation and notes by Edmund Law.

Knight, Gowin. *An Attempt to Demonstrate That All the Phaenomena in Nature May be Explained by Two Simple Active Principles, Attraction and Repulsion: Wherein the Attractions of Cohesion, Gravity, and Magnetism, are Shewn to be One and the Same; and the Phaenomena of the Latter are More Particularly Explained.* London, 1748. 95 pp.

[La Mettrie, Julien Offray de.] *L'homme-machine.* Leyde: De l'imprimerie d'E. Luzac fils, 1748. 10 prelim. leaves, 109 pp.

——. *L'Homme Machine: a Study in the Origins of an Idea.* Critical Edition, with an Introductory Monograph and Notes by Aram Vartanian. Princeton: Princeton University Press, 1960. 264 pp.

Langrish, Browne (d. 1759). M.D., educated as a surgeon, licentiate of the College of Physicians, and in 1734 elected Fellow of the Royal Society.

——. *The Croonian Lectures on Muscular Motion* . . . Read before the Royal Society in the year MDCCXLVII. Being a Supplement to the Philosophical Transactions for That Year. London: Printed for R. Davis, 1747.

——. *A New Essay on Muscular Motion. Founded on Experiments, Observations, and the Newtonian Philosophy.* London, 1733. 103 pp.

La Ramée, Pierre de, *see* Ramus, Peter

Law, Edmund (1703-87). Bishop of Carlisle; educated at St. John's College, later fellow of Christ College, both in Cambridge, where he became friends with Waterland, Jortin and Dr. John Taylor; favored religious toleration; edited the 1777 edition of Locke's *Works*.

——. *An Enquiry into the Ideas of Space, Time, Immensity, and Eternity; as also the Self-Existence, Necessary Existence, and Unity of the Divine Nature. In Answer to a Book lately publish'd, by Mr. Jackson, entitled, The Existence and Unity of God Proved from His Nature and Attributes . . . To which is added, A Dissertation upon the Argument A Priori for Proving the Existence of a First Cause, By a Learned Hand* [i.e. Daniel Waterland]. Cambridge: Printed for W. Thurlbourn, 1734. 196, 98 pp.

Layton, Henry (1632-1705). Voluminous theological writer; with the exception of *Arguments and Replies*, all his works are undated and were issued without a title page; all were published anonymously.

[——.] *Arguments and Replies, in a Dispute concerning the Nature of the Humane Soul. Viz. Whether the Same Be Immaterial, Separately Subsisting and Intelligent: Or Be Material, Unintelligent and Extinguishable at the Death of the Person*. London, 1703. 112 pp.

[——.] *Observations upon Dr. Nicholl's Book, Intituled, A Conference with a Theist, Being a Proof of the Immortality of the Soul*. [1703.] 124 pp.

[——.] *Observations upon a Sermon, Intituled, A Confutation of Atheism from the Faculties of the Soul; aliàs, Matter and Motion Cannot Think, Preached April 4, 1692* [by Richard Bentley]. *By Way of Refutation*. [1692.] 19 pp.

[——.] *Observations upon a Short Treatise, Written by Mr. Timothy Manlove: Intituled, The Immortality of the Soul Asserted, and Printed . . . at London, 1697.* [1697.] 115 pp.

[——.] *Observations upon a Treatise, intitl'd Psychologia: Or, An Account of the Nature of the Rational Soul* [by John Broughton]. [1703.] 132 pp.

[——.] *A Search after Souls, and Spiritual Operations in Man*. [1693?-94?] 2 vols.

Lee, Henry. *Anti-Scepticism: Or, Notes upon Each Chapter of Mr. Lock's Essay concerning Humane Understanding. With an Explication of All the Particulars of Which He Treats, and in the Same Order. In Four Books*. London: Printed for R. Clavel and C. Harper, 1702. 15 prelim. leaves, 140, 201-342 pp.

Leibniz, Gottfried Wilhelm. *A Collection of Papers*. See under Clarke, Samuel

——. *Essai de theodicée, par la bonté de Dieu, la liberté de l'homme et l'origine du mal*. A Amsterdam: Chez I. Troyel, 1710. 2 vols. in one.

Leng, John (1685-1727). Bishop of Norwich; educated at St. Paul's School, and Catharine Hall, Cambridge; eventually fellow and tutor at the latter.

——. *Natural Obligations to Believe the Principles of Religion, and Divine Revelation; in XVI Sermons, preached in the Church of St. Mary le Bow, London, in the Years 1717 and 1718. At the Lecture Founded by the Honourable Robert Boyle, Esq; . . .* London: Printed for R. Knaplock, 1719. 8 prelim. leaves, 512 pp.

Locke, John. *The Works of John Locke*. A New Edition, Corrected. London: Printed for T. Tegg [et al.], 1823. 10 vols.

——. *The Correspondence of John Locke*. Edited by E. S. De Beer. In Eight Volumes. Oxford: Clarendon Press, 1976-(in progress). The Clarendon Edition of the Works of John Locke.

——. *An Essay concerning Human Understanding*. Edited, with an Introduction, by John W. Yolton. Everyman's Library, 332, 984. London: J. M. Dent, 1961 (revised printing, 1965). 2 vols.

——. *A Letter to the Right Reverend Edward Ld Bishop of Worcester, concerning Some Passages Relating to Mr. Locke's Essay of Humane Understanding; In a Late Discourse of His Lordships, in Vindication of the Trinity*. London: Printed by H. Clark, for A. and J. Churchill, 1697. 227 pp.

Maclaurin, Colin. *An Account of Sir Isaac Newton's Philosophical Discoveries*. In Four Books. Published from the Author's Manuscript Papers, by Patrick Murdoch. London: Printed for the Author's Children; and Sold by A. Millar [et al.], 1748. [8], xxi, [20], 392 pp.

Malebranche, Nicolas. *Oeuvres complètes de Malebranche*. Direction: André Robinet. Paris: J. Vrin, 1958–70. 20 vols. and index. Editors of individual vols. vary, and include Geneviève Rodis-Lewis.

——. *The Search after Truth*. Translated from the French by Thomas M. Lennon and Paul J. Olscamp. *Elucidations of the Search after Truth*. Translated from the French by Thomas M. Lennon. Philosophical Commentary by Thomas M. Lennon. Columbus: Ohio State University Press, 1980. xxxii, 861 pp.

Mandeville, Bernard. *A Treatise of the Hypochondriack and Hysterick Passions vulgarly call'd the Hypo in Men, and Vapours in Women; in which the Symptons, Causes, and Cure of Those Diseases are Set Forth after a Method entirely New* . . . London: Printed and sold by D. Leach, 1711. xxiv, 280 pp.

——. ——. In Three Dialogues. The Third Edition. London: Printed for J. Tonson, 1730. xxii, 380 pp.

Martin, Benjamin (1704–82). Mathematician, instrument maker and general compiler.

——. *The Philosophical Grammar: Being a View of the Present State of Experimental Physiology, or Natural Philosophy* . . . In Four Parts: I. Somatology. II. Cosmology. III. Ærology. IV. Geology . . . London: Printed for J. Noon, 1735. xxx, 322, [13] pp.

[Mayne, Zachary, supposed author.] *Two Dissertations concerning Sense and the Imagination. With an Essay on Consciousness*. London: Printed for J. Tonson, 1728. 4 prelim. leaves, 231 pp.

Mead, Richard. *A Mechanical Account of Poisons; in Several Essays*. London: Printed by R. J. for R. Smith, 1702. 183 pp.

Meikle, James (1730–99). Surgeon and devotional writer; served in the Royal Navy.

——. *Metaphysical Maxims; Or, Thoughts on the Nature of the Soul, Free Will, and the Divine Prescience*. Edinburgh: Printed by G. Caw, 1797. 142 pp.

Melville, Thomas. "Observations on Light and Colours." In *Essays and Observations, Physical and Literary, Read before a Society in Edinburgh*, [i.e. Medical Society of Edinburgh] *January 3 and February 1752*. Vol. 2 (1756), pp. 2-90.

Michell, John (1724–93). B.D., astronomer, educated at Queen's College, Cambridge; member of the Royal Society from 1760; a violinist, he entertained William Herschel, Priestley, and Henry Cavendish.

——. *A Treatise of Artificial Magnets; in which is shewn, An Easy and Expeditious Method of Making Them, Superior to the Best Natural Ones; and, also, a Way of Improving the Natural Ones and of Changing or Converting their Poles. Directions are likewise given for making the Mariner's Needles in the Best Form*. Cambridge: Printed by J. Bentham, and Sold by W. and J. Mount, 1750. 81 pp.

Monboddo, James Burnett, Lord (1714–99). Scottish judge, self-styled Lord Monboddo; educated at Aberdeen; highly interested in science; in many ways anticipated Darwin and Kant.

——. *Antient Metaphysics; Or, The Science of Universals*. Edinburgh: Printed for T. Cadell, London, and J. Balfour, Edinburgh, 1779–99. 6 vols.

——. *Letters to Richard Price*. See Knight, William Angus, infra

Morgan, Thomas (d. 1743). Deist, of Welsh origin; dismissed from the ministry for his unorthodox views, he then studied medicine and took part in the controversy on behalf of the 'free-thinkers'.

——. *Physico-Theology; Or, A Philosophical-Moral Disquisition concerning Human Nature, Free Agency, Moral Government, and Divine Providence*. London: Printed by T. Cox, 1741. vii, 353 pp., 8 leaves.

——. *Philosophical Principles of Medicine, in Three Parts. Containing, I. A Demonstration of the General Laws of Gravity, with Their Effects upon Animal Bodys. II. The More Particular Laws which obtain in the Motion and Secretion of the Vital Fluids, Applied to the Principle Diseases and Irregularitys of the Animal Machine. III. The Primary and Chief Intentions of Medicine in the Cure of Diseases, problematically propos'd and mechanically resolv'd.* London: Printed by J. Darby and T. Browne, and Sold by J. Osborne [et al.], 1725. lviii, 440 pp.

Newton, Isaac. *Opticks; Or, A Treatise of the Reflections, Refractions, Influxions, and Colours of Light. Also, Two Treatises of the Species and Magnitude of Curvilinear Figures.* London: Printed for S. Smith and B. Walford, 1704. 144, 211 pp.

——. ——. The Second Edition, with Additions. London: Printed by W. Bowyer for W. Innys, 1717. 382 pp.

——. ——. Based on the Fourth Edition, London, 1730. With . . . an Introduction by Sir Edmund Whittaker, a Preface by I. Bernard Cohen, and an Analytical Table of Contents Prepared by Duane H. D. Roller. London: G. Bell, 1931. cxxii, 406 pp.

——. *Philosophiae naturalis principia naturalis.* Imprimatur S. Pepys, Reg. Soc. praeses, Julii 5, 1686. Londini: Iussu Societatis Regiae ac Typis J. Streater; Prostat apud Plures Bibliopolas, Anno 1687. 383, 400-510 pp.

——. ——. Editio secunda, auctor et emendatior [à Roger Cotes]. Cantabrigiae: 1703. 13 prelim. leaves, 484 pp., 4 leaves.

——. *The Mathematical Principles of Natural Philosophy.* Translated into English by Andrew Motte. To which are added, *Newton's System of the World; A Short Comment on, and Defence of the Principia, by William Emerson* . . . A New Edition (with a Life of the Author . . .) Carefully Revised and Corrected by William Davis. London: Printed for Sherwood, Neely and Jones [et al.], 1819. 3 vols.

——. *Unpublished Scientific Papers of Isaac Newton;* a Selection from the Portsmouth Collection in the University Library, Cambridge. Chosen, Edited and Translated by A. Rupert Hall and Marie Boas Hall. Cambridge: University Press, 1962. xx, 415 pp.

Norris, John. *An Essay towards the Theory of the Ideal or Intelligible World. Design'd for Two Parts. The First, Considering It Absolutely in it self, and the Second in Relation to the Human Understanding.* London: Printed for S. Manship [et al.], 1701–4. 2 vols.

——. *A Philosophical Discourse concerning the Natural Immortality of the Soul. Wherein the Great Question of the Soul's Immortality Is Endeavour'd to be Rightly Stated, and Fully Clear'd. Occasion'd by Mr. Dodwell's late Epistolary Discourse.* In Two Parts . . . London: Printed for S. Manship, 1708. 127 pp.

Pemberton, Henry. *A View of Sir Isaac Newton's Philosophy.* London: Printed by S. Palmer. 1728. 25 prelim. leaves, 407 pp.

Pope, Alexander. *An Essay on Man.* Edited by Maynard Mack. London: Methuen, 1951. 186 p. The Twickenham Edition of the Poems of Alexander Pope, vol. III, part I.

Porterfield, William. "An Essay concerning the Motions of the Eyes." In *Medical Essays and Observations of the Philosophical Society of Edinburgh;* 2d edition, corrected (1737–38), vol. 3.

——. *A Treatise on the Eye, the Manner and Phaenomena of Vision.* Edinburgh: Printed for A. Millar at London, and for G. Hamilton and J. Balfour at Edinburgh, 1759. 2 vols.

Price, Richard. *A Free Discussion of the Doctrines of Materialism* . . . *See* under Priestley, Joseph

——. *The Nature and Dignity of the Human Soul.* A Sermon Preached at St. Thomas's, January the First, 1766, for the Benefit of the Charity-School in Gravel-Lane, Southwark. London: Printed for A. Millar [et al.], 1766. 29 pp.

Priestley, Joseph. *Disquisitions relating to Matter and Spirit; To which is added, The History of the Philosophical Doctrine concerning the Origin of the Soul, and the Nature of Matter; with its Influence on Christianity, especially with Respect to the Doctrine of the Pre-existence of Christ.* London: Printed for J. Johnson, 1777. xxxix, 356 pp. An appendix, usually considered vol. 2 of this work, is entitled *The Doctrine of Philosophical Necessity.*

——. *The Doctrine of Philosophical Necessity Illustrated; Being an Appendix to the Disquisitions relating to Matter and Spirit. To which is added, An Answer to the Letters on Materialism, and on Hartley's Theory of the Mind.* London: Printed for J. Johnson, 1777. xxxiv, 206 pp.

——. *An Examination of Dr. Reid's Inquiry into the Human Mind, on the Principles of Common Sense; Dr. Beattie's Essay on the Nature and Immutability of Truth; and Dr. Oswald's Appeal to Common Sense in Behalf of Religion.* London: Printed for J. Johnson, 1774. lxi, 371 pp.

——. *A Free Discussion of the Doctrines of Materialism, and Philosophical Necessity, in a Correspondence between Dr. Price and Dr. Priestley. To which are added, by Dr. Priestley, An Introduction, Explaining the Nature of the Controversy, and Letters to Several Writers who have Animadverted on his Disquisitions relating to Matter and Spirit, or his Treatise on Necessity . . .* London: Printed for J. Johnson and T. Cadell, 1778. xliv, 428 pp.

——. *Hartley's Theory of the Human Mind. See* under Hartley, David

——. *The History and Present State of Discoveries relating to Vision, Light, and Colours.* London: Printed for J. Johnson, 1772. v, [6], xvi, 812, [12] pp.

Ramus, Peter. *The Logike of the most excellent philosopher P. Ramus, Martyr. Newly translated, and in diuers places corrected, after the mynde of the Author. Per M. Roll. Makylmenaeum . . .* London: Imprinted by T. Vautroullier, 1574. 101 pp.

Raphson, Joseph. *Demonstratio de Deo; sive, Methodus ad cognitionem Dei naturalem brevis ac demonstrativa. Cui accedunt Epistolae quaedam miscellaneae. De animae natura et immortalitate, De veritate religionis Christianae, De universo, etc.* London, 1710.

Reid, Thomas. *Essays on the Intellectual Powers of Man.* Edinburgh: Printed for J. Bell [et al.], 1785. xii, 766 pp.
Contents: *I. Preliminary. II. Of the Powers we have by means of our external Senses. III. Of Memory. IV. Of Conception. V. Of Abstraction. VI. Of Judgment. VII. Of Reasoning. VIII. Of Taste.*

Reynolds, Edward (1599–1676). Bishop of Norwich, educated at Merton College, Oxford; a Conformist at the Restoration.

——. *A Treatise of the Passions and Faculties of the Soul of Man. With the severall Dignities and Corruptions thereunto belonging.* London: Printed by F.N. for R. Bostock, 1650. 553 pp.

Robinet, Jean Baptiste René. *Vue philosophique de la gradation naturelle des formes de l'etre; ou, Les essais de la nature qui apprend à faire l'homme.* A Amsterdam: Chez E. van Harrevelt, 1768. 260 pp.

Robinson, Bryan (1680–1754). Physician and writer; educated at Trinity College, Dublin; fellow of the College of Physicians in Ireland, and president of the Irish Royal College of Surgeons.

——. *A Treatise of the Animal Œconomy: Viz., Of the Motion of the Fluids thro' the Vessels . . .* Dublin: Printed by G. Grierson for C. Rivington, London, 1732. iv, 283 pp.

Rohault, Jacques. *Rohault's System of Natural Philosophy, Illustrated with Dr. Samuel Clarke's Notes Taken Mostly out of Sir Isaac Newton's Philosophy.* With Additions . . . Done into English by John Clarke. London: Printed for J. Knapton, 1723. 2 vols. Translated from Samuel Clarke's Latin Version (1697) of the author's *Traité de physique* (1671).

Rotheram, John. *An Essay in the Distinction between the Soul and Body of Man*. Newcastle upon Tyne: Printed by T. Saint for J. Robson, 1781. 56 pp.

Rowning, John (1701?-71). Physicist and mathematician, educated at Magdalene College, Cambridge; author of papers in the Philosophical Transactions of the Royal Society.

——. *A Compendious System of Natural Philosophy; with Notes, containing the Mathematical Demonstrations, and some Occasional Remarks*. Cambridge, 1734-38. 3 vols.

——. ——. The Eighth Edition, Corrected, with Additions. London: Printed by J. Rivington for J., F. and C. Rivington, 1779. 2 vols.

Shepherd, Richard (1732?-1809). Versifier and theologian; voluminous writer; educated at Corpus Christi College, Oxford; member of the Royal Society from 1781.

[——.] *Reflections on the Doctrine of Materialism; and the Applications of that Doctrine to the Pre-existence of Christ. With an Appendix, Briefly Stating the Substance of a Correspondence between Dr. Priestley and Dr. Price, on that Subject; as far as that correspondence affects the preceding Reflections*. By Philalethes Rusticans. London, 1779. xx, 256 pp.

Smith, John (1618-52). Fellow of Queen's College, Cambridge, and a Cambridge Platonist.

——. *Select Discourses, Treating, 1. Of the True Way or Method of Attaining to Divine Knowledge. 2. Of Superstition. 3. Of Atheism. 4. Of the Immortality of the Soul. 5. Of the Existence and Nature of God. 6. Of Prophecy. 7. Of the Difference between the Legal and the Evangelical Righteousness, the Old and the New Covenant, &c. 8. Of the Shortness and Vanity of a Pharisaick Righteousness. 9. Of the Excellency and Nobleness of True Religion. 10. Of a Christians Conflicts with, and Conquests over, Satan*. [Compiled by John Worthington] *As also, A Sermon preached by Simon Patrick at the Author's Funeral. With a Brief Account of His Life and Death*. London: Printed by J. Flesher for W. Morder, 1660. liii, 526 pp.

Strutt, Samuel. *A Defence of the late learned Dr. Clarke's Notion of Natural Liberty: in Answer to Three Letters Wrote to Him by a Gentleman at the University of Cambridge, on the Side of Necessity. Together with Some Remarks on Mr. Locke's Chapter of Power*. London: Printed for T. Green, 1730. 68 pp.

[——.] *A Philosophical Enquiry into the Physical Spring of Human Actions, and the Immediate Cause of Thinking*. London: Printed for J. Peele, 1732. 53 pp.

Stuart, Alexander. *Three Lectures on Muscular Motion. Read before the Royal Society in the Year MDCCXXXVIII: As Appointed by the . . . Design of . . . William Croone, M.D.; . . . Being a Supplement to the Philosophical Transactions for that year; Wherein the Elasticity of Fluids, and the Immediate Cause of the Cohesion and Elasticity of Solids are proved by Experiments, &c., and Shewn to arise from the Same Principles as Gravity: with a general Scheme of Muscular Motion, Founded on Anatomy, Experiments, &c*. London: Printed for T. Woodward and C. Davis, 1739. liv pp.

Toland, John. *Letters to Serena: Containing, I. The Origin and Force of Prejudices. II. The History of the Soul's Immortality among the Heathens. III. The Origin of Idolatry, and Reasons of Heathenism. As also, IV. A Letter to a Gentleman in Holland, showing Spinosa's System of Philosophy to be without any Principle or Foundation. V. Motion essential to Matter; in Answer to some remarks by a Noble Friend on the Confutation of Spinosa. To all which is prefix'd, VI. A Preface; being a Letter to a Gentleman in London, sent together with the foregoing Dissertations, and declaring the several Occasions of writing them*. London: Printed for B. Lintot, 1704. 25 prelim. leaves, 239 pp.

——. *Christianity Not Mysterious; Or, A Treatise Shewing, That there is nothing in the Gospel contrary to Reason, Nor Above it: And that no Christian Doctrine can be properly call'd A Mystery*. London, 1696. xxxii, 176 pp.

[Tucker, Abraham.] *Freewill, Foreknowledge, and Fate. A Fragment*. By Edward Search [pseud.]. London: Printed for R. & J. Dodsley, 1763. xxxi, 268 pp.

Vicary, Thomas. *The Anatomie of the Bodie of Man*. The Edition of 1548 as re-issued by the Surgeons of St. Bartholomew's in 1577. With a life of Vicary, notes . . . Edited by Fredk. J. Furnivall and Percy Furnivall. Early English Text Society's Extra Series, no. 53. London: Published for the Early English Text Society by N. Trübner, 1888. viii, 336 pp.

Voltaire, Jean François Marie Arouet de. *Elemens de la philosophie de Neuton. Mis à la portée de tout le monde*. A Amsterdam: Chez J. Desbordes, 1738. 399 pp.

——. *Letters concerning the English Nation*. London: Printed for C. Davis and A. Lyon, 1733. 253 pp.

[Watts, Isaac.] *Philosophical Essays on Various Subjects, Viz. Space, Substance, Body, Spirit, the Operations of the Soul in Union with the Body, Innate Ideas, Perpetual Consciousness, Place and Motion of Spirits, the Departing Soul, the Resurrection of the Body, the Production and Operations of Plants and Animals. With some Remarks on Mr. Locke's Essay on the Human Understanding. To which is subjoined, A Brief Scheme of Ontology; Or, The Science of Being in general, with its Affections*. By I. W. London: Printed for R. Ford [et al.], 1733. xii, 403 pp.

Whitehead, John (1740?-1804). Physician and biographer of John Wesley.

——. *Materialism Philosophically Examined; Or, The Immateriality of the Soul Asserted and Proved, on Philosophical Principles; in Answer to Dr. Priestley's Disquisitions on Matter and Spirit* . . . London: Printed and Sold by J. Phillips, 1778. vii, 178 pp.

Whytt, Robert (1714-66). Scottish physiologist, professor of theory of medicine at University of Edinburgh; President of the Royal (Scottish) College of Physicians; studied under Boerhaave, also in Paris and Leyden.

——. *Observations on the Nature, Causes, and Cure of those Disorders which have been commonly called Nervous, Hypochondriac, or Hysteric. To which are prefixed, Some Remarks on the Sympathy of the Nerves* . . . Edinburgh: Printed for T. Becket [et al.], 1765. 520 pp.

——. *An Essay on the Vital and Other Involuntary Motions of Animals*. Edinburgh: Printed by Hamilton, Balfour and Neill, 1751. x, 392 pp.

——. ——. The Second Edition, with Corrections and Additions. Edinburgh: Printed for J. Balfour, 1763. x, 437 pp.

——. *Physiological Essays. Containing, I. An Inquiry into the Causes which Promote the Circulation of the Fluids in the Very Small Vessels of Animals. II. Observations on the Sensibility and Irritability of the Parts of Men and Other Animals; occasioned by Dr. Haller's late Treatise on These Subjects*. Edinburgh: Printed by Hamilton, Balfour and Neill, 1755. vii, 223 pp.

Willis, Thomas (1621-75). M.D., taught medicine in Oxford, one of the founders of the Royal Society.

——. *Cerebri anatome, nervorumque descriptio et usus*. Londini: Impensis J. Martyn et J. Allestry, 1664. 19 prelim. leaves, 456 pp.

[Wimpey, Joseph.] *Remarks on a Book, intitled, An Enquiry into the Nature of the Human Soul* [by Andrew Baxter]. *Wherein the Immateriality of the Soul is Evinced from the Principles of Reason and Philosophy*. In a Letter. London, 1741.

Windle, William. *An Enquiry into the Immateriality of Thinking Substances, Human Liberty, and the Original of Motion. Particularly in Answer to a late Pamphlet, intitled, A Philosophical Enquiry into the Physical Spring of Human Actions and Immediate Cause of Thinking* [by Samuel Strutt]. London: Printed by J. Bettenham, 1738. 124 pp.

Witty, John. *The First Principles of Modern Deism confuted. In a Demonstration of the Immateriality, Natural Eternity, and Immortality of Thinking Substances in General; and in Particular, of Human Souls; Even from the Supposition that we are Intirely Ignorant of the Intrinsic Natures of the Essences of Things*. London: Printed for J. Wyatt, 1707. xxii, 301 pp.

Wollaston, William. *The Religion of Nature Delineated*. [London?] 1722. 158 pp. Very few copies of this edition were printed.

——. ——. [Third Edition.] London: Printed by S. Palmer, and Sold by B. Lintot [et al], 1725. 219 pp. The notes in these editions are said to be by John, Samuel Clarke's brother.

Worster, Benjamin. *A Compendious and Methodical Account of the Principles of Natural Philosophy: As They are Explain'd and Illustrated in the Course of Experiments, Perform'd at the Academy in Little Tower-Street*. London: Printed for the Author, and Sold by W. and J. Innys, 1722. viii, 239 pp.

Wotton, William. *A Letter to Eusebia: Occasioned by Mr. Toland's Letters to Serena*. London: Printed for T. Goodwin, 1704. 75 pp.

PERIODICALS

The Annual Register; Or, A View of the History, Politics and Literature; for the Year 1758–1800. London: Printed for J. Dodsley [etc.] Still being published.

Bibliotheque choisie, pour servir de suite à la Bibliotheque universelle [et historique] Par Jean LeClerc. Tomes 1-28. A Amsterdam: Chez H. Schelte, 1703-13. Continued as *Bibliothèque ancienne et moderne*.

Bibliothèque raisonnée des ouvrages des savans de l'Europe. Tomes 1-50; pour les mois juillet/sept. 1728-avril/juin 1753. A Amsterdam: Chez les Wetsteins & Smith.

The Guardian. Nos. 1-175; March 12-October 1, 1713. London: Printed for J. Tonson. Published daily; by Addison, Steele, and others.

The London Journal. no. 1-999; August 6, 1719-March 17, 1744. London. August-December 24, 1719 issues called The Thursday's Journal.

The London Review of English and Foreign Literature. Vols. 1-12, no. 1; Jan. 1775-July 1780. By W. Kenrick [et al.] London: Printed by Cox and Bigg.

The Monthly Review; Or, New Literary Journal. Vols. 1-81, May 1749-December 1789; [2d series] Vols. 1-108, January 1790-November 1825. London: Printed for R. Griffiths [etc.] Founded and for many years edited by Ralph Griffiths.

Philosophical Transactions of the Royal Society. Vols. 1-12, no. 142, March 1665-February 1679; vol. 13, no. 143-vol. 177, Jan. 1683-December 1886. London.

In the interim, March 1679 through December 1682, Henry Oldenburg published the society's Philosophical Collections. In 1877, the journal split into two sections, A and B, and is still being published.

The Spectator. [By Joseph Addison, Richard Steele, and others.] March 1, 1711-December 6, 1712; June 18-September 29, 1714. London. Many times reprinted.

SECONDARY SOURCES

Anderson, Robert Fendel. *Hume's First Principles*. Lincoln: University of Nebraska Press, [1966]. xiv, 189 pp.

Attfield, Robin. "Clarke, Collins, and Compounds." *Journal of the History of Philosophy* 15, no. 1 (Jan. 1977): 45-54.

Ayers, Michael R. "Mechanism, Superaddition, and the Proof of God's Existence in Locke's Essay." *The Philosophical Review* 90, no. 2 (Apr. 1981): 210-51.

Bennett, J. A. "A Note on Theories of Respiration and Muscular Action in England, c. 1660." *Medical History* 20, no. 1 (Jan. 1976): 59-69.

Berman, David. "Anthony Collins and the Question of Atheism in the Early Part of the Eighteenth Century." *Proceedings of the Royal Irish Academy*, Section C, 75 no. 5 (1975): 85-102.

Boas, George. *The Happy Beast in French Thought of the Seventeenth Century*. Contributions to the history of primitivism. Baltimore: Johns Hopkins Press, 1933. vii, 159 pp. Reprinted in 1966 by Octagon Books, New York.

Bunge, Mario, ed. *The Critical Approach to Science and Philosophy; in honor of Karl R. Popper*. New York: Free Press of Glencoe, [1964]. xv, 480 pp.

Chapuis, Alfred. *Le monde des automates; étude historique et technique*. Paris: [E. Gélis], 1928. 2 vols.

Cruttwell, Patrick. "Physiology and Psychology in Shakespeare's Age." *Journal of the History of Ideas* 12, no. 1 (Jan. 1951): 75-89.

Ferg, Stephen. "Two Early Works by David Hartley." *Journal of the History of Philosophy* 19, no. 2 (Apr. 1981): 173-89.

Ferguson, James P. *The Philosophy of Dr. Samuel Clarke, and Its Critics*. New York: Vanguard Press, [1974]. 292 pp.

Gysi, Lydia. *Platonism and Cartesianism in the Philosophy of Ralph Cudworth*. Bern: H. Lang, 1962. xi, 163 pp.

Hayek, F. A. *Studies in Philosophy, Politics, and Economics*. Chicago: University of Chicago Press, [1967]. x, 356 pp. Includes reprint of "The Theory of Complex Phenomena."

——. "The Theory of Complex Phenomena." In Bunge, Mario, ed., *The Critical Approach to Science and Philosophy, q.v.*

Heimann, P. M., and J. E. McGuire. "Newtonian Forces and Lockean Powers: Concepts of Matter in Eighteenth-Century Thought." *Historical Studies in the Physical Sciences*, third annual volume (1971): 233-306.

Jacob, Margaret C. *The Newtonians and the English Revolution, 1689-1720*. Ithaca, N.Y.: Cornell University Press, [1976]. 288 pp.

——. *The Radical Enlightenment: Pantheists, Freemasons, and Republicans*. Early Modern Europe Today. London: Allen & Unwin, [1981]. xiii, 312 pp.

Jardine, Lisa. *Francis Bacon: Discovery and the Art of Discourse*. Cambridge: University Press, [1974]. viii, 267 pp.

Jaynes, Julian. "The Problem of Animate Motion in the Seventeenth Century." *Journal of the History of Ideas* 31, no. 2 (Apr./June 1970): 219-34.

Knight, William Angus. *Lord Monboddo and Some of His Contemporaries*. London: J. Murray, 1900. xv, 314 pp. Contains selections from Monboddo's correspondence.

Koslow, Arnold. "Ontological and Ideological Issues of the Classical Theory of Space and Time." In Machamer, Peter K. and Robert G. Turnbull, eds. *Motion and Time, Space and Matter: Interrelations in the History of Philosophy and Science*. Columbus: Ohio State University Press, [1976], pp. 224-63.

Koyré, Alexandre. *From the Closed World to the Infinite Universe*. Baltimore: Johns Hopkins Press, 1957. x, 313 pp.

Laird, John. *Hume's Philosophy of Human Nature*. London: Methuen, [1932]. ix, 312 pp.

McMullin, Ernan. *Newton on Matter and Activity*. Notre Dame, Ind.: University of Notre Dame Press, [1978]. viii, 160 pp.

Merchant, Carolyn. *The Death of Nature: Women, Ecology, and the Scientific Revolution*. New York: Harper & Row, [1980]. xx, 348 pp.

Mijuskovic, Ben Lazare. *The Achilles of Rationalist Arguments: the Simplicity, Unity and Identity of Thought and Soul from the Cambridge Platonists to Kant; a Study in the History of an Argument*. Archives internationales d'histoire des idées, Series minor, 13. The Hague: M. Nijhoff, 1974. 142 pp.

Mill, John Stuart. *A System of Logic, Ratiocinative and Inductive; Being a Connected View of the Principles of Evidence and the Methods of Scientific Investigation*. London: John W. Parker, 1843. 2 vols.

Mossner, Ernest Campbell, editor. "Hume's Early Memoranda, 1729-40: the Complete Text." *Journal of the History of Ideas* 9, no. 4 (Oct. 1948): 492-518.

O'Higgins, James. *Anthony Collins, the Man and His Works*. Archives internationales d'histoire des idées, 35. The Hague: M. Nijhoff, 1970. x, 267 pp.

Roe, Shirley A. *Matter, Life, and Generation: Eighteenth-Century Embryology and the Haller-Wolff Debate*. Cambridge: University Press, [1981]. x, 214 pp.

Rosenfield, Leonora Cohen. *From Beast-Machine to Man-Machine; the Theme of Animal Soul in French Letters from Descartes to La Mettrie*. New York: Oxford University Press, 1940. xxviii, 353 pp.

Schofield, Robert E. *Mechanism and Materialism: British Natural Philosophy in an Age of Reason*. Princeton: Princeton University Press, 1970. vi, 336 pp.

Sloan, Philip R. "Descartes, the Sceptics and the Rejection of Vitalism in Seventeenth-Century Physiology." *Studies in the History and Philosophy of Science* 8, no. 1 (1977): 1-28.

Thackray, Arnold E. *Atoms and Powers; an Essay on Newtonian Matter-Theory and the Development of Chemistry*. Harvard Monographs in the History of Science. Cambridge: Harvard University Press, 1970. xxiii, 326 pp.

Vartanian, Aram. *Diderot and Descartes; a Study of Scientific Naturalism in the Enlightenment*. The History of Ideas Series, no. 6. Princeton: Princeton University Press, 1953. vi, 336 pp.

Von Wright, Georg Henrik. *Explanation and Understanding*. Ithaca, N.Y.: Cornell University Press, [1971]. xvii, 230 pp.

White, Peter J. "A Study of the Psychology of Cognition in John Locke's *Essay*." [Toronto], 1972. 362 pp. Unpublished Ph.D. thesis, York University.

Whyte, Lancelot Law, ed. *Roger Joseph Boscovich, S.J., F.R.S., 1711-1787; Studies of His Life and Work on the 250th Anniversary of His Birth* . . . London: Allen & Unwin, [1961]. 230 pp.

Wilson, Margaret D. "Superadded Properties: the Limits of Mechanism in Locke." *American Philosophical Quarterly* 16, no. 2 (Apr. 1979): 143-50.

Wordsworth, Christopher. *Scholae Academicae: Some Account of the Studies at the English Universities in the Eighteenth Century*. Reprints of economic classics. New York: A. M. Kelley, 1969. xii, 435 pp. Facsim. reprint of the 1877 edition.

Yolton, John W. "Act and Circumstance." *Journal of Philosophy* 59, no. 13 (June 21, 1962): 337-50.

——. "Agent Causality." *American Philosophical Quarterly* 3, no. 1 (Jan. 1966): 14-26.

——. "Ideas and Knowledge in Seventeenth-Century Philosophy." *Journal of the History of Philosophy* 13, no. 2 (Apr. 1975): 145-66.

——. *John Locke and the Way of Ideas*. Oxford Classical and Philosophical Monographs. London: Oxford University Press, 1956. x, 235 pp.

——. "My Hand Goes out to You." *Philosophy* 41, no. 2 (Apr. 1966): 140-52.

——. "On Being Present to the Mind: a Sketch for the History of an Idea." *Dialogue* 14, no. 3 (Sept. 1975): 373-88.

Zafiropulo, Jean, and Catherine Monod. *Sensorium Dei, dans l'hermétisme et la science*. Collection d'études anciennes. Paris: Société d'Edition "les Belles Lettres," 1976. 390 pp.

Index

Index

Educated at the University of Cincinnati and Oxford University, **John Yolton** is professor of philosophy and dean of Rutgers College at Rutgers University. Among his books are *John Locke and the Way of Ideas* and *Locke and the Compass of Human Understanding*; he edited *The Locke Reader* and the Everyman edition of Locke's *Essay Concerning Human Understanding*. Yolton serves on the editorial board of the journal *Eighteenth-Century Studies*.